A
LEADER
IN THE
MAKING

A LEADER

IN THE

MAKING

ESSENTIALS TO BEING A LEADER
AFTER GOD'S OWN HEART

by Joyce Meyer

Harrison House
Tulsa, Oklahoma

A Leader in the Making —
Essentials to Being a Leader after God's Own Heart
ISBN 1-57794-219-1
Copyright © 2001 by Joyce Meyer
Life In The Word, Inc.
P. O. Box 655
Fenton, Missouri 63026

Published by Harrison House, Inc.
P. O. Box 35035
Tulsa, Oklahoma 74153

CONTENTS

Introduction

Some people who become leaders have natural leadership qualities. Other people who don't have those qualities become excellent leaders through training. But even natural leaders don't come ready-made; we all need a little work.

God called me into the ministry many years ago, but I didn't jump out of bed one morning ready to assume a leadership position and rise to the top by the next week. Oh, I thought I was ready, but I wasn't. The problem was that the fruit of the Spirit wasn't visible in my life[1] — the fruit wasn't evident in my character. There was no stability, faithfulness, patience, joy, love, kindness, gentleness nor meekness. And there was zero humility. I was full of me — concerned with my own wants, acting any way I wanted to act. If I had been in a leadership position at that time, instead of bringing the best out of people as a leader should do, I would have made me and everyone around me miserable. Yet God called me to be a leader. I used to wonder sometimes why He doesn't call people who are fixed up and ready to lead. I believe the reason is that He can't find anyone like that.

It is amazing how many gifted people there are who are just sitting on the sidelines of life doing nothing. You may be one of them. I can tell you that whether God uses you or not is dependent upon much more than just the gift or talent He has given you. It has everything to do with character — with maturity, with the fruit of the Spirit, with how we behave and with our heart attitude.

In this study when I refer to the **heart** of a person, I'm referring to the approach a person has toward God, people and circumstances. We can almost exchange the word **heart** with the word **attitude**. I believe that God uses people who are not always the most talented, but who have the best heart attitude, a right heart toward Him.

Many people try to lead, but they have never gone through the training process. They haven't matured or developed their character, and they have the wrong heart attitude. I don't believe that those kinds of people will ever become the leaders God wants them to be. To become strong leaders, there are things we need to experience while keeping a right heart attitude.

Why would we ever want to go through what it takes to develop the potential that God has given us? One reason is that we will never be fulfilled unless we develop that potential.

Some people who want to reach their potential don't know where to begin. Other people know where to begin but don't know how to move from there to the place where they are supposed to finish. If you fit either of those categories, you will learn from this book how to reach your goals and fulfill God's good plans for you. And you will learn what it takes to develop the qualities of a leader.

Before writing this book, I read the book *The Making of a Leader* by Frank Damazio and found the information so helpful, especially in the areas of heart conditions, character development, preparing for leadership, tests of leadership and leadership qualities, that I was inspired to expand upon some of it in this teaching. I believe his book will greatly benefit you. I highly recommend it and have included it in the recommended reading list at the end of this book.

Even though the teaching in this book is directed toward leaders and people who want to become leaders, it contains practical direction for everyday living that anyone who wants to experience all that God has for them can apply. Even if you think you **don't** want to be in leadership, God may have a different idea in mind. You never know what God has planned for you in the future. He may have more in store for you than you think! After all, most of us want to lead something, even if it is only the dog! We have a natural desire to be in charge.

A leader is not necessarily someone who has a large ministry or is in a position that influences thousands of people's lives. A leader is someone who is on top of things in his or her realm of influence. In this book I share what God has taught me over the years as He has guided me from my impatient beginnings in my first realm of influence, that of ministering to a few people in our home Bible study over a period of time, to the much larger realm today of ministering to thousands of people through our Life In The Word conferences and ministry outreaches. My husband, Dave, and I are doing what we are called to do. And in developing the gifts God has given us, we are fulfilling our potential. I am seeing my dreams and visions fulfilled. I don't believe this is something that God has in store for just a handful of people. I believe it is His will for all people to fulfill their potential.

God wants to do more with your life than you could ever imagine. As you read this book, I encourage you to be sure to keep your mind and heart completely open to hearing what He wants to tell you.

GOD WANTS TO DO MORE WITH YOUR LIFE THAN YOU COULD EVER IMAGINE.

PART 1

PREPARATION
FOR LEADERSHIP

CHAPTER 1

DEVELOP YOUR POTENTIAL:
NOBODY STARTS AT THE FINISH LINE, PART 1

"That person is a born leader."

We hear this statement often.

Are leaders born or are they made?

It is true that some people do seem to be born with an abundance of leadership gifts and qualities. But it is also true that some of the best leaders in the kingdom of God are those whom the world would probably disregard as even qualifying for leadership. All that these type of people need is someone to recognize their potential and help them develop it. Often they turn out to be some of the most precious and effective people in leadership.

Whether you are a born leader or you have to work at becoming one, my purpose in writing this book is to help you recognize your potential as a leader and show you how to develop it.

Some people who work for my husband and me in our ministry come under the category of born leaders. They just have that innate ability to get things done. They have the strong, aggressive type of personality that seems to instinctively know how to motivate others to work together.

But we also have people on our management team I personally would never have thought could ever become managers. Yet when we were in need in a certain area, they seemed to be the ones God was pointing to for that position, so we gave them that chance. We continued to work with them until some of them have become the best managers we have.

One of these people is a woman named Charlotte. When she first came to work for us, she was so fearful that she could not even talk to me without breaking down and crying. Anytime we tried to get her to do anything other than what she was used to doing, she would become frightened and say, "I don't know if I can do that. I'm afraid I'll make a mistake."

Finally, one day I felt that the Lord was telling me to call her into my office and say to her, "Charlotte, God wants me to tell you that it's time to grow up. You've got to stop crying and being afraid of everything."

She later told me that she went home in tears because I had hurt her feelings. But when she prayed about it, God told her, "Joyce is right. It is time for you to grow up and start accepting more responsibility."

She said yes to the Lord and to us, and now she has developed into one of our finest leaders. She has learned to accept more and more responsibility — all because she quit being afraid and started developing her potential.

That happened because we were determined not to give up on her. Like Charlotte, there are many people who have tremendous potential but need someone who will work with them and not give up on them.

Aren't you glad that God did not give up on you? Well, guess what? He may put someone else in your life He does not want you to give up on.

Sometimes the people who are the biggest thorns in our side are the very ones God wants us to be patient with and help develop just as He was patient with us and is helping us develop into all that we can be.

OUR NUMBER ONE JOB

The development of personal potential is each person's number one job.

We all have undeveloped potential, but we will never see it manifested until we believe God and believe that we can do whatever He says we can do in His Word. Unless we take a chance and step out in faith believing that with God nothing is impossible,[1] He cannot do the work in us that He wants to do to develop our potential.[2]

· I believe you are reading this book by divine appointment. Even if nobody else in the world believes in you, God does. With that confidence, you can do whatever He wants you to do. Without it, no matter what He wants you to do, you will be unable to do it because you are not in agreement with Him. ·

· When we don't agree with God, we are, in essence, agreeing with the devil. We are saying the devil is right when he tells us through negative thoughts or someone else's comments that we are worthless and can do nothing. ·

> IF NOBODY ELSE IN THE WORLD BELIEVES IN YOU, GOD DOES. WITH THAT CONFIDENCE, YOU CAN DO WHATEVER HE WANTS YOU TO DO.

It is very important with whom we agree. Jesus said that if any two agree on earth about anything, it will be done for them by His Father in heaven.[3]

When I was going through a difficult period in my life, the Lord reminded me of this verse and told me that if I could not find anyone else to agree with me, I could always agree with the Holy Spirit.[4] He is on the earth too if He lives inside of us. We agree with Him by agreeing with what we know the Word says is true in a particular situation.

GIVE SHAPE TO YOUR POTENTIAL

Noah Webster's *1828 American Dictionary of the English Language* defines *potential* as "existing in possibility, not in act."[5]

Potential cannot manifest without form. Like concrete, it must have something to be poured into, something to give it shape and make it useful. What is the form into which potential is poured? Decisions. To develop potential properly, we must have a plan and pray over that plan, we must have a purpose and we must be doing something.[6]

I believe that many people are unhappy because they aren't doing anything to develop their potential. In fact, many of them never develop their potential because they don't do anything except complain that they're not doing anything!

If you want to see your potential developed to its fullness, don't wait until everything is perfect. Do something **now**. Start laying your hand to whatever is in front of you. You cannot start at the finish line. You must start at the starting block like everybody else.

Many people want to start at *A*, blink their eyes twice and be at *Z*. It doesn't work that way.

Give your potential some form. Do something with it. You will never find what you are capable of doing if you never try anything. Don't be so afraid of failing that you never take a chance. Don't stay in the safety zone doing nothing, thinking that as long as you do nothing you are safe. You may be safe, but you will never succeed at developing your full potential or feeling fulfilled in what you are doing. Step out into what you feel God is leading you to do, and you will soon discover what you can and cannot do.

> **GOD IS NOT GOING TO MAKE YOU SPEND YOUR WHOLE LIFE DOING SOMETHING YOU HATE.**

So many people are frustrated about not knowing what their gifts are or what God has called them to do with their life. All you have to do to find out what your call is, is to start doing a few things related to an area in which you are interested. God is not going to make you spend your whole life doing something you hate. Although I have children and grandchildren whom I love and enjoy very much, I have also discovered that my gift and calling is not working with small children. But there are people who love to do that. My daughter Sandra is one of them.

· There is someone who is anointed for everything that needs to be done. **The smart leader knows what he can do and what he cannot do and surrounds himself with people who do well what he cannot do at all.**·

DEVELOP YOUR SEED

· I believe God puts seeds in us. Even Jesus is referred to in the Bible as a Seed.[6] We often talk about all the rights, privileges and victories that are ours in Christ, along with all the other blessings like peace, righteousness and joy. I believe all of those things come into our spirit as a seed when we receive Jesus as our Savior. (If you have never done that, and you would like to, there is a prayer you can pray at the end of this book.)·

One reason some people never have manifested in their lives what the Bible tells us we can have is that they never develop their seed. It never gets out of the seed stage because it just sits in them; they don't do anything with it.

I have experienced a lot of victory in my life. I come from an abusive background where I endured many years of sexual, verbal and mental abuse, failed relationships, hurts and emotional pain before I married my husband, Dave. I was quite a mess when I got into a serious relationship with the Lord. I can say that what I read in the Bible has worked in my life. But I can also say that it had to be developed. None of it fell on me like ripe fruit from a tree. I had to take potential and turn it into reality — by developing it.

The Necessity of Development

As defined in Webster's 1828 dictionary, *development* is "an unfolding; the discovering of something secret or withheld from the knowledge of others; disclosure; full exhibition."[7]

What you and I have in us is great, but it is not going to do any good if we do not take it and give it some form and shape that is going to help us and everybody else.

In 1 Peter 4:10 TEV we are told that we are to develop and **use** our gifts as a blessing to one another. That is why God gives us gifts, so we can be a blessing to others.

There is no excuse for any of us ever being bored or lonely because there is always someone out there who needs what we have. All we have to do is find them and start releasing our gifts for their benefit.

A real estate developer may have plans in his office for a new subdivision, but no one will ever see those plans become reality unless the developer takes them and does something with them. The same is true for us in the church. How many of us have good ideas and great plans but never do anything with them? Many of us are good at dreaming but are no good at all at making a practical, dedicated effort to develop our potential and manifest our dreams in our lives.

What lies between potential development and manifestation? Nothing so spiritual that nobody can figure it out, but just simple, everyday things like time, determination and hard work.

•Nobody can be determined for us. We must be determined. If we are not determined, the devil will steal from us everything we have. But although we must be determined, we must not go to the extreme and become workaholics. We need balance in this area just as in every other area of our lives.•

Later on in this book I will describe the time when the Lord spoke to my husband, Dave, and told him it was time for us to go into television ministry when we were just getting comfortable with being on the radio. Obviously, we had the potential to do that, but it had to be developed, and that kind of development does not come by sitting in a rocking chair taking it easy!

I have a saying, "If you're going to hang out with God, there ain't no retirement!" Whatever our age or situation, taking potential and transforming it into reality requires an investment of time, determination and a willingness to work hard.

NO RETURN WITHOUT INVESTMENT

Many people are not willing to invest anything with the hope of reaping a return from that investment somewhere down the road. Their philosophy is, "If I'm going to do anything right now, I want some pay **right now**. I want something back **right now**."

In my own life, I started out in the ministry teaching twenty-five people who sat around together on my living room floor. I invested five years of my life into teaching those people with little or no financial return at all and often not much appreciation, just a lot of hard work. But those five years were developmental years for my teaching ministry today.

Not long ago my older son, David, who has started to teach and preach some, asked me if I had any notes on a certain subject. I have three file cabinets with three long drawers each that are full of message after message on a variety of subjects. Those files represent twenty-two years of hard work. So often people look at something like my ministry and they wish they had it. But they wouldn't want to invest the time and hard work it took to build it.

Most of us have no problem with wishbone; it's backbone that we are lacking.

YOU ARE FULL OF POTENTIAL

The undeveloped, wasted potential in this world is pathetic. Everyone was created to do something great — great in its own realm. Each of us has the potential to become great at something — a great wife, a great mom, a great seamstress, a great husband, a great father, a great businessman. But whatever we do, we should not have little ideas, dreams or visions.

> **EACH OF US HAS THE POTENTIAL TO BECOME GREAT AT SOMETHING.**

Little things are important, and we should never despise the day of small things.[8] But we ought to have big ideas, dreams and visions because we serve a big God. I would rather have a big dream and see half of it come to pass than to have a little dream and see all of it come to pass.

I believe that when God created all of us, He formed and fashioned each person, breathed the breath of life into us[9] and then took a little part of Himself and placed it within each of us.[10] One of us may have a musical gift, another may have a speaking gift, another a writing gift. The problem comes when we try to take the gift God has given us and use it to do what someone else is doing instead of developing our own potential.

Each one of us is full of potential. We have a part of God in us. We are not a mistake. We don't have to spend our lives on the back burner. We are not too old or too young. We have God-given dreams and visions. But the dreams and visions God gives us for the future are possibilities not "positivelys." (That's the way God spoke it to me a long time ago.) •With Him, nothing is impossible, but it also takes our cooperation and willingness through determination, obedience and hard work to develop what He has put in us.•

IT ALL STARTS WITH A SEED

The manifestation of our God-given dreams and visions does not appear overnight. It grows from a seed planted in our heart by God and nourished and nurtured by us day after day until it gradually springs forth as fruit in our lives.

It is similar to a seed that is planted in a woman's womb at the time of conception. The baby doesn't appear immediately. There is a nine-month development period.

We often see patterns in the way God does things, and God uses the pattern of birthing in many areas of our lives. He starts with a seed, which He plants in us in the form of a thought, a dream, a desire. In order for that seed to grow and develop, we must nourish and nurture it, being careful to watch over it and protect it because the devil is a master at stealing seeds. Then one day that seed springs forth as the manifestation we desired.

That is what Jesus meant when He said that the devil comes only *to steal, and to kill, and to destroy. . . .*[11] Jesus also said that Satan *is a liar . . . and the father of lies. . . .*[12] Between stealing and lying, he keeps the majority of the human race from ever doing much of anything.

> BY DEVOTING THE TIME AND EFFORT IT TAKES TO DEVELOP WHAT GOD HAS PLACED IN YOU, YOU WILL EXPERIENCE THE JOY OF FULFILLMENT.

I am living proof that anybody can fulfill the call of God on their life if they want to. In the natural I don't have a lot of gifts and talents. But I have a mouth, and I am using it for the glory of God. As a result, I have the joy of fulfillment because I have devoted the time and effort it takes to develop what God placed in me.

We all have potential but not all have a willingness to work hard. When a twenty-year-old is a concert pianist and you hear them playing beautifully, you know immediately that they spent years practicing while their peers were playing games, running around with their friends and doing fun things that young people love to do. That concert pianist may have lost a lot of good times, but instead, spent the time developing their potential. They've developed something that will bring them joy the rest of their life.

Many people will never experience that kind of joy because they are not willing to pay the price for it. They would rather have a "right now" good time.

It concerns me that so many people spend their time satisfying their flesh and, as a result, end up empty inside.

You will enjoy the fulfillment of your potential when you develop it. And the way to do that is by keeping at it, refusing to quit and never giving up.

KEEP ON KEEPING ON

*And let us not be weary in well doing:
for in due season we shall reap, if we faint not.*

Galatians 6:9 KJV

One time I became frustrated because it seemed the seed of a dream I had inside of me would never bear fruit. At the time I was teaching a little Bible study and not doing much else. It was a time of real discouragement for me, but every time I turned around it seemed that God was giving me this Scripture in Galatians 6:9.

It came to me on greeting cards. It was on my calendar. I drew it out of my Promise Box. The preacher spoke on it. I mean, every time I turned around I was hearing or seeing it.

During this time I had my first encounter with the ministry of a prophet who came to our church. In his presentation he picked me out of the audience and said, "The Lord says to you, 'Be not weary in well doing, for in due season you will reap if you faint not.'"

I got so mad at God. I thought, **I do not want to hear that Scripture one more time. I already am weary, and I don't want to reap something later on; I want to reap it now!**

After the meeting was over, and I had calmed down a bit, I was walking through the graveled parking lot kicking rocks. Finally I stopped and said, "All right, God. What are You telling me?"

He said (not in an audible voice but in my heart), "Joyce, just keep on keeping on and you'll get there."

Nobody can promise you that you will arrive at your destination in a week or a year or after one trip around the mountain. The Israelites wandered in the wilderness around the mountain called Mount Seir for forty years making what was actually an eleven-day journey.[13]

You may have to go through one difficult trial or test, or it may be ten or twenty. You may have to put up with one obnoxious person or deal with three unlovely people. But you don't have to go through it in your own strength and ability. God will give you His grace to help you make it through. His grace is His ability and strength to help us do what we could not do without Him, and it is freely given to all of us who have received His Son Jesus in our heart.[14]

If you are ever going to develop the potential God has put in you, you must make up your mind that you are not going to quit, no matter what, until you see manifested what God has placed within you.

Have you been convinced that your life will never change? Remember, the devil will tell you that because he wants you to quit, to give up and believe that you are always going to be in the same mess. But don't be trapped by misbeliefs that stem from his lies. There is one kind of person he can never defeat — one who is not a quitter!

RUN THE RACE TO WIN

Do you not know that in a race all the runners compete,
but [only] one receives the prize? So run [your race]
that you may lay hold [of the prize] and make it yours.

Now every athlete who goes into training conducts himself
temperately and restricts himself in all things. They do it to
win a wreath that will soon wither, but we [do it to receive
a crown of eternal blessedness] that cannot wither.

1 Corinthians 9:24,25

How are you running your race? You need to be running it to win.

The devil doesn't want you to win because he knows that if you win, you will become a world changer. Your life will change, which will cause many other lives to change. If you develop your potential, you are not only going to have a positive effect on your life, but on someone else's life. That person will then go on and develop their potential and effect other lives, and so on and so on.

In this passage the apostle Paul says two things about running the race that make us feel uncomfortable. First, he says that those who run to win **conduct themselves temperately.** That means they cannot allow themselves to do everything they want to do. Second, he says that they **restrict themselves in all things.** That means they live a balanced life. There is no area of their life in which they are out of control.

To some of us, leading a balanced life may mean something as simple as going to bed at a decent hour so we won't be tired the next day. It may mean cleaning our house even though we don't feel like it. These are simple, practical things, but they reveal how much or how little we are in control of our life.

In the body of Christ today there are a lot of people who are trying to cast out devils who have never taken authority over a sink full of dirty dishes!

> POTENTIAL IS A PRICELESS TREASURE, LIKE GOLD. ALL OF US HAVE GOLD HIDDEN WITHIN, BUT WE HAVE TO DIG TO GET IT OUT.

According to the Bible, a leader has got to get their own house (or life) in order first before they can go out and set other people's houses (or lives) in order.[15]

There are many ways to prepare to be a leader. Getting your life in order is one of them. It involves making some changes on your part. But with God's help and your hard work and determination, you can break old habits that are hurting and hindering you and form new habits — ones that are healthy and will help you make progress toward developing your potential and reaching your goals.

Potential is a priceless treasure, like gold. As you will see next, **all of us have gold hidden within, but we have to dig to get it out.**

CHAPTER 2

DEVELOP YOUR POTENTIAL:
NOBODY STARTS AT THE FINISH LINE, PART 2

There is a gold mine hidden in every life.

A young man found a vein of gold in a mountain. He tried to get it out himself but kept failing repeatedly. He felt like giving up, but instead he went into town and asked a mining agency to come take a look at it. The mining company surveyed the mountain and the vein of gold and wanted to buy it. They offered the young man a large amount of cash if he would sell it to them.

The young man thought about it and decided that rather than selling it to the mining company, he would keep it and learn all he could about mining. Over the next year he studied practically day and night. He read every book on mining he could lay his hands on, took every course on it he could find and talked to every person who would give him any information about it. He did nothing else for that entire year but learn about mining. He laid aside everything else in his life in order to devote his entire attention to learning how to mine gold.

At the end of that year, he went back to the mountain and began to dig out the gold. It was tremendously hard work, but in the end he had millions and millions of dollars.

Here is the lesson. Many people, perhaps most people, would have taken one look at that mountain and the hard work required to get the gold out of it, and they would have taken the offer of the quick and easy money. They wouldn't have wanted the hassle, the aggravation; they wouldn't have wanted to give up a year of their life to study when they could have been having a good time. Instead they would have taken the "right now" thing.

FIND THE GOLD MINE HIDDEN IN YOUR LIFE.

How many people never have what they could have had because of that kind of mindset? The young man could have done that too, but if he had, he never would have enjoyed the full benefits of that vein of gold.

Does that say anything to you? Does it light a fire in you? Does it move you to strip off everything else that's been hindering you from staying focused on developing your potential? Like that young man, it may take some effort, but if you stay focused, you will eventually hit gold — the gold of enjoying the benefits of living a totally fulfilled life.

STAY FOCUSED

Wherefore seeing we also are compassed about with
so great a cloud of witnesses, let us lay aside every weight,
and the sin which doth so easily beset us, and let us run
with patience the race that is set before us.

Hebrews 12:1 KJV

This verse tells us that if we are going to run our race, we must lay aside every weight and run the race with patience. I've heard this point summarized in this way: Running our race with no hindrances means stripping for the contest.

In the days when this verse was written, the writer was drawing a parallel that was much better understood than it is today. In those days, runners conditioned their bodies for a race just as we do today. But at the time of the race, they stripped off their clothing so that when they ran there would be nothing to hinder them. They also oiled their bodies with fine oils.[1]

In the same way, we need to be well oiled or anointed with the Holy Spirit[2] if we are going to win our race. We also need to remove anything from our lives that would hinder us in running the race set before us.

· There are many different hindrances to running a race. Too many commitments will keep us from developing our potential. Letting other people control us will keep us from developing our potential. Not knowing how to say no will keep us from developing our potential.¹ Getting overly involved in someone else's goals and vision or becoming entangled in someone else's problems instead of keeping our eyes on our own goals will keep us from fulfilling our potential.

I have found that the devil can come up with a thousand ways every week to entangle me and get me off into something that is going to prevent me from doing what I am supposed to be doing. They all seem like emergencies, and it seems they all have to be handled by me because I am the only one who can do so.

If we are going to do what God has called us to do, we are going to have to stay focused because the world we live in is filled with distractions and entanglements.

We try to read our Bible, and somebody stops by. We try to pray, and the phone rings. There is distraction after distraction. Sooner or later we have to learn to say no. We have to be determined that nothing is going to hinder us from fulfilling God's plan and purpose for us.

Sometimes we may have to engage in a bit of holy anger and say, **"No, world! You are not going to do this to me any longer. I am not going to live on this crazy merry-go-round with no way off of it. I know what I am supposed to do, and I am going to do it. If you don't like it, talk to God. He is the One Who put this vision in me, and I am not going to frustrate myself all my life just to please you."**

BE LIKE THE ANT

Therefore I do not run uncertainly (without definite aim).
I do not box like one beating the air and striking without an adversary.

But [like a boxer] I buffet my body [handle it roughly, discipline it by hardships] and subdue it, for fear that after proclaiming to others the Gospel and things pertaining to it, I myself should become unfit [not stand the test, be unapproved and rejected as a counterfeit].

1 Corinthians 9:26,27

Paul says here that if we are going to win the race, we must subdue our body. In this sense, the body refers to all the carnal, fleshly passions.

In verse 27 Paul is speaking about self-control, self-denial, restraining the appetite and mortifying the flesh. He says that he "buffets" (**BUFF**-its) his body. He does not say that he "buffets" (buf-**FAYS**) his body!

Self-discipline is the most important quality in any life. Do you know what self-discipline is? It is keeping ourselves going in the right direction without someone making us do so. It is getting ourselves up in the morning because we know we should. How can anybody be a leader if he can't even get himself up out of bed each day? How can we lead anyone else if we can't even make ourselves clean our own house?

It concerns me that there are so many people today who want to occupy important positions but who don't want to accept the duties and responsibilities that go with those positions.

> TO EXPERIENCE THE FULFILLMENT OF YOUR DREAMS AND VISIONS IN THE FUTURE, STAY FOCUSED ON FULFILLING YOUR POTENTIAL NOW.

Many people spend their whole lives frustrated because they have never developed their potential. Without the development of their potential, they will never see the fulfillment of their dreams and visions.

There are so many frustrated people in the church that it is almost unbelievable. We Christians are supposed to be the most fulfilled people on the face of the earth. We are supposed to be a light to the world, living epistles read by others.[3] People are supposed to look at us and say, "That is what life is supposed to be like."

We are supposed to make others hungry just by looking at us — hungry to have what we have. The problem is that somehow there has been passed down to us the wrong idea that everything in life is supposed to be easy. We have gotten so used to automatic dishwashers and washing machines and dryers that we think all we should have to do is push a button and get what we want. Even then, we consider that a hard day of work, and we complain about having to push the button or get the clothes out of the permanent press cycle in time so that we won't have to iron them!

In Proverbs 6 we read about the ant, *which, having no chief, overseer, or ruler, provides her food in the summer and gathers her supplies in the harvest* (vv. 7,8).

We need to be like the ant. We need to be the kind of people who are self-motivated and self-disciplined, those who do what is right because it is right, not because someone may be looking or because someone is making us do it.

CONTROL YOUR EMOTIONS

He who is slow to anger is better than the mighty,
he who rules his [own] spirit than he who takes a city.

Proverbs 16:32

As this Scripture indicates, a person who operates in self-control is pretty powerful. But no one will ever develop into a leader if they cannot manage their emotions, especially the emotion of anger.

The Bible has a great deal to say about this subject. For example in the Old Testament we read: *He who foams up quickly and flies into a passion deals foolishly. . .* (Proverbs 14:17). *Good sense makes a man restrain his anger, and it is his glory to overlook a transgression or an offense* (Proverbs 19:11). *Do not be quick in spirit to be angry or vexed, for anger and vexation lodge in the bosom of fools* (Ecclesiastes 7:9).

In the New Testament we are told in James 1:19,20: *Understand [this], my beloved brethren. Let every man be quick to hear [a ready listener], slow to speak, slow to take offense and to get angry. For man's anger does not promote the righteousness God [wishes and requires].*

Part of righteousness, or the right way of being what God wishes and desires, is that we fulfill our potential, and unless we restrain our anger, we will never be able to find fulfillment.

Take Moses, for example. Moses was supposed to lead the Israelites out of Egypt into the Promised Land, but he was denied that privilege by God because he reacted with his unrestrained temper, disobeying God.[4]

We all want to have big ministries, but we don't always want to operate under the guidelines of self-control. We would rather allow our fleshly nature to dictate our lives. If we are ever going to become leaders, we must keep our passions under control. That doesn't mean we have to be perfect or that we can never make mistakes. Although the Holy Spirit will give us power to control our emotions, we may still lose our temper from time to time. But as soon as we do so, we should immediately confess it and repent of it, which means saying, "I'm sorry, God. Forgive me," and then move on.

A disciplined, self-controlled life not only requires time, determination and hard work, it also requires self-denial, which involves putting off our old ways. But the rewards are worth the effort.

PUT ON A NEW NATURE

Strip yourselves of your former nature [put off and discard your old unrenewed self] which characterized your previous manner of life and becomes corrupt through lusts and desires that spring from delusion.

Ephesians 4:22

Even when we think we have our negative emotions under control, something will happen to set them off. Nobody can guarantee us that they will never show up again. We may think we have gotten a breakthrough in this area and that we will never lose control again — and then we do that very thing, usually when we least expect it to happen.

‹ When we receive Jesus as our Savior, we receive the nature of God. › What the Bible calls the "old man" died with Christ on the cross when He died. Those who have received Jesus as Savior are seen by God as having died with Jesus by virtue of their faith in Him. They are given a new nature and instructed to choose to operate in it.[5]

The "old nature" represents our old ways of doing things, and the "new nature" represents the new way in which we now may behave through the help of the Holy Spirit. The choice is still ours; the "old nature" does not totally disappear, but we have available to us another, much better choice.

I might have two coats in my closet: one that is old, outdated and ragged, and another that is new, stylish and beautiful. I could wear the old one if I chose to, but if I have the choice of a new and beautiful one, why would I choose the old ragged one?

Prior to accepting Jesus as Savior, we had no choice, so to speak. We had only one nature: a fleshly, selfish one. After accepting Jesus, another choice is made available to us. The "old man" does not die, but we are dead to it. Our desires change, and we want to please God by behaving in a way that will honor Him. I recommend reading Romans chapter 6 for a more complete understanding about this issue of the old nature and the new nature.

Another thing we must do to reach the fulfillment of our potential is have patience.

BE PATIENT

Consider it wholly joyful, my brethren, whenever you are enveloped in or encounter trials of any sort or fall into various temptations.

Be assured and understand that the trial and proving of your faith bring out endurance and steadfastness and patience.

But let endurance and steadfastness and patience have full play and do a thorough work, so that you may be [people] perfectly and fully developed [with no defects], lacking in nothing.

James 1:2-4

Why do we get angry? Often it is because people do not do what we want them to do as fast as we want them to do it. If we had more patience, we would not get upset. Without patience we will never come to the fulfillment of our potential.

If we are lacking in patience, we must let God develop it in us. In this book one thing we look at is how leaders are developed through tests and matured as God builds character in them.

James tells us in the Bible that we are to be exceedingly joyful when we fall into all kinds of trials and temptations, knowing that the trying of our faith brings out patience.[6]

I have found that before tribulation brings out patience, it brings out a lot of other undesirable things. But those are the things that need to be brought out of us. Otherwise, we go around putting on a show because we have all kinds of junk in us that has never surfaced and been dealt with. The reason it's never been dealt with is that instead of going **through** some difficulties, we figure out a way to avoid them.

Going THROUGH DIFFICULTIES INSTEAD OF AVOIDING THEM WILL SAVE YOU A LOT OF AGONY.

'In Isaiah 43:2 the Lord tells us that He will be with us as we go through the water and through the fire. That means that there are some trials and tests that we cannot avoid, some hard things we have to go **through.**'

The Bible talks about purification, sanctification, sacrifice and suffering. Those are not popular words; nonetheless, they are in the Bible, and if we want to fulfill our potential, we must be prepared to go through such things.

There were times when I had to face loneliness and hard work, times when I wanted to give up and quit. God kept putting people in my path I didn't want to deal with, but He placed them there because I needed them. They were the sandpaper I needed to rub off my rough edges.

Has God put someone or something in your life that is sandpaper to you? If so, you will someday learn that what you thought was your greatest enemy turned out to be your best friend, simply because it was what God used to change you.

‹ God must change us to use us — we must become Christlike in character; we must follow His example and learn His ways. ‹

I struggled with the process of change for a long time, but I finally realized that God was not going to do things my way. He did not want an argument from me; He only wanted to hear, "Yes, Lord — Your will be done."

I soon learned that I could run from one difficult person or situation, and there would be two more to replace them around the next corner. I urge you to learn the lesson quicker than I did. If you do, it will save you a lot of agony. When you wrestle with God, you will always lose the contest.

You and I may as well settle down and deal with what God has placed in front of us. We all want to love the unlovely, but none of us wants to be around anybody who is unlovely. But that is part of our training in patience, and it has a purpose.

MAKE THE BEST OF LIFE

Do not, therefore, fling away your fearless confidence,
for it carries a great and glorious compensation of reward.

For you have need of steadfast patience and endurance, so that
you may perform and fully accomplish the will of God, and thus
receive and carry away [and enjoy to the full] what is promised.

Hebrews 10:35,36

Who do we need to be patient with? We need to be patient with ourselves because sometimes we are slow in learning. We need to be patient with God because He doesn't always move in our timing. And we need to be patient with other people because it is not their fault that we are not where we should be.

If our dream is not coming to pass, sometimes we get angry with everybody and everything. We must be patient with life and learn to take each day as it comes, living it to the fullest extent.

That is one of the characteristics of a leader — the ability to take life as it comes and to make the very best of it.

The reason we have to do that is because some days we are going to get lemons. But if we are smart, we will make lemonade from those lemons.

BALANCE IN WORK AND FUN

But Jesus answered them, My Father has worked [even] until now,
[He has never ceased working; He is still working]
and I, too, must be at [divine] work.

John 5:17

Jesus said here that both He and His Father worked and are still working. Later on in John 9:4 He told His disciples, *We must work the works of Him Who sent Me and be busy with His business while it is daylight; night is coming on, when no man can work.*

If you and I really believe that Jesus is coming back soon, then why in the world do we want to spend three-fourths of our time entertaining ourselves?

"But, Joyce," you might ask, "don't you believe in having fun?"

Yes, I believe in having fun. I believe in laughing, having a good time, resting and leading a balanced life. In fact, I preach all those things quite often, especially to ministers who have a hard time maintaining a balanced life. So I am not saying that we are to be workaholics. But I am saying that sometimes we get out of balance the other way.

How do we balance the two? In all things we need to use wisdom.

Equal Opportunity

Then the kingdom of heaven shall be likened to ten virgins
who took their lamps and went to meet the bridegroom.

Five of them were foolish (thoughtless, without forethought)
and five were wise (sensible, intelligent, and prudent).

For when the foolish took their lamps,
they did not take any [extra] oil with them;

But the wise took flasks of oil along
with them [also] with their lamps.

While the bridegroom lingered and was slow in coming,
they all began nodding their heads, and they fell asleep.

But at midnight there was a shout,
Behold, the bridegroom! Go out to meet him!

Then all those virgins got up and put their own lamps in order.

And the foolish said to the wise, Give us
some of your oil, for our lamps are going out.

Matthew 25:1-8

All ten of these virgins had the same opportunity. Half of them took extra oil with them, while five of them did not.

· Lazy people will never do anything extra. They may do what they have to do to get by, but they will never go beyond the basic requirements of life. ·

When the bridegroom stayed longer than expected, all the virgins fell asleep. But at midnight there was a shout that the bridegroom was coming. All the virgins began to get their lamps ready to go out to meet him. But the five foolish virgins did not have enough oil, so they said to the five wise virgins, "Give us some of your oil."

That happens every time. The foolish are always wanting what the wise have worked so hard to get. Usually when they don't get it, they end up feeling sorry for themselves.

For years I felt sorry for myself because I had been abused as a child, because I didn't have everything I wanted, because I didn't get to go to college and on and on. Finally, God dealt with me and said, "Joyce, you can be pitiful or you can be powerful, but you cannot be both."

Five of the virgins in Matthew chapter 25 were pitiful, and they lost out because they hadn't kept their lamps filled with oil. All ten of the virgins had the same opportunity, but when the bridegroom came, the five virgins without the oil missed their opportunity to go with him because they were out trying to buy some oil for their lamps.

> GOD IS AN EQUAL-OPPORTUNITY EMPLOYER. EVERYONE HAS AN EQUAL OPPORTUNITY TO BE BLESSED AND USED BY HIM.

God is an equal-opportunity employer. It doesn't matter to Him what kind of background we came from, what kind of parents or family life we had, what color or gender we are, what kind of education we have, what our physical handicaps may be. None of those things make any difference to Him. In Him, we all have equal opportunity. Anyone who will follow His guidelines and do what He tells them to do can be blessed and used by Him.

God has put the same potential in us that He has put in anybody else. If we will work with God to develop that potential, we can do just as great a thing as the next person.

All of us can dream. Every one of us has an equal opportunity. Each of us can have hope. Remember, we serve a God Who says that with Him all things are possible. Every day we can wake up brimming with hope that today things are going to change for the better. We can say, "I am going to change; my life is going to change and my finances are going to change."

Be patient with yourself. Keep pressing on and believe that you are changing every day. Don't be satisfied with being anything less than all you can be.

Be All That You Can Be

*For it is like a man who was about to take a long journey, and
he called his servants together and entrusted them with his property.*

*To one he gave five talents [probably about $5,000], to another two, to
another one — to each in proportion to his own personal ability. . . .*

Matthew 25:14,15

In verses 14 through 29 of the same chapter as the story of the ten
virgins, Jesus went on to tell the story of a man who was going on a
long journey, so he called his servants together and gave them different
amounts of money to handle, **depending upon their abilities.**

No, we do not all have the same talents and abilities. We cannot all
do the same things, but we can all be what God has called us
individually to be. I cannot be what you are, and you cannot be what I
am, but we can each be all that God wants us to be.

When God gave Moses leaders to help him with his task of
governing the Israelites, some were to be rulers over thousands, some
over hundreds, some over fifties and some over tens.[7]

Not everyone is anointed, or filled with the inner strength of the
Holy Spirit, to lead thousands. Some are anointed to lead hundreds or
fifties or tens. But whatever you are anointed to do, if you will be
obedient to do it, you will find personal fulfillment in it. And as long as
you have that sense of personal fulfillment and satisfaction, knowing in
your heart that you are doing what God has called and anointed you to
do, you will not have to compare yourself with anybody else; you will
not have to be in competition with anyone else.

Whatever you are called to do, do it with excellence. Do it in a
superior way. If you are called to lead fifty, then be an outstanding leader
of fifty. Don't try to lead a thousand because if you do, you will make a
fool of yourself. Likewise, if you are called to lead a thousand, don't try
to ignore your real call and lead fifty just because you don't want to do
the hard work and take the responsibility. If you do, you will never be
fulfilled or satisfied.

If I were still trying to have a small ministry in Fenton, Missouri, I
would not be fulfilled or satisfied. Yes, there is a lot of work and

responsibility in a huge ministry like mine. There is also a lot of financial responsibility.

Speaking to thousands of people on television every day is an unbelievable responsibility. I know that I don't always say everything just right. I have to make sure that I am *rightly dividing the word of truth*[8] for all those people, as the Bible says we should do, and not teaching them something that is wrong or unbalanced. Because it is such a huge responsibility, I have to trust God a great deal. But I would be miserable if I refused to do it because I wanted something easier. It might be easier on my flesh, but it would be harder on my spirit, or my heart. I would go around sick inside all the time.

There are a lot of people who are sick inside because they are not fulfilled. They are not being all they can be and are not doing all they know they are supposed to be doing. They are letting the devil and/or other people talk them out of their calling and their blessing.

That's what happened to one of the servants in the passage in Matthew chapter 25. The man who was going on the journey gave talents to three of his servants before he left. While he was gone, one invested what he was given and received it back with interest, so when the man returned and found out what the servant had done with the talent, he said, "Well done, good and faithful servant. You have been faithful over little, so I will make you ruler over much."

The second man did the same thing and was told the same thing by the man. But the third man went and buried his talent in the ground because he was afraid. When the man found out what that servant had done, he was so upset with him that he took away the talent he had and gave it to the servant who had the ten talents.[9]

Many people are like that third servant. They hide their talent because they are afraid — afraid of responsibility, afraid of judgment, afraid of what people will think. They are afraid to step out, afraid they might fail, afraid of criticism, afraid of other people's opinions, afraid of being misunderstood. They are afraid of the sacrifice and hard work involved.

I do not want you to be afraid to take the talent God has given you and use it for His glory. I don't want you to end up unhappy, unfulfilled and dissatisfied because you are compromising what God has placed in you.

I hope that by the power of the Holy Spirit I am lighting a fire inside you so that you will take a stand against our enemy Satan and be determined to press on toward the high calling of God in Jesus Christ,[10] always abounding in His service, knowing that your labor is not in vain.[11]

CHAPTER 3

STABILITY RELEASES ABILITY, PART 1

In Chapters 1 and 2 we saw that the development of our personal potential is our number one job. Everyone has more potential than they use. Possibility does not mean something that is positively going to happen. It means that it can happen, if we add the other ingredients with it.

I liken potential to a cake mix. Just because I have a cake mix on my kitchen shelf does not guarantee that I am going to have a cake. There are a few things that I must do to get the potential cake from the shelf to an actual cake on the table.

Each of us has potential because God shares Himself with us. He puts gifts and talents within us. But, like the potential in the cake mix, those gifts and talents must be taken and developed.

Dave and I take a lot of pictures, but we are not very good at getting them developed. Sometimes there are rolls and rolls of film lying around the house, and I don't even know what's on them, so what good do they do me? Unless I have them developed, they are a waste of time and money.

There is a lot of wasted potential in the church because people are not developing what God has given them. That is why I urge you to take whatever gifts and talents you have and develop them. You can change your life and make a difference in someone else's life.

We also saw in Chapters 1 and 2 that between potential and the manifestation of that potential lies **effort.** Ecclesiastes 5:3 says, *For a dream comes with much business and painful effort. . . .*

I believe I am a classic example of what God can do with somebody who, in the natural, doesn't appear to have much going for them but who is willing to put out the effort required to develop their potential.

I am not putting myself down, but the truth is, as I mentioned before, I do not have a lot of gifts and talents. I am not creative or artistic or musical. But I can talk. I have a gift of communication both verbally and in writing. So I am taking that gift and developing it for God's service. I am doing what God put in my heart.

Sometimes Dave and I discuss what we see ahead for Life In The Word Ministries and what we see ahead for us. We feel that God just wants us to keep on doing what we are doing, keep doing more of what we're doing, and keep doing it well and with excellence.

I have many goals and ideas on how to spread the Gospel more effectively, but I don't go beyond my gifts and calling. If I did, it would only cause frustration.

> **TO REMAIN STABLE, SIMPLY KEEP DOING WHAT GOD HAS CALLED YOU TO DO.**

I hear from God on a regular basis; He speaks to me in my heart and in His Word about different things. But sometimes I go for a long time without receiving a direct word from Him saying "Do this" or "Do that" about the ministry.

But that doesn't bother me because I know I am doing what He wants me to do. If He wants me to keep on doing that until Jesus comes,[1] then that is what I am going to do. I am endeavoring to remain stable — to simply keep doing what God has called me to do.

As we will see later, reaching that point with anything we are called to do requires a testing process that builds character and develops stability.

Anyone can acquire stability; it is not limited to those in ministry. **It is imperative not only for a good leader but for every person to develop stability because God wants to do more with our life than we could ever imagine possible.**

DISPLAY STABILITY

I am calling up memories of your sincere and unqualified faith (the leaning of your entire personality on God in Christ in

absolute trust and confidence in His power, wisdom, and goodness),
[a faith] that first lived permanently in [the heart of] your
grandmother Lois and your mother Eunice and now,
I am [fully] persuaded, [dwells] in you also.

That is why I would remind you to stir up (rekindle the embers of,
fan the flame of, and keep burning) the [gracious] gift of God,
[the inner fire] that is in you by means of the laying on of
my hands [with those of the elders at your ordination].

For God did not give us a spirit of timidity (of cowardice, of craven
and cringing and fawning fear), but [He has given us a spirit]
of power and of love and of calm and well-balanced
mind and discipline and self-control.

2 Timothy 1:5-7

I have a feeling that in these last days[2] there is going to be a
resurrection of some teaching that has not been popular for quite a while
but which, nonetheless, we all need to hear. I think we are going to have
to be reminded (as Paul was doing here in this passage with his young
disciple Timothy) of being willing to sacrifice or to suffer to fulfill the
call of God on our life. Everything we have to do is not going to feel
good all the time.

There is a right kind of suffering that is taught in the Bible. Now
obviously we are not talking about poverty, disease and personal disaster.
But if you and I are going to do what God wants us to do, we are going
to have to suffer in the flesh to do it.

Timothy was a young minister who was feeling like giving up. The
fire that he once had within him was beginning to grow cold. The
apostle Paul was writing to him to encourage him and even to correct
him about the attitude he was allowing to take control of him.

There was a lot going on in the church in those days. There was a
great deal of persecution. Timothy had some fears, and they were
beginning to get to him.

We all go through those periods of frustration and fear in our life
and ministry. We all experience those times when it seems that
everything is kind of crashing down upon us. We all feel at times that we
just can't keep going on anymore.

Has the devil ever told you in your mind that you just can't do what you are doing any longer?

Well, I want you to know that I hear that too — on a regular basis, especially when I am out on the road, going from town to town, living in hotels and staying up late at night ministering and preparing for the next day. Sometimes when I wake up in the morning, I am so tired from preaching and studying I will hear the devil say in my mind, "You can't do this anymore. You just can't do it any longer."

I was so glad to find out that it was the devil because for a long time I thought it was me. Now that I know it is the devil and that, as we saw before, *he is a liar . . . and the father of lies,* I can say, "**Satan, you're a liar. I can do this because God is my strength.**"

When I return home and get a little rest, I am ready to go back out and do it all again.

Timothy was at the place I get to sometimes. He was worn out and ready to give up. So Paul had to write the passage in 2 Timothy 1:5-7 to him to remind him of the faith that he had inherited from his grandmother, Lois, and his mother, Eunice. He urged him to *stir up* and *rekindle the embers,* to *fan the flame* and *keep burning . . . the [gracious] gift of God,* the fire that was within him. He told him in verse 7 that God had not given him a *spirit of fear; but of power, and of love, and of a sound mind,* as the *King James Version* puts it. But *The Amplified Bible* translates this last phrase as a *calm and well-balanced mind and discipline and self-control.*

> **TO SEE A RELEASE OF OUR POTENTIAL, WE MUST DISPLAY STABILITY.**

So what was Paul really saying to young Timothy? He was saying, "Timothy, straighten up. Don't go by how you feel. You may feel like giving up, but I want to see some **stability** in you."

If we ever want to see a release of our potential, we must display stability.

STABILITY THROUGH OBEDIENCE

Webster's II New College Dictionary defines *stability* as "1. Resistance to sudden change, dislodgment, or overthrow. 2. **a.** Constancy of character or purpose: STEADFASTNESS. **b.** Reliability: dependability."[3]

If we have stability, we do what is right when it feels good and when it doesn't feel good — we pray when we feel like praying and when we don't feel like praying; we give when we feel like giving and when we don't feel like giving; we give away not only what we want to give away, but what we don't want to give away, if God tells us to do so.

If you and I are going to have such stability, we are going to have to be obedient when we feel like it and when we don't feel like it.

I don't know about you, but I have made up my mind that I am going to be stable. I am going to do what I believe God has told me to do in my heart and in His Word, no matter what.

We've already seen that the Bible tells us that God has not given us a spirit of fear, but of power, love and a sound, well-balanced mind.

I love *The Amplified Bible* translation of that verse because it tells me something I might not have known otherwise. It tells me that the Spirit of God on the inside of me is a spirit of discipline and self-control.

STOP THE EMOTIONAL YO-YO

But the fruit of the [Holy] Spirit [the work which His presence within accomplishes] is love, joy (gladness), peace, patience (an even temper, forbearance), kindness, goodness (benevolence), faithfulness,

Gentleness (meekness, humility), self-control (self-restraint, continence). . . .

Galatians 5:22,23

According to this Scripture, self-control is a fruit of the Holy Spirit. If we want to be leaders, we must be able to control ourselves. We must also be trustworthy. God must be able to trust us. Trustworthiness is a by-product of stability.

Nothing irritates me more than to have people on my staff or my ministry team who are up and down all the time so that I never know what they are going to do. I call them "high maintenance" employees. Such people irritate me because I have to deal with them constantly.

The reason we have to be constantly dealing with people like that is because they follow their emotions rather than following the leadership of the Holy Spirit within them. If they don't learn to follow the Holy Spirit through the inner knowing He gives and by reading and obeying the Word, they will never develop into what God wants them to be.

TRUSTWORTHI-NESS IS A BY-PRODUCT OF STABILITY.

Leaders have to be in control of themselves and discipline themselves. They have to be able to recognize when they are going in a wrong direction and make the appropriate corrections themselves without someone else having to do it for them.

That kind of emotional stability, self-control and self-restraint is not limited to leaders; it is something we all need to develop more of in our lives.

I remember the years when I was what I call a "Christian yo-yo." I was continually up and down. If Dave did what I liked, I was happy. If he didn't do what I liked, I would get mad.

I have grown since those days. Dave still doesn't always do the things I like, but now it doesn't upset me the way it used to. The reason it doesn't upset me as much now is that I have learned to exercise self-control.

You may have a great marriage, as Dave and I do now (after I went through some major changes with the help of the Holy Spirit), but you are never going to be married to anyone who is going to do what you want all the time. If you are the type who is happy every time your mate does what you like and unhappy every time your mate doesn't do what you like, then you are going to be the way I used to be — up and down all the time.

God does not want us to be up and down. He wants us to be stable.

I hope you are hungry for stability because if you are, you can be helped by what you read in this book.

FOCUS ON WHAT YOU BELIEVE

If you and I are ever to develop stability in our lives, our flesh is going to suffer once in a while because we are going to have to choose to do what is right, even when we don't feel like it.

More than any other single thing, believers tell me how they feel:

"I feel that nobody loves me."

"I feel that my spouse doesn't treat me right."

"I feel that I am never going to have any happiness or success in my life."

"I feel . . . I feel . . . I don't feel . . . ," and on and on it goes.

It seems that we are feeling or not feeling all the time. As Christians, instead of concentrating on how we **feel,** we need to be focusing on what we **believe.**

To be honest, I don't always feel anointed, but I believe I am. I don't always feel like preaching and teaching, but I get up and do it anyway. Why? Because it is my responsibility. I am a leader. People are depending on me.

> AS CHRISTIANS, INSTEAD OF CONCENTRATING ON HOW WE <u>FEEL</u>, WE NEED TO BE FOCUSING ON WHAT WE <u>BELIEVE</u>.

How can we be leaders if we are going to follow our feelings? We have to go by what we believe is right. If we wait to **feel** like doing what is right, we may never get around to it.

If we're going to be a leader, we can't just go with how we feel; we have to do what's right.

We all have flesh, and we have to be able to divide between soul and spirit.[4] We must be able to distinguish whether it is our soul — our mind, will and emotions — leading us or whether it is the Holy Spirit leading us. If it is our soul trying to lead us, then we must have the strength and determination to say no and then choose to go with the Spirit.

That is what the Bible means by stability — the ability to exercise self-discipline and self-control.

MANAGE YOUR EMOTIONS

As we consider the qualifications for leadership, it is amazing how often we find reference to self-discipline and emotional control. In fact, it is so important that I wrote an entire book on this subject entitled *Managing Your Emotions.*[5]

In this book I explain that since our emotions are never going to go away, we must learn to manage them rather than letting them manage us.

We always want unpleasant or troublesome things to go away. If something is bothering us or causing us problems, we want to get prayer and have somebody cast that thing out of our lives and make it leave us alone.

God, on the other hand, wants us to grow up and realize that there are some things in this life that we must learn to control ourselves. One of those things is our emotions.

For example, just because I feel like smacking someone up the side of the head does not mean that I am to allow myself to do that. I cannot do everything I feel like doing.

Not too long ago I told my husband, "Dave, do you know what I feel like doing? I feel like running away from home!"

> **LEADERS DON'T RUN AWAY FROM THINGS THEY DON'T LIKE. THEY STAY AND DEAL WITH THEM.**

At that time I felt that everything in my life was caving in on me. There were problems at the office, problems in the home, problems everywhere I looked. I thought, **I want to get out of here. I don't want anybody talking to me. I want to go some place where nobody knows me or recognizes me. I just want everyone to leave me alone. I wish I could run away from home.**

But I knew I wouldn't do that because I couldn't. **I am a leader, and leaders do not run away from things they don't like. They stay and deal with them.**

If you and I are to be leaders, we must realize that we will not be able to do or say everything that is on the inside of us.

That is especially true in marriage.

My husband, Dave, and I are a team; we run a home and a ministry together. Even though we have totally different personalities, we have to dwell with one another in peace and walk in love with each other as good examples. I think we get along wonderfully considering the amount of time we spend together and all the decisions we make together.

Ours is not a marriage in which we each get in our little car in the morning and go off to work after spending fifteen minutes together. We don't come home in the evening and spend another hour and a half together before bedtime, then get up the next day and do the same thing. No, we are together all the time, constantly, day and night. When you do that with your spouse, you had better be married to someone you can get along with very well!

To tell the truth, as much as I love Dave, there are probably at least fifty times a week when I have to shut my mouth even though I really **feel** like saying something that would cause trouble. But I know by the Holy Spirit within me that if I say anything to Dave right then, we are going to have a problem. So I exercise self-control and keep my mouth shut. There are many times, I am sure, when Dave does the same thing for me.

We have both learned that, as we cannot say and do everything that we want to say and do in order to have a successful marriage, the same principle applies to our being leaders in the kingdom of God.

If you are going to be a leader, you are not going to be able to say everything you want to say, do everything you want to do, go everywhere you want to go, eat everything you want to eat, stay up as late as you want to stay up or get up when you feel like getting up.

You are going to have to exercise self-control.

You are going to have to say to your flesh, "You **are** going to line up with what is right, whether you like it or not!"

For the leader, there is a higher calling involved. There is something more important than satisfying the flesh, something more important than feeling good all the time.

To be able to follow the Spirit rather than the desires of the flesh, you have to really **want** to be a leader.

DESIRE FOR LEADERSHIP IS GOOD

The saying is true and irrefutable: If any man [eagerly]
seeks the office of bishop (superintendent, overseer),
he desires an excellent task (work).

1 Timothy 3:1

It is a good thing to desire leadership. There is nothing wrong with wanting to be a leader. But according to the following passage, there are some qualifications that must be met if a person is to be a leader in the kingdom of God.

Let's look at some of these scriptural requirements for spiritual leadership.

BE ABOVE REPROACH

Now a bishop (superintendent, overseer) must give no grounds for accusation but must be above reproach, the husband of one wife, circumspect and temperate and self-controlled; [he must be] sensible and well behaved and dignified and lead an orderly (disciplined) life; [he must be] hospitable [showing love for and being a friend to the believers, especially strangers or foreigners, and be] a capable and qualified teacher.

1 Timothy 3:2

A spiritual leader must give no grounds for accusation. They must be above reproach. That means that they must behave so well that people cannot find any reason to accuse them of wrongdoing or bring any kind of accusation against them.

Dave and I cannot occupy positions of spiritual leadership, teaching other people how to live their lives, if we are out in public displaying ungodly behavior. If we are going to lead, we must be examples to others. We cannot teach people to do something and then not do it ourselves.

That was what the Pharisees did, which is why Jesus called them hypocrites. They taught others what to do, but they did not do it themselves.[6]

Also notice that the leader must be circumspect, temperate, self-controlled and **sensible.** I love that last requirement. The biggest problem with many people, including some in the body of Christ, is that they are just plain goofy. Sometimes it seems that when people get born again and filled with the Holy Spirit, or filled with God's power and ability to fulfill His will for our life, some of them think they have to throw all common sense out the window. Just the opposite is true. If a person is going to build a ministry, he is going to have to have a lot of plain old common sense, as we are told in Proverbs 24:3,4 TLB: *Any* *enterprise is built by wise planning, becomes strong through* **common sense,** *and profits wonderfully by keeping abreast of the facts.*

Notice also in 1 Timothy 3:2 that a leader must be well behaved and dignified, leading an orderly and disciplined life. There it is again: **discipline.**

We must be hospitable and friendly, especially to foreigners or those who are outsiders. For example, in any kind of social gathering like a party, a church service or other function, we need to go out of our way to make people outside of our family and friends feel comfortable and accepted.

Finally, in this verse we are told that a leader must be a capable and qualified teacher. This involves teaching by example. People want to see Christians who live good, clean lives. They want to be able to trust someone, and it is our job to pass along the principles of godly living to others.[7] One area where this must be done is in the home.

TAKE CARE OF OUR HOUSEHOLD

Not given to wine, not combative but gentle and considerate, not quarrelsome but forbearing and peaceable, and not a lover of money [insatiable for wealth and ready to obtain it by questionable means].

He must rule his own household well, keeping his children under control, with true dignity, commanding their respect in every way and keeping them respectful.

For if a man does not know how to rule his own household, how is he to take care of the church of God?

1 Timothy 3:3-5

That is a mouthful. It is a full-time job to keep our children respectful. We really have to work at it. We have to continually say, "I am not going to put up with that kind of attitude and behavior. You are going to show respect."

Sometimes in the natural it is easier just to let kids get by with things than it is to endure what we have to go through to correct them.

When Dave used to punish our kids by making them stay in for two weeks, I felt like he was punishing me, not them. I would say,

"Couldn't we just take away their allowance or something? If they have to stay in the house for two weeks, you go off to work, but I have to stay here with them."

In order to raise children right, sometimes we have to suffer. We have to go through some hard things that we would rather not go through. I believe that is one reason kids are having the problems they are today because we as parents are so busy we don't want to take the time to properly deal with correcting our children; it's just too much trouble.

Paul says that if a person does not know how to rule his own household, how is he going to be able to take care of the church? Now when Paul talks about ruling our household, he's not talking about authoritarian, controlling or iron-fisted rule. **The successful leader is capable of guiding, leading and nurturing their household with godly wisdom, love and understanding.**

Pass the Test

He must not be a new convert, or he may [develop a beclouded and stupid state of mind] as the result of pride [be blinded by conceit, and] fall into the condemnation that the devil [once] did.

Furthermore, he must have a good reputation and be well thought of by those outside [the church], lest he become involved in slander and incur reproach and fall into the devil's trap.

In like manner the deacons [must be] worthy of respect, not shifty and double-talkers but sincere in what they say, not given to much wine, not greedy for base gain [craving wealth and resorting to ignoble and dishonest methods of getting it].

They must possess the mystic secret of the faith [Christian truth as hidden from ungodly men] with a clear conscience.

And let them also be tried and investigated and proved first; then, if they turn out to be above reproach, let them serve [as deacons].

1 Timothy 3:6-10

Here Paul warns against putting a person into a leadership position too quickly because we need to be prepared. Preparation involves going through some tests, some hard, dry places. Hard times change us. They develop our character. They mature us. They force us to look to God instead of to ourselves, to people or to things. Without preparation, we will become filled with pride and end up with disastrous results.[8]

Paul emphasizes that in the Scripture above. He says that those who seek positions of leadership must be put to the test and proven before they can be given responsibility in the church. If they pass the test, then they can serve as leaders of the people and fulfill the call of God upon their lives.

If you are frustrated right now because of an unfulfilled call of God upon your life, I can tell you where you are: You are in the testing ground. What God does with you later on fully depends upon how you pass the test you are being put to right now.

> TO BE STABLE, WE MUST MAKE UP OUR MIND THAT WE WILL DO WHAT IS RIGHT WHETHER IT FEELS GOOD OR NOT.

Later in this book we will consider in detail some of the tests that we must go through in order for God to develop character in us. One of those is the stability test, which is not easy to pass.

In order to be stable, we have to make up our mind that we are going to do right whether it feels good or not. We are going to have to read the Bible and do what it instructs us to do whether we like it or not, whether we want to or not, whether we feel like it or not.

If we are going to stay in the flow of the Holy Spirit, we have to do what He tells us to do in our heart and through the Word. We are not a board member who gets to vote on it; we are required to be obedient to it.

CHAPTER 4

STABILITY RELEASES ABILITY, PART 2

Because the Lord God helps me, I will not be dismayed;
therefore, I have set my face like flint to do
his will, and I know that I will triumph.

Isaiah 50:7 TLB

We have seen that every one of us must be the kind of person God can trust. If we are not stable, then we cannot be trusted by God or anyone else.

In our ministry, I want people working with me whom I can trust to do what they are expected to do, people who have been tested and proven so that I can know what they are going to do in any given situation.

For example, one time I was scheduled to hold a meeting in a certain city. Because of an airline flight cancellation, my team and I ended up having to drive so that we arrived in town just two hours before the meeting was supposed to begin. We had many things to do to get ready for that meeting, things like setting up our equipment and running sound tests.

In all that hurried time, I did not hear one word of complaint from that team of people. I did not see evidence of a single bad attitude. We were actually laughing and having fun. That was possible because we had people helping us who knew what to do and how to do it with a good attitude, people who were stable.

I am so glad that God has given me stable employees and coworkers, stable friends, a stable family and a stable husband. Stability is probably the keynote of Dave's life. All those early years of our marriage and ministry when I was up and down emotionally, screaming at Dave and the kids and getting extremely upset about our bills and money, Dave was always right there, both feet firmly planted on the ground, as stable as a rock.

In fact, Dave was so stable I used to get upset with him. I would complain, "You don't feel anything. You don't have any emotions. You wouldn't know one if it slapped you in the face."

When we are unstable and erratic, we get aggravated at the stable people in our lives. We want them to get upset along with us. The very fact that they are stable convicts us that we are not.

In those days I would be at the kitchen table counting up the money and adding up the bills, and there would always be more bills than money, so I would get all upset.

Dave would be in the living room with the kids, watching television and playing games with them. I would get so mad at him I would say, "Why don't you come in here and do something?"

"What do you want me to do?" he would ask. "You've already told me how much money we have and how much the bills are. You quit your job to prepare for the ministry because that is what God told you to do. We are committed to do what He says and trust Him. We are tithing. He takes care of us. Every month He provides what we need to keep going. Do we have to go through all this again?"

Then he would say, "Joyce, you want me to come and be miserable with you, and I'm not going to do it. You're just mad because I'm having fun. You can come and have fun too if you want to. If you want to stay away and be miserable, that's up to you. There is nothing I can do to make you happy, and I am not going to let you make me miserable."

I can still remember the rage I felt. It would come over me so strongly that I just wanted to do **something.** But all I could do was fume.

If we want to be leaders, all of that kind of thing has to die. We have got to quit going around and around the same mountain. We have got to quit taking the same test and failing it again and again. But no matter how many times we fail, God will never "flunk" us out of His school. We just have to do retakes until we get it right.

I had a call on my life, and God was telling me, "Joyce, I love you. I have put My gifts within you. I have great things in mind for you. But for them to come to pass, you must get stable."

God does not want us to change every time our circumstances change. He wants us to always be the same, just as He is.

> NO MATTER HOW MANY TIMES WE FAIL, GOD WILL NEVER "FLUNK" US OUT OF HIS SCHOOL. WE JUST DO RETAKES UNTIL WE GET IT RIGHT.

Stability Is Unchanging

Jesus Christ (the Messiah) is [always] the same, yesterday, today, [yes] and forever (to the ages).

Hebrews 13:8

What is the main thing that we love so much about Jesus? There are many answers to that question, of course, such as the fact that He died for us on the cross so we wouldn't have to be punished for our sins; then He rose again on the third day.[1] But in our daily relationship with Him, one of the things that we appreciate most about Him is the fact that we can count on Him not to change.

We love Jesus and are able to trust Him because He is never changing. He has said in His Word, "This is the way I was, and this is the way I'm always going to be."[2] If you can count on anything, you can count on Jesus never changing. He can change anything else that needs to be changed, but He always remains the same.

That is the kind of friends I want, the kind of employees I want and the kind of person I want to be. That is the kind of leader I want to be. I want to have that kind of stability in my life, so that people can know they can count on me.

There was a time in my life when my emotions had control over me. I was not managing them; they were managing me. In those days, I didn't know what I know now.

Not only could others not count on me, but there were times when my emotions had such control over me that I couldn't even count on myself. I never knew what I was going to do. I would get up each day wondering what I was going to do that day, what I was going to be like.

Jesus is not that way. You could say that He has emotional maturity. Part of that maturity is that He is **always** the same — stable, unchanging, dependable, trustworthy. That kind of emotional maturity should be our goal.

MAKE DECISIONS BASED ON THE LEADING OF THE HOLY SPIRIT, NOT ON FEELINGS.

Being emotionally mature means making decisions based on the leading of the Holy Spirit, not on our feelings. But it doesn't come naturally.

Just knowing these things is not going to make our emotions go away. But we have a God Who is able. When we come to the place where we want to stop giving in to our emotions, we can trust Him to help us mature and be emotionally stable just like His Own Son Jesus.

That doesn't mean we become emotionless. God gave us emotions so we could enjoy life. A life without feelings would be a terribly dull life. Being emotionally stable just means that we have a balanced emotional life. As believers in Jesus, it is rightfully ours; it becomes part of our spiritual inheritance when we turn our life over to Him.[3]

So the next time your emotions flare up, I encourage you to rise up and say to them, "**No, you have run me long enough. Now I'm taking over and taking control of you in the strength and power of the Holy Spirit.**"

GOD IS GOOD — ALL THE TIME

Every good gift and every perfect (free, large, full)
gift is from above; it comes down from the Father of all
[that gives] light, in [the shining of] Whom there can be no variation
[rising or setting] or shadow cast by His turning [as in an eclipse].

James 1:17

What is James saying in this verse? He is saying that God is good, period. He is not good sometimes; He is always good. He is not good plus something else; He is just good.

James is also saying that God is unvarying. With God there is no turning, no variation. We have seen that His Son Jesus never changes. In

John 10:30 we are told that Jesus and God are the same. If Jesus never changes, God never changes; whether in the form of the Father, His Son Jesus or the Holy Spirit, He is always the same.

God is always the same — He is always just good. If we are having a hard time, God is still good. If something bad happens to us, God is still good. God is a good God, and He wants to do good things for us. He doesn't do good things for us because we are good and we deserve them; He does good things for us because He is good.

> GOD WANTS TO DO GOOD THINGS FOR US, NOT BECAUSE WE ARE GOOD AND DESERVE THEM, BUT BECAUSE <u>HE</u> IS GOOD.

The world still needs to learn that truth. So do some in the church.

STABILITY IS PROGRESSIVE

And [further], You, Lord, did lay the foundation of the earth in the beginning, and the heavens are the works of Your hands.

They will perish, but You remain and continue permanently; they will all grow old and wear out like a garment.

Like a mantle [thrown about one's self] You will roll them up, and they will be changed and replaced by others. But You remain the same, and Your years will never end nor come to failure.

Hebrews 1:10-12

How comforting it is to know that although everything else in the world may change, God always remains the same. How could we put the trust in God He wants from us if we did not believe that He is always faithful, that somehow He always comes through to meet our needs, whatever they may be?

God **always** loves us unconditionally. He doesn't love us if we are good and then stop loving us if we are bad. He always loves us. He is always kind, always slow to anger, always full of grace and mercy, always ready to forgive.

What would happen in our lives and in the lives of those around us if we were like God? What would happen if we were always loving, always slow to anger, always filled with grace and mercy, always ready to forgive? What would happen if we, like God, were always positive, peaceful and generous?

We're not supposed to be emotionally up and down like a yo-yo. We're supposed to be stable. Our problem is that we are always changing.

My husband and I have been married for more than thirty years, and every single day of our marriage Dave Meyer has gotten out of bed in a good mood. Not only that, but he's not out of bed more than five minutes before he's singing.

In the beginning I was just the opposite. I wanted him to be quiet so I could think. I wanted to get all my problems figured out first. Thank God, I have changed.

When Dave and I were first married, I had all kinds of problems as a result of the abuse I had suffered in my early life. Since I had never known any kind of stability, I didn't even know what it was.

You may have been raised by unstable people. If so, like me, you may have to learn that the erratic, emotional life you have always been used to is not the norm. It is not what God wants for you.

God wants you to come into a place of stability. You will never be able to enjoy life as you were meant to do until you become stable.

> YOU WILL NOT ENJOY LIFE AS YOU WERE MEANT TO UNTIL YOU BECOME STABLE.

Dave tells me that he remembers how I was before I began to become emotionally stable. He says, "I can remember driving home from work at night thinking to myself, **Well, I wonder what Joyce will be like tonight."**

You may be like Dave. You may be married to a person who is unstable. If so, you know that such people are hard to live with. It is hard on relationships when people are so unstable that no one can count on them or even know what they are going to be like from one moment to the next.

That is not to say that we never have bad days. I don't think everybody can be like Dave. But he has been an example for me, and by living with him and learning from him, I have come a long, long way. I believe that now I am stable about 99 percent of the time. I still have a little more fire in me than he does, so if I get mad, it may take me a while longer to get back to normal again. But now it takes me two or three minutes, when it used to take me two or three weeks! So I thank God for the progress I have made.

I know that anyone can change if I can because I had a bad case of instability. But I kept making progress until I became a stable person. That is one thing God desires for each of us — stability. He does not expect us to become perfect at it overnight, but He wants to help us to become more and more like Him day by day.

THE LORD IS A ROCK

He [God] *is the Rock, His work is perfect, for all His ways are law and justice. A God of faithfulness without breach or deviation, just and right is He.*

Deuteronomy 32:4

In the Old Testament, Moses did not become the leader God used to deliver the Israelites out of bondage overnight. Later on we will talk more about him in his position of leadership. In this passage, he is speaking to the Israelites about the Lord. He is telling them what he learned that God is really like.

He was telling them that God is a Rock, that He is unchanging and undeviating, or stable, that He is great and unfailing, that He is faithful and just, perfect and right in all His doings.

According to the *Jamieson, Fausset and Brown Commentary,* the word "rock" in this Scripture is **"expressive of power and stability. The application of it in this passage is to declare that God had been true to His covenant with their** [the Israelites] **fathers and them. Nothing that He had promised had failed . . . the metaphor of a 'rock' as a refuge, or to represent the divine faithfulness and stability of purpose, occurs more than once in this song** [Deuteronomy, chapter 32, is referred to as the Song of Moses], **and frequently in other parts of Scripture."**[4]

God is called the Rock in this passage and in other parts of the Bible because He is solid and stable. He is never moved by the things that move us. It seems the "natural" flow of the flesh to have emotional ups and downs, to be moved by our circumstances and feelings. As we have seen, the Lord changes not; He cannot be moved. To become a strong leader, we should follow His example.

THE ROCK AS OUR EXAMPLE

For they are a nation void of counsel,
and there is no understanding in them.

O that they were wise and would see through
this [present triumph] to their ultimate fate!

How could one have chased a thousand, and two
put ten thousand to flight, except their Rock had
sold them, and the Lord had delivered them up?

For their rock is not like our Rock,
even our enemies themselves judge this.

Deuteronomy 32:28-31

> GOD IS OUR
> ROCK, BUT
> HE IS ALSO
> OUR EXAMPLE.

When I read this last verse I got tickled. I thought about the ad on television for a certain insurance company which shows an image of a big rock and says, in essence, "Get this insurance and you can have a piece of the rock."

As much as I believe in the wisdom of having insurance, I can tell you that their rock is not like our Rock. The temporal rock the world offers us is not like the Rock of Ages.

Our Rock is a place of refuge. He is stable, steadfast, faithful, dependable, always there, always the same, always good and loving, always kind and merciful. He will never leave us nor forsake us. And we are supposed to be molded and transformed into His image.[5] He is our Rock, but He is also our Example. We are to be the way that He is.

THE ROCK OF FAITH — A SOLID FOUNDATION

Now when Jesus went into the region of Caesarea Philippi,
He asked His disciples, Who do people say that the Son of Man is?

*And they answered, Some say John the Baptist; others
say Elijah; and others Jeremiah or one of the prophets.*

He said to them, But who do you [yourselves] say that I am?

Simon Peter replied, You are the Christ, the Son of the living God.

*Then Jesus answered him, Blessed (happy, fortunate, and to be envied)
are you, Simon Bar-Jonah. For flesh and blood [men] have not
revealed this to you, but My Father Who is in heaven.*

*And I tell you, you are Peter [Greek, **Petros** — a large piece of rock],
and on this rock [Greek, **petra** — a huge rock like Gibraltar]
I will build My church, and the gates of Hades
(the powers of the infernal region) shall not overpower it
[or be strong to its detriment or hold out against it].*

Matthew 16:13-18

When Peter said that Jesus was the Christ, the Son of the living
God, that was a statement of faith. In making that statement, Peter
was displaying faith.

I don't think Peter just casually or nonchalantly made that statement.
I think he said it with a surety and a certainty that impressed Jesus
because He immediately turned to Peter and told him that he was
blessed. Then He went on to say that it was upon that rock, that solid
foundation of faith, that He would build His church.

Jesus was saying to Peter, "If you maintain this faith, it will be a rock-
like substance in your life upon which I will be able to build My kingdom
in you. Your potential will be developed to the place that even the gates
of hell will not be able to prevail against you."

But this promise was not just for Peter alone. Jesus is saying the same
thing to you and me. The problem is that we don't always have faith.
Sometimes we believe, and sometimes we doubt.

FROM FAITH TO FAITH

*For therein is the righteousness of God revealed from
faith to faith: as it is written, The just shall live by faith.*

Romans 1:17 KJV

It has long been a goal of mine to learn how to live from faith to faith.

A number of years ago the Lord revealed to me, "Joyce, you go from faith to doubt to unbelief, and then back to faith to doubt to unbelief."

The trouble with the church today is that we have too much mixture and not enough stability. That mixture is evident in our speech, as we see in James 3:10: *Out of the same mouth come forth blessing and cursing. These things, my brethren, ought not to be so.*

Some time ago God spoke to me about a person I was dealing with whom I was around a good bit of time. This person had a lot of problems in her life. She would be positive for a while. She would say things like, "Oh, praise God, I believe the Lord is going to heal me. Yes, God's going to take care of it. He is going to meet all my needs."

She would do that for two or three days. Then she would get discouraged and depressed and become really negative and critical. She would start saying, "Nothing good is ever going to happen to me. Everybody else gets blessed, but not me. My family members who are unbelievers are more blessed than I am." On and on she would go in that negative vein.

We would minister to her and get her all pumped back up again, but a few days later she would be back down again.

She was like so many of us are sometimes — like a flat tire. We get all pumped up and roll along fine for a while, but then the next thing you know we are flat again.

One day God spoke to me and said clearly in my heart, "What you are seeing is exactly why My people operate at zero power level. They keep mixing positives and negatives. They are positive, which is power, for a while. Then they start to throw in a bunch of negatives, which deletes the power, so that they end up right back at zero."

I don't know about you, but I don't want to operate at zero power. I don't want to have a positive confession for two or three days and a negative one for two or three days so that I am back to zero again.

I think this is one of the reasons that people in the body of Christ sometimes get confused. They think, "I don't understand. I try to do all the right things, but it never seems to produce positive results." The reason is that they negate their positive actions by negative speech.

I'm not saying that I never get negative and that I never complain, but I quickly put a stop to it instead of allowing it to continue for a long time like I used to do. Nobody can say that they never make a mistake like that. But we need to start getting more stable if we want God to trust us with leadership. We need to be dependable, reliable and trustworthy so people know they can trust us and count on us, and so God knows it too.

> **WE NEED TO BE DEPENDABLE, RELIABLE AND TRUSTWORTHY SO PEOPLE KNOW THEY CAN COUNT ON US, AND GOD KNOWS HE CAN TRUST US WITH LEADERSHIP.**

STABILITY IN FAITH AND TRUST

Trust in, lean on, rely on, and have confidence in Him at all times. . . .

Psalm 62:8

We are not to have faith and trust in God once in a while or occasionally or from time to time, but **at all times.** We must learn to live from faith to faith, trusting the Lord when things are good, and when things are bad.

It is easy to trust God when things are going good, but when things are going bad and we decide to trust God, that is when we develop character.

And the more character we develop, the more our ability can be released. That is why I say that **stability releases ability.**

The more stable we become, the more our ability is going to be released because the potential in us now has some character to carry it.

A lot of people have gifts that can take them places where their character cannot keep them. Gifts are **given,** but character is **developed.**

I could always talk. Even in school I could talk enough to make the teacher think I knew everything about everything she was teaching, when I really didn't know anything.

I have always been a communicator and a convincer. But in order for God to allow me in the pulpit to preach to millions every day, not only did I have to have a gift, I also had to have character so God could trust what I was going to say. Otherwise, He could not allow me to teach that many people because I might say one thing one day and something else the next day.

It is by disciplining our emotions, our moods and our mouths that we become stable enough to remain peaceful whatever our situation or circumstances, so that we are able to walk in the fruit of the Spirit — whether we **feel** like it or not.

> GIFTS ARE GIVEN; CHARACTER IS DEVELOPED. YOU MUST DEVELOP CHARACTER SO GOD CAN TRUST THE WAY YOU WILL USE YOUR GIFTS.

The more stable we become, the more ability can be released through us.

At All Times

I will bless the Lord at all times; His praise shall continually be in my mouth.

Psalm 34:1

Notice that the psalmist says he will bless the Lord — **at all times.**

Besides praising the Lord like this Scripture says, there are several other Scriptures that tell us things to do at all times — resist the devil **at all times,**[6] believe God **at all times,**[7] love others **at all times**[8] — not just when it's convenient or it feels good.

One of my favorite things to do when I've finished doing a conference is to go to a restaurant, sit down and have a good meal. I work hard and that's my way of relaxing. One time, we called a restaurant and asked for a reservation for about fifteen people. They sounded like they'd taken our reservation. But when we got there, the place was jam-packed crowded, and we got in and were told, "We don't take reservations."

I felt the irritation rise in me, and I thought, **Well, why didn't you tell us that on the phone?** Then I told myself, **Joyce, you just got done preaching a conference; just be nice.**

You know it's amazing how sometimes when you talk about what you believe, Satan will come around and test you on it.

We waited forty-five minutes to be seated. They gave us a big, long table, and the waitress took our drink orders. Soon she returned carrying a large tray with all the drinks on it. It was so crowded in there that day that she caught the corner of her tray on the wall trying to get between the wall and our table, and she dropped the tray and dumped all the drinks on my husband.

Dave had on his best suit, and now it was soaked in water, iced tea and pop. At that point we could have blown up and said, "What's the matter with you? Can't you do your job right? Now you've ruined our clothes. I'm never coming to this place again!" But Dave was so nice to the waitress about the whole ordeal. He said to her, "Don't worry about it. It was a mistake. I understand. I used to work at a restaurant, and one time I dumped malts inside a customer's car. He had on a really nice suit and was taking his date out. I know how you feel. Don't worry about it."

Then he went to the manager and said, "I don't want her to get in trouble. The place is overly crowded. She's doing a good job. She's doing the best she can. It wasn't her fault." He just went to the extreme to be nice.

Soon the waitress came back with the second tray of drinks, and you could tell she'd been crying. She said to us, "I just feel so bad. This is my first week, and this is my first big table, and I just feel so bad because I dumped the drinks all over you." Then she leaned a little bit across the table, and she looked right at me and said, "I think I'm just nervous because you're in here. I watch you on television every day."

I tell you, in my heart I started going, **Oh, thank You, God, thank You, thank You, thank You, that we didn't act bad about this!**

What would it have done to her, what would it have said to her about God, about leaders, about television evangelists, if she would have heard me preach every day on television and then seen Dave and me blow up and have a fit over her spilling the drinks on him?

Did I feel like having a fit about it? Yes. The Bible never says that sin dies. It says that since Christ died for our sin we should consider ourselves dead to sin.[9] If we are waiting for sin to die, we are going to be waiting a long time. When I say "waiting for sin to die," I mean waiting not to be tempted by sin. We will always be tempted — the Bible says so — but Jesus taught His disciples to pray that they would not come into the temptation when it did come.[10]

The flesh does not die; we have to kill it, as we read in Colossians 3:5: *So kill (deaden, deprive of power) the evil desire lurking in your members [those animal impulses and all that is earthly in you that is employed in sin]. . . .* We kill it by not giving in to it.

You don't lose the potential you've developed when you fall into sin, but you do hinder progress — not only your progress, but the progress of those around you.

What a mess we would have had if we had given into our flesh instead of being stable in that situation. People would have said, "If that's the way Christians are, I don't want anything to do with Christianity. If that's the way they act, I don't need any part of it. I've got enough trouble of my own. I can act like that without getting saved."

That is why God works with us to develop character in us before He looses us on people — because if we don't have any stability, we are going to ruin His reputation, not help it.

PART 2

THE HEART
OF A LEADER

CHAPTER 5

NEGATIVE CONDITIONS OF THE HEART, PART 1

Let not yours be the [merely] external adorning with [elaborate]
interweaving and knotting of the hair, the wearing of jewelry, or
changes of clothes;

But let it be the inward adorning and beauty of the hidden person of
the heart, with the incorruptible and unfading charm of a gentle and
peaceful spirit, which [is not anxious or wrought up, but] is very
precious in the sight of God.

1 Peter 3:3,4

One of the most important things to God is the heart of a leader,
what the Bible calls the hidden person of the heart. The *King James
Version* calls it *the hidden man of the heart.*[1] When we look at one another,
what we see is not necessarily the way things really are. We can talk and
act like everything is great, but inside we may be hurting, and everything
in our life may be wretched and miserable.

I believe that God is more concerned about our heart than He is
our performance because if our heart is right, our performance will
eventually catch up with that. But if we go around doing the right things
with a wrong heart, what we do won't mean anything to God.

One of the most life-transforming things for me as a leader in the
body of Christ is what God has shown me about the inner life, the
hidden man of the heart. What goes on in us? What kind of heart do we
have? What are we really like inside? What is our thought life like? What
kind of attitude do we have? What goes on behind closed doors? **If we
want to be a good leader, we have to look deeper into those things
that nobody knows about but God and us.**

Years ago, God began to deal with me about the importance of the inner life. It takes us a while to catch on to that importance because we are all so appearance oriented. We go through life trying to keep up outward appearances, forgetting that there is another whole part of us that cannot be seen, but it is a part of us that God sees and is very much in contact with. While the world is busy trying to conquer "outer space," we should strive to conquer "inner space."

> **WHILE THE WORLD IS BUSY TRYING TO CONQUER "OUTER SPACE," WE SHOULD STRIVE TO CONQUER "INNER SPACE."**

When God began to deal with me about this subject, I began to study it, and at that time I did a series of teachings on it. It is kind of sad to me because the series did not sell very well. People would grab up tapes on healing, prosperity and success, but not about maturity, humility and obedience.

I once did a tape series on obedience but had to give it the title "How to Be Radically and Outrageously Blessed." That album sells very well because people want to be blessed. But if I had called it "How to Be Radically and Outrageously Obedient," very few would have bought it. The fact is that if you want to be radically and outrageously blessed, then you've got to be radically and outrageously obedient.

The truth is, we all want results, but we don't want to do what is required to get those results. Because of that, many people just go around and around the same mountains all their life, never getting anywhere.

In his letter in 1 Peter 3, the apostle Peter is using the example of jewelry, makeup and clothes, but that's really not the issue here. He is telling us that we are not to be so concerned with how others see us but with what we really are deep down inside. We need to learn how to live deeper than being concerned only with a superficial, outward appearance.

In Luke 5, Peter and his men had been fishing all night and had caught nothing, so they had brought their boats in and were cleaning their nets and putting them away for the night. Jesus came walking along the banks of the shore, and when He saw them, He came up to them and said, . . . *Put out into the deep [water], and lower your nets for a haul* (v. 4).

A lot of people in the church are fishing and catching nothing, so to speak, because they are not launching out into the deep. As a result, they are not satisfied with their life because they are not living deep enough.

LIVE IN THE RIGHT WAY

The passage in Luke 5 is one of the Scriptures that God used to really begin to change my life. He let me know that He is not the least bit interested in outward things like fancy titles or how many invitations we receive to go and speak somewhere. He wants leaders who have a right heart. He wants us to be in ministry because we want to help people and not because we want to be famous. Leaders are not called to be famous; we are called to hard work, to servanthood, to sacrifice, etc. Ministry is spelled W-O-R-K.

Yes, there are wonderful benefits that go with the office in which we walk, as Paul pointed out in his letter to the church in Corinth.[2] But all of our works are going to have to pass through the fire[3] because it's not what we do; it's why we do it.

When we leave this earth and pass in front of Jesus' eyes of fire, I believe every work is going to be judged on its purity, whether our motive for doing it was right or not. Therefore, we must let the Holy Spirit examine our hearts and show us any wrong attitude that is in us — and let Him root that thing out and change us.[4]

Change us to what? Change us to live in a right way that is going to bless God and be pleasing to Him. If we don't live like that, then everything else we're doing is totally wasted.

If we refuse to let God deal with our flaws, we open a door for the enemy. Satan gets into our lives through our flaws. God desires to prevent him from having any part in us, and He needs our cooperation. When Jesus said in John 14:30 that Satan had no part in Him, He meant that He was giving him no opening through flaws that were not dealt with. Jesus always obeyed the Father, and He did it promptly and entirely.

A good example is found in Ephesians 4:26,27. We are instructed not to let the sun go down on our anger; if we do, we give the devil an opportunity. Those living by emotions will stay angry until they **feel** like getting over it. Those who live by the Word of God will refuse to stay angry simply because God told them not to do so in His Word. It is not difficult to observe why some people have victory in their lives, while others have very little or none.

A Gentle and Peaceful Spirit

Peter said in 1 Peter 3:4 that God wants us to have a gentle and peaceful spirit, one that is not anxious or wrought up. That means He does not want us to be upset all the time. He wants us to be peaceful inside continually, to walk in peace. To do that in the world we live in is a full-time job. But it is possible to do that when we have a heart after God, when we ask Him to put His heart or His Spirit in us so that we might feel what He feels and want what He wants and hate what He hates. He hates sin, but He loves the person who commits the sin.

In Acts 13:22 we read that David was a man after God's own heart. We know that David made some pretty serious mistakes.[5] He sinned, repented and got right with God again. He paid a price for his sins, but he still had a heart after God.

I do not particularly want to be known as a famous lady preacher, but as somebody who walks in love and who has a heart after God.

That is what we all need to have. It is imperative that the condition of the heart of a leader be right because a leader ministers out of their heart. The heart is the center of a person, their spirit, their mind, their inner self.

We don't have to be perfect to minister, but we can't give somebody something we don't have.

How can we minister victory to others if we don't have any victory in our life? How can we minister peace to others if we have no peace within ourselves? Our circumstances are not always going to be peaceful, but with God's help, we can learn to be peaceful while we are going through them.

Peace in the Midst of the Storm

In Mark 4:35-41 we read how a storm arose when Jesus and His disciples were in a ship crossing the Sea of Galilee. The disciples got all upset, but Jesus calmly rebuked the storm, speaking peace to it, and it quieted down.

Do you know why He was able to speak peace to the storm? **Because He never let the storm get on the inside of Him.** The disciples could not calm the storm because they were as disturbed as it was. Remember, you can't give away something you don't have. Jesus gave them peace because He had peace to give them. He had a peaceful heart within Him.

I tell you, I want to be the kind of person who has a soothing effect on people when I get around them. I want to be the kind of person who can walk into a strife-filled room, and I don't have to be in there but a few minutes, and all of a sudden everyone starts to calm down.

When Jesus walked around on the earth, He had something going out of Him — the anointing or the virtue of God, which is the power of God. Something was constantly emanating from Him that brought healing and hope and salvation to people's lives. It wasn't just something that God put on Him; there was a foundation there of how He was living His life.

Yes, He was anointed, but that anointing was not going to be released if He didn't live His life right. And that's exactly why He never let the devil upset Him. He didn't let the storms of life get on the inside of Him. He kept His heart peaceful, calm and loving. As we saw earlier, we are to be like Him.

Guard Your Heart

In Proverbs 4:23 KJV we are told, *Keep thy heart with all diligence; for out of it are the issues of life.* That statement is for every believer, but for someone who wants to be a leader it is crucial. We must be diligent about keeping our hearts peaceful. In Philippians 4:6,7 we are told how to do that, *Do not fret or have any anxiety about anything, but in every circumstance and in everything, by prayer and petition (definite requests), with thanksgiving, continue to make your wants known to God. And God's peace . . . which transcends all understanding shall garrison and mount guard over your hearts and minds in Christ Jesus.*

That means that we should guard our hearts like a soldier guards a city to keep out invaders. That is important because there are a lot of things in our hearts that should not be there. If we allow God to do so, He will begin to expose those things and root them out, so we can have and maintain a peaceful heart.

CONDITIONS OF THE HEART

Amaziah was twenty-five years old when he began to reign,
and he reigned twenty-nine years in Jerusalem. . . .

He did right in the Lord's sight, but
not with a perfect or blameless heart.

2 Chronicles 25:1,2

When God speaks to us about our heart or He asks for our heart, He is asking for our entire life, the entire personality, character, body, mind, emotions in the spirit of a person. The heart is the real person, not the person everybody sees. The church and the world are looking for someone who is real.

Many people wonder why some things have not been working. It's because they've been too concerned with the exterior life and not nearly enough with the interior life. In this section of the book, we are going to look at the things concerning the interior life, or the conditions of our heart.

Actually, there are many conditions of the heart. Some are positive, and some are negative. Of course, many people do have a right heart. They love God with all their heart, and they really want to do the right thing in every situation. But there are others who have a wrong heart, and they do the right thing but with the wrong motive.

In 2 Chronicles 25:1,2 we read about a king who had a negative condition of the heart. In this passage King Amaziah did all the right things, but his heart was not right. Therefore, God was not pleased with him. That's a scary thing. We can do the right thing, and yet it still will not be acceptable to God because we do it with a wrong heart. Let's take giving, for example.

In 2 Corinthians 9:7 we are told that God loves a cheerful giver, one who does not give out of compulsion or with a bad attitude but out of a willing heart. God wants us to give cheerfully. In fact, it says that God loves a cheerful giver so much that He is absolutely unwilling to do without one.

Someone has said that although God wants us to give with a cheerful, willing heart, He will take our gift even if we are stingy and unwilling. He may take our money, and He may use it for His kingdom, but that is not the heart attitude He wants us to have when we give.

There is a physical heart and a spiritual heart, and the two are parallel. Physically speaking, the heart is the most important bodily organ. Spiritually speaking, I believe the heart is the most important aspect of the spiritual body. And it is the most important thing the believer or the leader can give to God. That is why the condition of our heart is so important.

> **A WRONG HEART ATTITUDE, RATHER THAN A LACK OF ABILITY OR POTENTIAL, PREVENTS MOST PEOPLE FROM PROGRESSING AND ENJOYING LIFE.**

The heart attitude is the major issue of a leader. It should be the major issue of every believer. It is not lack of ability or potential that prevents most people from making progress and enjoying fulfillment in life; I believe it is wrong heart attitudes. That is why we are going to look at them first.

1. An Evil Heart

> *The Lord saw that the wickedness of man was great in the earth, and that every imagination and intention of all human thinking was only evil continually.*
>
> *And the Lord regretted that He had made man on the earth, and He was grieved at heart.*
>
> *So the Lord said, I will destroy, blot out, and wipe away mankind, whom I have created from the face of the ground. . . .*
>
> *But Noah found grace (favor) in the eyes of the Lord.*
>
> Genesis 6:5-8

In this passage we see three things about people that displeased God: wickedness, evil imaginations and evil thinking. Because those things described the condition of man's heart on the earth at that time, God decided to destroy all mankind. But Noah found grace and favor in His eyes.

Noah must have been a man with a right heart; otherwise, he would have been destroyed along with all the other people of his day.

I believe the lesson we can draw from this story is that many people today are being destroyed for the simple reason that their hearts are wrong. They are not being careful what they are doing with their imagination.

We cannot imagine how many areas of our lives would get straightened out if we would just get our hearts right with God. Our hearts may not be filled with the kind of evil thoughts, imaginations, etc. of the people in Noah's day, but a bad attitude or wrong thinking can also be labeled evil imaginations and evil thinking. That's why we need to have a right attitude because attitude is basically everything. If we have a bad attitude and a bunch of "stinking thinking," we are going nowhere in life.

We will cover this in depth later on, but we need to have a tender heart. We need to hear and heed the voice of conscience so that the moment we realize we have a bad attitude about anything or anyone, we can do something about it. That is why we are told to keep guard on our heart because out of it flow the issues of our life.

Most of the time we don't keep a close enough guard on our heart. We let into it too much junk and nonsense. We need to remember the computer rule: **Garbage in, garbage out.** We need to realize that we are not going to take in garbage and produce glory. We have got to be careful not only about our actions but also about our imagination, our intent, our motivation, our attitude. If we are not careful to keep these things in check, we may end up with an evil heart.

2. A Hard Heart

> *Therefore, as the Holy Spirit says: Today, if you will hear His voice,*
>
> *Do not harden your hearts, as [happened] in the rebellion
> [of Israel] and their provocation and embitterment
> [of Me] in the day of testing in the wilderness.*
>
> Hebrews 3:7,8

As we see in this passage referring to the Israelites in the wilderness, a hard heart causes rebellion. A person with a hard heart cannot believe God easily. That can cause them to fall into the next heart condition we are going to discuss.

3. A Wicked, Unbelieving Heart

> *[Therefore beware] brethren, take care, lest there be in*
> *any one of you a wicked, unbelieving heart [which refuses*
> *to cleave to, trust in, and rely on Him], leading you to*
> *turn away and desert or stand aloof from the living God.*

Hebrews 3:12

In Chapter 12 of Hebrews, verses 7, 8 and 12, we see two wrong conditions of the heart — a hard heart and a wicked, unbelieving heart. This second condition is a major problem because everything we receive from God comes through believing. To receive from Him, we must come to Him in simple, childlike faith and just believe.[6]

We call ourselves believers, but the truth is, there are a lot of "unbelieving believers."

I will share something with you. This is one area in which I used to have a hard time. There were some things I didn't have any problem believing. But there were some other things that I just couldn't seem to believe, and I didn't know what my problem was. After several years, God began to reveal to me the reason for my problem in believing. It was because of the hardness of my heart, which was a consequence of the abuse I had suffered during my childhood.

People who are abused usually develop a hardness about them on purpose as a defense mechanism. It is the only way they can survive what they are going through. They get to the point where nothing can touch them. They have been hurt so much that they develop the attitude that no matter what anybody does to them, it does not bother them.

That was the way I was. When God tried to touch me and get me to believe and trust Him, I had a hard time doing so because my heart had been so hardened. I had practiced not trusting anyone for years — now God was asking me to trust Him.

We need to come to the place in our faith where we believe and we believe easily; we're not slow to believe, but we're quick to believe.

Moses reached the place where he was not quick to believe.[7] There are a lot of wonderful things we can say about Moses. In no way, shape or form am I trying to downgrade him. He was a marvelous leader. I don't know how he managed to lead those millions of people through those forty years in the wilderness. I would have given up on them the first time around the mountain. But as we saw earlier, after a certain period of time, Moses did get himself in trouble with God so that the Lord had to forbid him from leading the Israelites into the Promised Land.

Moses got to the place where he was slow of heart to believe. He was tired and worn out. And when we get tired, it is harder to believe God. That's why we have to stay sharp spiritually if we are going to be quick to believe and to walk in faith day by day. We must be careful to go from faith to faith and not begin to mix in any doubt and unbelief.[8]

Many times the dreams and visions God would like to reveal to us never come to pass because as soon as He begins to show them to us we start saying, "Oh, I doubt that." Yet, in Hebrews 3:12 God calls such a lack of faith a wicked, unbelieving heart — and He wants it out of us. He wants us to be full of simple, childlike faith.

Many years ago, when I began my relationship with God, there was a heavy emphasis in the church on healing and the manifestation of the gifts of the Spirit, especially the giving of individual prophetic words. It seemed that everyone was going around prophesying to everyone else, saying, "Thus saith the Lord . . ."

It seemed to me that many times it wasn't something God was doing; people were trying to force something to happen that was simply not going to take place. I ended up getting so turned off by all those things that I developed a hard, unbelieving heart, which made it hard for me when God was ready to start using me in healing and in the gifts of the Spirit. I would see people healed in my services, and I would actually have a hard time believing it. I would think to myself, **I wonder if they really did get healed.**

Since that time I have come a long way. Because I didn't want to have a hard, unbelieving heart, I prayed about it for a long, long time until I had developed a believing heart.

One reason I had such a hard time believing, even after I had become a minister, was that I had been taught all my life to be suspicious. I had been told repeatedly, "Don't trust anybody. Everybody is out to get you. Anybody who gives you something wants something from you." When you have that pounded into your head all the formative years of your life, you can't get rid of it overnight.

A person with a hard heart usually has difficulty showing people mercy when they fail. Hard-hearted people tend to be demanding and legalistic. They have been hurt and wounded emotionally.

Remember that Jesus wants to restore your soul.[9] Part of your soul is your emotions. I encourage you to let Jesus into those areas of your life that no one could ever reach except Jesus Himself. I finally did that, and even though it was hard, it has been well worth it.

One thing is sure. We will never get to where we need to be if we refuse to admit where we are. Phoniness, pretense and acting like we have something we don't have won't work. It is the truth that sets us free.[10]

If you have a problem in this area, repent and ask God to cleanse you of it. Ask Him to change you into a person after His heart, a person who has the same kind of heart that He has.

4. A Deceived Heart

> *Take heed to yourselves, lest your [minds and] hearts be deceived*
> *and you turn aside and serve other gods and worship them,*
>
> *And the Lord's anger be kindled against you, and He shut up*
> *the heavens so that there will be no rain and the land will not*
> *yield its fruit, and you perish quickly off the good land*
> *which the Lord gives you.*
>
> Deuteronomy 11:16,17

There are many things that can become a god to us. Even a ministry can become a god. Having the ministry and seeing it grow can become more important than God Himself. We must never forget that it is the Lord Who places the vision for ministry in our hearts. It is He Who calls us and gives us the desire. He must always maintain the first and most preeminent place in our lives. If we put before Him the thing that He has blessed us with, it offends Him.

In the passage above, God is telling us that if we do not have a right heart before Him, we are not going to get blessed. It is not a matter of rebuking devils. We sometimes think everything in our life would be fine if the devil would just leave us alone. That is not so. We have it backwards. If we would live right, then the devil would not bother us. He might pester us, but he would have no real power over us, just as he had no real power over Jesus.

> *Therefore you shall lay up these My words in your [minds and]*
> *hearts and in your [entire] being, and bind them for a sign*
> *upon your hands and as forehead bands between your eyes.*

> *And you shall teach them to your children, speaking of them when*
> *you sit in your house and when you walk along the road,*
> *when you lie down and when you rise up.*

> *And you shall write them upon the doorposts*
> *of your house and on your gates,*

> *That your days and the days of your children may be multiplied*
> *in the land which the Lord swore to your fathers to give them,*
> *as long as the heavens are above the earth.*

Deuteronomy 11:18-21

Do you get a revelation of what these people were supposed to do? They were supposed to write Scriptures on the doors of their houses, on their gates, on their foreheads, on their hands and on their arms. They were supposed to talk about them all day, everywhere they went — sitting down, lying down and walking around. Why were they told to do all this? Because God knew that it is only knowing the Word that keeps a people from having a deceived heart, which is what Jesus was saying in John 8:31,32: . . . *If you abide in My word [hold fast to My teachings and live in accordance with them], you are truly My disciples. And you will know the Truth, and the Truth will set you free.*

If we don't really care enough about the Word of God to abide in it, we are going to be in for trouble in these last days. Exterior fluff is not going to be enough to get us through. We have to be deeply serious about learning the Word. When we know the Word, God will protect us and keep us. Otherwise, we are going to be sucked up in deception.

Make no mistake, we should all pray not to be deceived and seek to know any areas where we might be deceived. We are deceived when we believe a lie. Satan lies to us continually. Without a thorough knowledge of God's Word, we don't even recognize they are lies.

Some people deceive themselves *by reasoning contrary to the Truth.*[11]

There were times in my life before I was as surrendered as I am now to the will of God, when He would place it on my heart to give something away that I wanted to keep. I learned from making mistakes that it was very easy to deceive myself when God asked for something I didn't want to let go of.

We make all kinds of excuses, including pretending that it could not have been God dealing with us, but was probably the devil just trying to make us miserable by asking for the things that are precious to us. We can quickly become "spiritually deaf" to the voice of God when He says something we don't want to hear.

A deceived heart won't do for leaders and those who intend to be victorious in life. We must learn to live openly and honestly, always walking in the light of God's truth.

5. A Proud Heart

> . . . *he who has a haughty look and a proud and*
> *arrogant heart I cannot and I will not tolerate.*
>
> Psalm 101:5

Has God ever had to deal with you about pride?

Several years ago when God first directed my attention to Andrew Murray's book on humility,[12] it was very hard for me to read because I had a proud heart. Although I had a call on my life, a gift of communication and a lot of potential, I also had a problem with pride. And a proud person does not want to admit that he has a problem with pride.

Many people are just stuffed full of potential, but if they don't get their heart right, they won't be able to develop it. Remember, our potential is possibilities but not positivelys.

God starts out using us but then as He wants to promote us, He has to keep changing us. He begins to show us what attitude has to go and what heart condition has to change.

I once did a series of teachings called "Pride and Humility." Nobody bought the tapes because those who needed them most were too proud to pick them up for fear someone would see them and realize they had a problem with pride.

How can you tell you have a problem with pride? Examine yourself. If you have an opinion about everything, you have a problem with pride. If you are judgmental, you have a problem with pride. If you can't be corrected, you have a problem with pride. If you rebel against authority, if you want to take all the credit and glory to yourself, if you say "I" too often, then you have a problem with pride.

It is so hard to let God get all of that stuff out of us, but it is vital to ministry and leadership. Interestingly, most people who are really equipped for leadership come prepackaged with a major spirit of pride. They just believe they are right. To do anything important, it is necessary to have that kind of assurance, but it is also necessary to have an attitude of humility to realize that we are not always right about everything and to be willing to take correction. If we do not have a certain degree of humility, we are headed for trouble. This point is well illustrated in the life of King Hezekiah in the Old Testament.

KEEP PRIDE UNDER CONTROL

Thus the Lord saved Hezekiah and the inhabitants of Jerusalem from the hand . . . of all his enemies, and He guided them on every side.

And many brought gifts to Jerusalem to the Lord and presents to Hezekiah king of Judah; so from then on he was magnified in the sight of all nations.

2 Chronicles 32:22,23

In answer to the prayers of King Hezekiah and the prophet Isaiah, the Lord intervened and saved Hezekiah and Judah from their enemies. As a result, Hezekiah began to be lifted up in the sight of the people.

God is not against that. If you become a leader, people will look up to you and honor you. They may want to do nice things for you. That is not all bad, but it is dangerous. As we see in this passage, people's admiration for a leader, or the leader's view of it, if not kept under control can lead to pride, as it did with Hezekiah:

> *In those days Hezekiah was sick to the point of death; and he prayed to the Lord and He answered him and gave him a sign.*
>
> *But Hezekiah did not make return [to the Lord] according to the benefit done to him, for his heart became proud [at such a spectacular response to his prayer]; therefore there was wrath upon him and upon Judah and Jerusalem.*
>
> *But Hezekiah humbled himself for the pride of his heart, both he and the inhabitants of Jerusalem, so that the wrath of the Lord came not upon them in the days of Hezekiah.*

2 Chronicles 32:24-26

Hezekiah developed a proud heart, and in his pride, he fell ill and almost died. But he humbled himself and repented and got it straightened out. Look at the results:

> *And Hezekiah had very great wealth and honor. . . . for God had given him very great possessions. . . . And Hezekiah prospered in all his works. And so in the matter of the ambassadors of the princes of Babylon who were sent to him to inquire about the wonder that was done in the land, God left him to himself to try him, that He might know all that was in his heart.*

2 Chronicles 32:27,29-31

It is interesting that when Hezekiah turned to God, the Lord began to honor, promote and bless him. That is exactly what happens to anyone who commits wholeheartedly to the Lord. Sooner or later their ministry starts increasing, and they start moving up. People begin looking up to them. But if they become proud, one of two things has to happen.

God has to deal with them about their pride. Like Hezekiah, either they quickly repent and come back to a place of humility, so God can continue to bless them in an amazing way, or they refuse to do so and begin to lose God's blessing and eventually their place of honor.

WHEN WE TURN
TO GOD AND
COMMIT WHOLE-
HEARTEDLY TO
HIM, THE LORD
WILL BEGIN TO
HONOR, PROMOTE
AND BLESS US.

This is a key issue. There is no one who is doing anything of importance for the Lord who is not attacked and tempted by the spirit of pride. That is why no one gets a right heart and always has a right heart; it takes effort to keep a right heart. We have to work at it all the time. And one of the most powerful things we have to guard against is a spirit of self-righteousness, which is rooted in pride.

You have to understand that our enemy Satan is going to use every opportunity he can to get us into an area where we've got a wrong heart. When that happens, we need to repent to God immediately.

If you and I want to stand before God one day and say, as Jesus did in John 17:4, *I have glorified You down here on the earth by completing the work that You gave Me to do,* then we must be careful to keep a right heart. Psalm 101:5 tells us that God cannot and will not tolerate anyone who has a haughty look and a proud and arrogant heart.

6. A Presumptuous Heart

*The man who does presumptuously and will not listen to the priest
who stands to minister there before the Lord your God or to the judge,
that man shall die; so you shall purge the evil from Israel.*

*And all the people shall hear and [reverently] fear,
and not act presumptuously again.*

Deuteronomy 17:12,13

In Old Testament days God dealt differently with His people than He does now. I am so glad to be living under the dispensation of grace. But if we look at how God dealt with sin under the Old Covenant, we can see how serious it is and be warned not to wink at it and put up with it.

In this passage, God was telling His people that if one of their leaders acted presumptuously, he was to be killed. As leaders, whatever we do, we are telling people by our actions that it is OK to do what we do. But God is saying to us, "If there is a presumptuous leader among you, I will not let them get by with their presumptuousness because if I do, everyone is going to think it is all right to act the way they are acting."

That is exactly why we must keep a right heart attitude if we want God to continue to use us. There is a great responsibility to leadership. There is more to ministry than just standing up in front of people and exercising spiritual gifts. Our lives must be right behind the scenes. We must always be on our guard against presumption.

Presumption causes disrespect and a rebellious attitude toward authority. A presumptuous person thinks he doesn't have to listen to those who have been placed in authority over him.

The dictionary defines *presuming* as "venturing without positive permission; too confident; arrogant; unreasonably bold."[13] Presumptuous people talk when they should be quiet. They try to dictate direction to those from whom they should be receiving counsel. They give orders when they should be taking orders. They do things without asking permission.

Presumption is a big problem. And it comes from a wrong heart, as we are told in 2 Peter 2:10,11 which speaks of . . . *those who walk after the flesh and indulge in the lust of polluting passion and scorn and despise authority. Presumptuous [and] daring [self-willed and self-loving creatures]! They scoff at and revile dignitaries (glorious ones) without trembling, whereas [even] angels, though superior in might and power, do not bring a defaming charge against them before the Lord.*

God does not want presumption. He wants humility.

7. A Hypocritical Heart

> *Therefore you have no excuse or defense or justification,*
> *O man, whoever you are who judges and condemns another.*
> *For in posing as judge and passing sentence on another, you*
> *condemn yourself, because you who judge are habitually practicing*
> *the very same things [that you censure and denounce].*
>
> Romans 2:1

Any person who judges and condemns other people for doing the same things he does has to be deceived. Yet to some degree, we all do that. We tend to look at ourselves through rose-colored glasses while looking at everyone else through a magnifying glass. We make excuses for our wrong behavior, while claiming that others who do the same things we do are deserving of judgment. That kind of attitude of heart is hypocritical.

A hypocrite is a phony. It is someone who puts on an act but doesn't have a right heart.

Some people do the dumbest things, and yet God still uses them. The reason God is able to use them despite their human errors is that they have a right heart. That is what He means when He says that we judge by outward appearance, but He looks on the heart[14] and that David was a man after His own heart.

God's Son Jesus also looked on the heart, which is why He said to the scribes and Pharisees of His day:

> *The scribes and Pharisees sit on Moses' seat [of authority].*
>
> *So observe and practice all they tell you; but do not do what they do, for they preach, but do not practice.*
>
> *They tie up heavy loads, hard to bear, and place them on men's shoulders, but they themselves will not lift a finger to help bear them.*
>
> Matthew 23:2-4

What was Jesus saying about these people? He was saying that their hearts were rotten.

> *They do all their works to be seen of men; for they make wide their phylacteries (small cases enclosing certain Scripture passages, worn during prayer on the left arm and forehead) and make long their fringes [worn by all male Israelites, according to the command].*
>
> *And they take pleasure in and [thus] love the place of honor at feasts and the best seats in the synagogues,*
>
> *And to be greeted with honor in the marketplaces and to have people call them rabbi.*
>
> Matthew 23:5-7

Jesus was saying that these people were hypocrites because they put on a big show of being holy while refusing to help anybody, yet helping people is what ministers and leaders are supposed to do.

These people were proud and haughty. They did good works only to be seen by the crowds and to be thought of as great and important. In Matthew 6:1,2,5, Jesus talked about all their hypocritical deeds, saying, . . . *Truly I tell you, they have their reward in full already.*

One time I was having my nails done in a shop I went to regularly. At the time I happened to be wearing a rhinestone Jesus pin. God prompted me to give it to a nurse there who was talking about ministering to cancer patients in the hospital, saying she was not allowed to preach to them openly but would like to be able to give them something.

The Lord spoke to my heart and told me to give her that pin so that when she wore it on her lapel as she bent over her patients, just the name of Jesus would minister to them. I hesitated because I felt the Lord wanted me to do that privately, and I couldn't do that in front of the girl who was doing my nails.

Suddenly the girl stopped and said, "Oh, I ran out of something. I have to run next door to get some more. I'll be right back."

I knew God was making a way for me to give that pin away privately and not make a big deal out of it, but my flesh wanted some credit. So instead of doing what God wanted me to do the way He wanted me to do it, I kept putting it off, reasoning to myself, **I think it would really bless this manicurist if she saw my generosity.**

So I waited until the girl came back. Then I took off the Jesus pin and made a big deal about giving it to the nurse. Just as I had envisioned, the ladies expounded on my generosity, going on and on about how kind it was of me to give my pin away. As I left the shop thinking how generous I had been, the Holy Spirit spoke to me in my heart and said, "Well, I hope you enjoyed that because it is all the reward you are going to get. Whatever reward you would have had from Me, you just traded it for that."

I often wonder what God would have done for me if I had been obedient and done what He told me to do and let Him have all the glory and credit.

We all have such opportunities to be blessed, but we trade them for little fleshly "zings" that make us feel important for a moment. For example, when the preacher in a service tells the audience to open to a certain passage of Scripture, we love to open our Bible and be proud of how we have it marked up in all different colors. We may have Scriptures underlined, with handwritten notes beside them. We secretly hope the people around us will notice and think well of us because we appear to have studied quite a lot. We want people to think we are spiritual, but we must realize that God is not impressed with how many Scriptures we have underlined.

OUR DEGREE OF SPIRITUAL MATURITY IS MEASURED BY HOW PROMPTLY WE OBEY GOD'S WORD AND HOW WE TREAT OTHER PEOPLE.

All of that kind of fleshly glory means nothing to God. He is looking for people with a right heart so He can bless us. Our degree of spiritual maturity is not measured by how many Scriptures we have underlined, nor even by how much we read the Bible, but by how much we promptly obey God's Word and by how we treat other people.

As soon as we start getting proud of ourselves and our accomplishments, God is obligated to show us our flaws. He does not do it to embarrass us or to make us feel bad about ourselves, but to keep us in a place where we are dependent upon Him and merciful with other people who also have faults.

8. A Despising Heart

And you say, How I hated instruction and discipline, and my heart despised reproof!

Proverbs 5:12

As leaders, you and I should be teachable. If we ever get to the point where we think we know everything, that is a sure sign we know nothing. We need to stop going around despising things. We even need to stop despising little things and saying things like, "I hate going to the grocery store. I hate driving in traffic. I hate my job." We are not supposed to hate anything but sin.

As leaders, we should be functioning in the love of God, yet we go through life with hate for a lot of other things mixed into God's love. If there is anything in our life we ought to get rid of, it is mixture. We need something pure coming from us.

Paul told us that to the pure in heart everything is pure.[15] In Matthew 5:8 KJV, Jesus said that the pure in heart will see God. I believe that means the pure in heart will have revelation knowledge. They will know what God wants them to do. They will have clear direction. They will hear from God very clearly because their heart is pure.

We are all tempted to hate things, just as we are prone to dread certain things. God has taught me that dread is a close relative of fear. We don't need to go around dreading doing the dishes, dreading getting up, dreading going to bed, dreading doing the laundry, etc. Satan uses our hatred and our fear and dread to deceive us into problems. That is another wrong heart condition that needs to go.

We are not to have a despising heart. We are not to despise other people, but we are also not to despise things.

Don't despise your job; be glad you have one. Thank God you are not in a soup line or living under a bridge. God blesses those who have a thankful heart.

In Philippians 4:6 we are told, *Do not fret or have any anxiety about anything, but in every circumstance and in everything, by prayer and petition (definite requests), with thanksgiving, continue to make your wants known to God.* Years ago I taught a message saying that when you ask God for something, you should thank Him ahead of time that you are going to get it because that will help release your manifestation. I believe that. I took the Scripture in Philippians 4:6 to mean just that, that when I prayed for something, I should start thanking God that it was on its way.

But one day God revealed a broader scope of that verse to me. He said, "No, what I am really saying there is that when you pray and petition Me for anything, make sure you are doing it from a foundation of a thankful heart." Then He went on to say, "If you are not thankful for what you already have, why should I give you more to complain about?"

In those days, I had a complaining heart, a murmuring, grumbling, faultfinding heart. I could find a thousand things to grumble about, but God does not want us to have a grumbling heart. As we saw earlier, He wants us to get to the place that we are living epistles, read of all men. From our lifestyle, people should be able to tell that there is something different about us, "Why are you so happy? Why are you so peaceful?

Why are you so loving?" We are supposed to be salt and light to the world.[16] Our lives are supposed to make people want what we have.

Our heart condition eventually shows us for what we really are. We can wear a T-shirt with Scripture on it. We can go to church and act very holy. We can drive into the parking lot with an "I love Jesus" bumper sticker on our car. We can get out and walk into the building wearing a Jesus pin on our lapel, carrying a big Bible under our arm and cassette teaching tapes in our bag. Once the service begins, we can jump and shout and do all the right things in public. But it is what goes on behind closed doors that really reveals the true attitude of our heart.

Years ago I heard a well-known Bible teacher say, "If you want to find a spiritual person, don't look in the church." He said that because in church you can't tell who is real and who is putting on.

He went on to say, "If you want to find out whether people are really spiritual, go to their home. See how they act in the morning when they first get up. See how they act with their family when things don't go right. See how they treat people who can't do them any good."

All this is important to me. I don't want to be a phony. I don't want to be a big famous preacher, the lady with the television ministry that everybody is excited about. I want to be real. I want to help people. I want God to be proud of me. And I want Him to be proud of you too. That is based on the attitude of our heart. We must learn to guard our heart with all diligence.

In Psalm 26:2 David said to God, *Examine me, O Lord, and prove me; test my heart and my mind.* We should all be bold enough to go to God in confidence and say, "Examine me, Lord. If there is anything in me that is not right, shine Your light on it. Help me to see it and get rid of it." We need to start praying that way on a daily basis. We need to ask God regularly to remove from our heart anything that will keep us from being what He wants us to be. One of the signs that we are ready for leadership is when we are ready to work with God to keep our heart right.

CHAPTER 6

NEGATIVE CONDITIONS OF THE HEART, PART 2

By the time you have reached this point in the book, you are beginning to realize how important the condition of our heart is in leadership. There is nothing more important to God than what kind of heart we have. To remove the negative conditions of the heart is not something that He has in store for leaders only; it is His will for every believer.

As we have seen, we can't give away what we don't have. In the same way, what we do have may not be something we should give away but something we should remove. When we are open and allow God to examine our heart attitudes, with His help, we can begin to change the ones that need to be changed.

Wrong heart attitudes can prevent us from making progress and enjoying promotion to the next level where God wants us to be. You may not have every negative heart condition that is being covered here, but this book is insurance to help make sure you never do.

Let's continue now to look at more negative conditions of the heart.

9. An Offended, Bitter, Resentful, Unforgiving Heart

> *The heart knows its own bitterness, and no stranger shares its joy.*
>
> Proverbs 14:10

This is probably one of the most dangerous heart conditions we can have because the Bible tells us very plainly that if we will not forgive other people, then God cannot forgive us.[1] If we do not forgive others, our faith will not work. And everything that comes from God comes by faith. If our faith doesn't work, we are in serious trouble.

When I preach on the subject of forgiveness, I always ask the audience to stand if they have been offended and need to forgive someone else. I have never had less than 80 percent of the congregation stand up.

POWER COMES FROM LOVE.

It doesn't take a genius to figure out why we are lacking the power we need in the body of Christ. Power comes from love, not from hatred, bitterness and unforgiveness.

"But you don't know what was done to me," people always say to try to excuse their bitterness, resentment and unforgiveness. Based on what the Bible says, it really doesn't matter how great their offense was. We serve a God Who is greater, and if we will handle the offense in the right way, He will bring us justice and recompense if we allow Him to do so.

In Isaiah 61:7 the Lord promises us, *Instead of your [former] shame you shall have a twofold recompense. . . .* A recompense is a reward. It is a payback for past hurts. It is like Workmen's Compensation. The Lord once told me, "Joyce, you work for Me, and as long as you are on My payroll, if you get hurt on the job, I will pay you back."

In Romans 12:19 we are told, *Beloved, never avenge yourselves, but leave the way open for [God's] wrath; for it is written, Vengeance is Mine, I will repay (requite), says the Lord.* Don't try to get people back for what they have done to you. Leave it in God's hands.

Jesus taught us that we are to forgive those who hurt us, pray for those who despitefully use us and bless those who curse us.[2] That is hard. But there is something harder — being full of hatred, bitterness and resentment. Don't spend your life hating someone who is probably out having a good time while you are all upset.

JOSEPH HAD A RIGHT HEART

In the Old Testament, Joseph was wrongly treated by his brothers because they were jealous of him. One day when the opportunity arose, his brothers sold him into slavery in Egypt where he ended up in prison for something he didn't do. It seemed as though everywhere Joseph went, he tried to do the right thing, but he was treated wrongly for it.[3]

That sometimes happens to all of us. When it does, I believe it is one of the tests we have to pass to be prepared for leadership. It is the forgiveness test, which we will discuss later. People are going to hurt us and do us wrong, and we have to forgive them if we want to be promoted to the next level of what God has for us.

"But it's not fair," we cry. We must remember that we serve a God of justice. He has promised to repay us and to make things right for us if we will just trust Him and not try to take matters into our own hands.

Joseph was treated unfairly. Even after his brothers mistreated him, he was falsely accused by his employer's wife and thrown into prison. There he helped others get out of prison, but they forgot all about him. Mistreatment seemed to be a lifelong problem for Joseph. Later, God redeemed him from prison and set him up as second in command over the entire nation of Egypt.[4]

It was then, during the time of famine, that Joseph's brothers came down from Israel to Egypt because they had heard there was grain there. When Joseph revealed himself to them, they were afraid because he was in a position of power to pay them back for what they had done to him.[5]

That must have been a great temptation for Joseph, but in it we see his heart. The story tells us why God was able to promote him so that everywhere he went and whoever he worked for, he ended up in a position of power. It was not because he was the smartest or the best looking; it was because he had a right heart.

Neither our education nor our background, neither our skin color nor anything else about us is as important to God as the condition of our heart. The Bible says that the eyes of God roam to and fro across the earth looking for someone in whom He can show Himself strong, someone whose heart is perfect toward Him.[6] Joseph was just such a person.

There was famine in the land and Joseph had the access to the food supply. His brothers and father were starving to death where they lived, so the brothers came to Egypt to try to get grain not knowing that Joseph was the one who was in charge of distributing the food. As we saw before, when his brothers recognized him in Egypt, they became afraid. Now that he was in a position of power, what might he do to get back at them for their treachery to him?

And they sent a messenger to Joseph, saying,
Your father commanded before he died, saying,

So shall you say to Joseph: Forgive (take up and away all
resentment and all claim to requital concerning), I pray you now,
the trespass of your brothers and their sin, for they did evil to you.
Now, we pray you, forgive the trespass of the servants of your
father's God. And Joseph wept when they spoke thus to him.

Genesis 50:16,17

Joseph must have had a tender heart, as we see by his response to his brothers' request for forgiveness:

Then his brothers went and fell down before him,
saying, See, we are your servants (your slaves)!

And Joseph said to them, Fear not; for am I in
the place of God? [Vengeance is His, not mine.]

As for you, you thought evil against me, but God meant it for good, to
bring about that many people should be kept alive, as they are this day.

Now therefore, do not be afraid. I will provide for and support
you and your little ones. And he comforted them [imparting
cheer, hope, strength] and spoke to their hearts [kindly].

Genesis 50:18-21

So here we see Joseph giving comfort and encouragement to the people who had hurt him badly. Instead of returning evil for evil, he was charitable, unselfish, speaking kind words to those who had harmed him, being good to those who did not deserve it. That is the heart of a true leader.

STEPHEN FORGAVE HIS TORMENTORS

In Acts 6 and 7 we read the story of Stephen who was called before the Jewish council and falsely accused of blaspheming God and Moses by preaching the Gospel. After he had delivered a sermon that angered the council, he was taken out and stoned. But even as they were stoning him, Stephen prayed for his enemies, saying, . . . *Lord Jesus, receive and accept and welcome my spirit! And falling on his knees, he cried out loudly, Lord, fix not this sin upon them [lay it not to their charge]! And when he had said this, he fell asleep [in death].*[7]

I am afraid that in that situation I would have been tempted to pick up a rock and throw it back. But that is not what Stephen did. He forgave his tormentors and prayed for them, saying in essence, "Forgive them, Lord, they don't understand what they are doing."

A large majority of the time those who injure us don't understand what they are doing. They are just operating out of selfishness. Years ago someone told me something that helped me. He said that 95 percent of the time when people hurt our feelings, that was not what they intended to do.

It is easy for us to be offended. But according to the Bible love is not easily offended.[8] God does not want us to have an offended heart. If we do, we will not be able to minister to others.

I can remember times years ago when I'd try to go preach while I was mad at Dave and I felt like death was all over me. It's the most awful feeling to try to minister when you are rip roaring mad at someone. That is why we must learn to overcome our feelings and develop a loving, forgiving heart. No matter what it costs us, no matter how much it hurts our flesh or how hard it is, we need to straighten things out between the person who offends us and ourselves before we can minister to others.

You may think this doesn't relate to you because you don't have a pulpit ministry. But every believer has a ministry. You may not be on a platform teaching, but you've got a ministry to your children, your spouse, your family, to God. How can we properly praise God with a wrong heart condition?

In Matthew 5:23,24 and Mark 11:25,26 Jesus taught that if we have something against anyone, we must go to the person and set things right between us before we can pray or worship the Lord.

In 2 Timothy 4:14-16 the apostle Paul wrote to his young disciple:

> *Alexander the coppersmith did me great wrongs.*
> *The Lord will pay him back for his actions.*

*Beware of him yourself, for he opposed and
resisted our message very strongly and exceedingly.*

*At my first trial no one acted in my defense [as my advocate]
or took my part or [even] stood with me, but all
forsook me. May it not be charged against them!*

Paul had gone through a lot to bring the Gospel to the early world. He had been persecuted, beaten and thrown in prison for preaching the Good News. Many times he had suffered because of opposition, as he describes in this passage.

What Paul was saying here was, "Alexander the coppersmith has done me great wrong, but I am not going to worry about it. I'm not going to get full of bitterness and hatred. I am going to let God handle it. He will take care of it."

How much better our lives would be if we would take that attitude toward so many things, if we would just cast our care on the Lord and allow Him to handle it for us.

Then Paul went on to tell how no one had come to his defense in his trial. I wonder how we would feel if we had suffered everything that Paul had gone through to bless so many others only to end up without a single soul even to stand up for us in our time of greatest need. Paul had risked his very life for others, yet they would not even be seen associating with him for fear they might be punished too.

What was Paul's response to all this? He prayed that their failure would not be laid to their charge. That shows us his heart.

We can go through the Bible and look at the great men and women of God, and it doesn't take us very long to see why they were called heroes of the faith. It wasn't because they were smarter than everybody else or because they had more going for them in the natural than others. It was simply because they had great hearts.

10. A Foolish Heart

The lips of the wise disperse knowledge [sifting it as chaff from the grain]; not so the minds and hearts of the self-confident and foolish.

Proverbs 15:7

The Bible tells us that we should have a wise heart, but it also says that a foolish heart is a wrong heart condition.

Those who are wise in heart use their lips to spread knowledge, but those who are foolish in heart speak whatever comes to their mind. I believe that sometimes one of the biggest problems with people is that they just do foolish things.

One time a lady came up to me after a meeting I had led in which I was talking about how I felt a godly woman should dress, and she said to me, "I just really feel like God wants me to share something with you."

"What's that?" I asked.

"Well," she said, "I know you probably don't realize it, but you wear your clothes just a little too tight."

I looked at that woman and thought, **This poor lady thinks she is hearing from God.**

"But how do you know she wasn't?" you may ask.

I know because if God had wanted to correct me about my clothes, He would have done it through my husband, one of my children or one of the leaders in my ministry. He would have chosen someone I knew and whose opinion I respected, not someone I had never met or even heard of before.

It was foolish of that woman to try to give me such a personal word from the Lord. It was also presumptuous.

That was what Aaron and Miriam were when they told Moses that he was not the only one who could hear from God.[9]

I have been around long enough to know I need correction from time to time and to know the person God is going to choose to give it to me. For example, our pastor recently shared with us a word about our ministry, and we received it from him because we know and respect him. Oral Roberts once shared some things with us, and we listened because it would have been foolish of us not to do so.

So many people ruin relationships and they ruin their ministry and show that they are not yet qualified for the leadership they want to be in when they do foolish things. One of the most foolish things you can do is think you are anointed to tell everybody else what they are supposed to do.

In Proverbs 8:15,16 wisdom is speaking, and she says, *By me kings reign and rulers decree justice. By me princes rule, and nobles, even all the judges and governors of the earth.* It is wisdom that exalts us to places of leadership. That tells me that if I want to be a leader, I must have wisdom. But I must also have something else.

People are constantly asking me, "How were you able to build a ministry like yours?" I share with them a ministry success principle, one of the most positive aspects of our ministry, the thing that has brought us to where we are today: use a lot of common sense!

Now I am not a mental giant, but I finally got a college degree. It was an honorary doctorate from Oral Roberts University. I would really have liked to have gone to college. My teachers recognized that I had a writing gift. But I was never able to get a college education because I had to work to take care of myself. I believe that honorary degree was part of my compensation package that the Lord gave me because I have served Him faithfully all these years. God will give you what somebody else tries to take away from you.

> GOD WILL GIVE YOU WHAT SOMEBODY ELSE TRIES TO TAKE AWAY FROM YOU.

But as wonderful as having that degree is, I have something even more wonderful and important going for me. I have a lot of just plain old **common sense.**

Sometimes when people feel strongly about something, that is all they preach about. That is wrong. There needs to be a balance. We need to use common sense even in our spiritual life.

In our ministry, Dave and I use common sense in everything we do. We don't buy things we don't have the money to pay for. We don't hire people if we can't afford to pay their salaries. We get rid of people in our organization who cause strife. We have enough common sense to know what to do to stay out of trouble. It really is not that hard; just do what you would want others to do to you.[10] Pay your bills on time, communicate properly, mix encouragement with correction so a person's spirit is not broken, etc.

If Christians would just use more common sense, things would be much better for them. Sometimes when people get saved and filled with the Holy Spirit, they think everything is going to come to them by means of a miracle. Getting saved simply means giving ourselves up to God by taking ourselves out of our own keeping and entrusting ourselves into His keeping. God does miracles, but He also expects us to do our part.

Instead of being foolish in heart, we need to be wise in heart. And one of the best ways to do that is by using the common sense God has given us.

11. A Double Heart.

> *Of Zebulun, 50,000 experienced troops, fitted out with all kinds of weapons and instruments of war that could order and set the battle in array, men not of double purpose but stable and trustworthy.*

> 1 Chronicles 12:33

In this passage, the writer is listing the brave men who came to David to help him wage war to make David king of Israel. As we see, these men were not double hearted but were stable and trustworthy.

The Bible says that we are to be wholehearted and single-minded. In Matthew 6:24 Jesus said, *No one can serve two masters; for either he will hate the one and love the other, or he will stand by and be devoted to the one and despise and be against the other. . . .*

Some years ago I served as associate pastor of a church in St. Louis. I loved it and my pastor very much, but the Lord told me to leave it and start my own ministry.

I knew that when the Lord calls you to do something, whether you want to do it or not, you had better do it because if you don't, everything else in your life is going to dry up.

I also knew that the thing I had been doing and enjoying very much at one time I was no longer enjoying because God was finished with it. And when God gets finished, we may as well get finished too. Yet I stayed on in that position for another whole year. During that time I experienced all kinds of things that I did not like. I was not happy at all, and I didn't know why. Nothing seemed to be right any longer. I felt like I was trying to put a square peg in a round hole.

Finally, the Lord spoke to me and said, "Take your ministry and go north, south, east and west." So I did. But for three years every time I would go to church I would grieve. I would hear about a pastors' retreat, and I would get depressed. I kept asking myself, "What is my problem? Did I miss God?"

My pastor felt the same way I did. On the one hand he could see that what I was doing was God's will for me, but on the other hand he still wanted me to be part of his church staff. We kept making arrangements so that I could have my own ministry but still be involved in the church I had just left.

Through all of this, God had to really deal with me. Finally, He said to me, "Joyce, I cannot do anything else in your ministry until you set your heart fully and completely on what I have called you to do."

I still didn't understand what was wrong with me. I kept asking, "If this is what I am supposed to be doing, why do I still feel so bad?"

Finally, I shared my problem with a man who had a prophetic ministry.

"If I heard from God and am doing His will, why do I still feel this way?" I asked.

"It's very simple," he said. "You have soul ties to that old job."

I realized he was right. I had invested five years of my life in that job, and my soul was deeply involved in it. God had told me to move on, but my soul was still tied to the place I had left behind. My basic problem was that I had a double heart. And as long as I was double hearted, I could not find any peace of mind.

That is why, when God called Abraham, He told him to get away from his country, his family, his relatives and everything he had known, and to go to a place that God would show him.[11] That is what Paul was talking about when he spoke of letting go of what lies behind and pressing on to what lies ahead.[12] That is what the Lord was telling Israel when He said through the prophet Isaiah, *Do not [earnestly] remember the former things; neither consider the things of old. Behold, I am doing a new thing! . . . do you not perceive and know it and will you not give heed to it? . . .*[13]

Our problem is that we always want to hold on to the past and still go into the future. That is what is meant by having a double heart.

In James 1:8 we read that a person who is of two minds is hesitating, dubious, irresolute, unstable, unreliable and uncertain about everything he thinks, feels or decides. The *King James Version* says, *A double minded man is unstable in all his ways.*

IF WE TRY TO HOLD ON TO THE PAST WHILE MOVING INTO THE FUTURE, WE WON'T HAVE ANY PEACE.

I don't think we should have a double heart. Instead, we should be decisive people. Leaders should be able to make decisions and then stick to them. If we make a decision and then continue to go back and forth in our mind about whether we did the right thing or not, we are unstable in our ways. We need to do the best we can to hear from God, then make a decision based on what He has said to us. Once we have decided something, we need to do it with all our heart. Whatever we decide to do, we need to do it wholeheartedly, putting our whole selves into it.

In Romans 12 the apostle Paul talks about the different gifts of grace that have been given to the individual members of the body of Christ. In that chapter he tells us that if we are a teacher, we should give ourselves to our teaching. If we are a giver, we should give ourselves to our giving. If we are an exhorter, we should give ourselves to our exhortation. In other words, don't get sucked up into everybody else's call that really is not the call on your life. Fight to stay centered in on what God is calling you to do. Don't be double-minded.

If you believe you have a call on your life, then believe it — consistently. Don't believe it on Monday, doubt it on Tuesday, believe it again on Wednesday and then by Friday be ready to give it up because your circumstances are not good. Whatever your call may be, do it the best you know how, believing that you have heard from God.

12. A Wounded Heart

> For I am poor and needy, and my heart
> is wounded and stricken within me.
>
> Psalm 109:22

Is it wrong to have a wounded heart? No, a wounded heart is not wrong, but you need to get it healed and go on.

In Old Testament days if a priest had a wound or a bleeding sore, he could not minister.[14] I think today we have a lot of wounded healers. By that I mean that there are a lot of people in the body of Christ today who are trying to minister to other people but who themselves still have unhealed wounds from the past. These people are still bleeding and hurting themselves.

Am I saying that such people cannot minister? No, but I am saying that they need to get healed. Jesus said that the blind cannot lead the blind because if they do, they will both fall into a ditch.[15]

There is a message in that statement. What is the use of my trying to minister victory to others if I have no victory in my own life? How can I minister emotional healing to others if I still have unresolved emotional problems from my past? In order to minister properly, we need to go to God and let Him heal us first.

I have found that when I get wounded, when someone hurts my feelings or when Dave and I have problems with each other, I cannot minister properly until I get that situation worked out because it takes away my strength and affects my faith. When I have unresolved problems in my life, I am not as strong as I could be, should be or would be without them.

I think we need to wake up and realize that God is not looking for wounded healers. He wants people with wounds that He can heal who will then go and bring healing to others. God loves to use people who have been hurt and wounded because nobody can minister to someone else better than one who has had the same problem or been in the same situation as that person.

Our new worship leader once shared with me that he had been having trouble with one of the big muscles in his back. He was doing five worship sessions in a row and was not used to standing that long with a guitar in his hands.

God has since healed him of that problem, but for a year and three months I had similar back pain. The minute I heard about his back hurting him, I started praying for him, believing God for healing with him because I knew what it was like to have a backache.

I am not saying that we have to have everybody's problem in order to minister to them. My point is that if we are still bleeding and hurting from our own wounds, we are not going to be able to come against other people's problems with the same kind of aggressive faith we would have if we had already worked through that problem ourselves.

The bottom line is that we need to let God heal us so He can use us to bring healing to other people.

WE NEED TO LET GOD HEAL US, SO HE CAN USE US TO BRING HEALING TO OTHERS.

13. A Faint Heart

> *When you go forth to battle against your enemies and*
> *see horses and chariots and an army greater than your own,*
> *do not be afraid of them, for the Lord your God,*
> *Who brought you out of the land of Egypt, is with you.*
>
> *And when you come near to the battle,*
> *the priest shall approach and speak to the men,*
>
> *And shall say to them, Hear, O Israel, you draw near this day to battle*
> *against your enemies. Let not your [minds and] hearts faint; fear not,*
> *and do not tremble or be terrified [and in dread] because of them.*
>
> *For the Lord your God is He Who goes with you*
> *to fight for you against your enemies to save you.*
>
> Deuteronomy 20:1-4

Fainthearted people are people who give up easily.

What happens when our heart faints? It just gives up. In our heart we say, "I can't do this. It's just too hard."

If we are going to fill a position of leadership in the kingdom of God, we must not do that. We cannot be wimpy or a quitter and be a leader of God's people.

You may think it strange that in one part of this book I say that in order to be a leader we must be tenderhearted, and in another part of the same book I say that we must be tough-hearted. It is possible to be tender and tough at the same time. The key is to know when to be tender and when to be tough. We must be tender toward people and tough toward the devil.

Before I learned the difference, I used to have a lot of problems with two Scriptures that seemed to be at variance. One seemed to say that I was to be as gentle as a lamb, while the other seemed to say that I was to be lionhearted, as bold as a lion.[16] I didn't have any trouble with the lion part, but I did have problems with the lamb part. I had a lot of natural lion in me, but it was the lamb part of me that needed to be developed.

It seems that most people are prone to be more like one or the other. You may be that way. You may be shy and timid, as gentle and meek as a lamb, preferring to avoid having to deal with anything hard or controversial. So God has to put a bit of lion in you. Or you may have a strong lion in you, as I did, and need to have some lamb qualities developed in you.

I was actually desperate for the lamb-like nature. Gentleness did not come easy to me, partly because I was not raised in a gentle atmosphere, and partly because my personality was not gentle by nature.

In Matthew 11:28-30 Jesus said:

> Come to Me, all you who labor and are heavy-laden
> and overburdened, and I will cause you to rest.
> [I will ease and relieve and refresh your souls.]
>
> Take My yoke upon you and learn of Me, for I am gentle (meek) and
> humble (lowly) in heart, and you will find rest (relief and ease
> and refreshment and recreation and blessed quiet) for your souls.
>
> For My yoke is wholesome (useful, good — not harsh, hard,
> sharp, or pressing, but comfortable, gracious, and pleasant),
> and My burden is light and easy to be borne.

Jesus is humble, gentle, meek and lowly, not harsh, hard, sharp and pressing. I was not like Jesus, but I wanted to be, so I went to the extreme of collecting little stuffed lambs and placing them all over my house. I had pictures of lambs and paintings of lambs. I had images of Jesus holding lambs, Jesus in the middle of lambs and carrying lambs on His shoulders. I had so many lambs in my house that it started to look stupid, so I had to clean a whole bunch of them out and keep only the ones I liked best.

Like Scriptures on the refrigerator, those lambs were there to remind me to be gentler. That is what we need to do to remind us not to be fainthearted. If we are too much like a lamb, we need to become more like a lion. If we are too much like a lion, we need to become more like a lamb.

I finally did a series of teachings called "The Lionhearted Lamb" because I began to get a revelation from God that if I did not have a lamb-like nature, I would not have the power of the Holy Ghost manifesting in my ministry. But at the same time I was told that the righteous are to be as bold as a lion. So then I understood that I needed to be meek, sweet and gentle toward people, but bold, tough and aggressive with the devil — because that is the way he is with us.

From time to time we all need to dig in our heels, set our face like flint and say, "I am not going to be fainthearted. I am not going to give up or quit, no matter how hard it gets or how long it takes."

In Deuteronomy 20:8 we read: *And the officers shall speak further to the people, and say, What man is fearful and fainthearted? Let him return to his house, lest [because of him] his brethren's [minds and] hearts faint as does his own.*

Here the Lord is saying to us, "If any of you is fainthearted, you will not be able to stand against the enemy."

A fainthearted person cannot take much. He has to have everything a certain way or he gives up and quits. He gets discouraged and depressed quickly. He gets his feelings hurt easily. Everything bothers him. He is touchy. If that describes you, I want you to know that you don't have to stay that way. The power of God is available to you to break that fainthearted spirit off your life.

In this verse the fainthearted person is told to go home before the battle begins because his faintheartedness might cause others to faint in the face of the enemy.

In Proverbs 24:10 we are told, *If you faint in the day of adversity, your strength is small.* The Bible never promises us that we will never have to face adversity. It promises us the strength we need to overcome that adversity.[17] With God's strength, we don't have to become fainthearted and give up, no matter what kind of adversity we are facing.

All of us have to resist against getting tired and giving up and quitting because we are being hassled by the devil. I am not afraid of the devil, but I do respect his power. I have gotten used to fighting against him. I have come to realize that it is just part of the Christian lifestyle.

You may be thinking, **But when am I not going to have to do that?**

Never. There will always be some challenge in our lives. Our reaction to it determines how hard it is on us.

The best way to fight the devil, especially in times of challenge and stress, is to just stay calm and not get rattled, to maintain a peaceful, gentle heart that is not anxious or wrought up in the sight of God. That is what will help defeat the devil, as we are told in Philippians 1:28: *And do not [for a moment] be frightened or intimidated in anything by your opponents and adversaries, for such [constancy and fearlessness] will be a clear sign (proof and seal) to them of [their impending] destruction, but [a sure token and evidence] of your deliverance and salvation, and that from God.*

So when the devil starts aggravating you, just remain constant. Be fearless. That will be a sign to him of his impending destruction. It will tell him that his days are numbered, and it will be a sign to God to move in your behalf and bring deliverance to you.

We are told in Hebrews 12:3, *Just think of Him Who endured from sinners such grievous opposition and bitter hostility against Himself [reckon up and consider it all in comparison with your trials], so that you may not grow weary or exhausted, losing heart and relaxing and fainting in your minds.*

Make up your mind right now that you are not going to be fainthearted.

Verse 5 of Hebrews 12 says, *And have you [completely] forgotten the divine word of appeal and encouragement in which you are reasoned with and addressed as sons? My son, do not think lightly or scorn to submit to the correction and discipline of the Lord, nor lose courage and give up and faint when you are reproved or corrected by Him.*

Another area in which we need not to be fainthearted is God's correction of us. When God is dealing with us and chastening us, sometimes He has to do it over and over. At such times it is easy for us to feel that we are never going to change, so we are tempted to just give up and quit.

I remember when the Lord had to deal with me again and again about things like my attitude, my pride and my mouth. I would get so discouraged and down on myself that Dave would say to me, "Why don't you stop that? You are discouraged with yourself or our circumstances most of the time."

In the early days of my ministry, when the money wasn't coming in as I thought it should, Dave would say to me, "Joyce, the money is not going to come in until you get stable about it."

In those days Dave was working in the engineering field and would receive a Christmas bonus each year, which we would put in the bank. That money was supposed to be kept for extra things we might need throughout the year, like a new tire if one went flat.

I was always so worried about that money, trying to keep it all in the bank because it was my security blanket. It wasn't so bad in the beginning of the year when almost the entire amount was still untouched, but as the fall came along and we were down to only a couple hundred dollars, every time something would happen to force us to take out some of what was left, I would get wildly upset.

I would start griping, "It never fails! Every time we get a few dollars ahead, something always comes along to take it away! I am so sick and tired of the stupid, stinking devil stealing our money." On and on I would go, ranting and raving and rebuking the devil.

Finally, one day Dave said to me, "I'll tell you when our finances are going to change. They are going to change when you don't have to have that money in the bank to lean on because you are leaning on God and trusting in Him, not that bank account."

The truth makes us mad sometimes, and I got so mad because deep down inside I knew it was true. I didn't want to hear that, and if I had to hear it, I didn't want to hear it from Dave.

So I took that money out of the bank and said to Dave, "All right, I hope you're satisfied now, you and God. Now we have nothing to fall back on financially!" After that, God started taking care of our financial needs.

That may sound funny now, but it wasn't funny when it was happening. I had some serious problems. I was not a good example of leadership in this area, but I am an excellent example of the fact that God can do an awesome work in us if we will just stick with Him and not give up and quit. But we must face the truth. And facing the truth about somebody else is not going to get the job done.

Leaders are not born; I believe they are made. You and I may have been born with some potential, but that potential has to be developed. The flesh has to be crucified. We have to be molded into the image of the

Lord, as we read in Romans 8:29, which tells us that God has predestined us from the beginning to be molded into the image and likeness of His Son Jesus.

Molding is no fun. In fact, it hurts. But it is so wonderful when it is over. So we should do as we are told in Galatians 6:9 and not get weary in well doing, knowing that we will reap if we do not faint. In other words, we will reap if we refuse to become or remain fainthearted.

CHAPTER 7

NEGATIVE CONDITIONS OF THE HEART, PART 3

Learning about negative heart conditions may not be comfortable, but it has a purpose. It actually shows us our problem areas so we can cooperate with the Holy Spirit in overcoming them. If you are finding that you have some of the negative heart conditions mentioned in this book, let me encourage you that you are not alone. We all have things we need to work on in our lives.

We cannot always avoid the opportunities that tempt us to get into wrong heart attitudes, but we can learn to avoid getting into them. And as believers, we know that God is with us, and that as we spend time alone with Him in prayer and reading His Word, He strengthens us daily to do what we need to do in order to fulfill His good plan for our lives.

Before we talk about the positive heart conditions for leadership, there are several more negative heart conditions we need to look at.

14. A Despiteful Heart

> *Rejoice not when your enemy falls, and let not your heart*
> *be glad when he stumbles or is overthrown,*
>
> *Lest the Lord see it and it be evil in His eyes and displease Him,*
> *and He turn away His wrath from him [to expend it upon you,*
> *the worse offender].*
>
> Proverbs 24:17,18

Having a despiteful heart simply means wanting to get people back for what they have done to us.

The writer of this passage is saying that if someone does us wrong, and later on we rejoice because they have problems, thinking that they deserve what they are getting, then the wrath that God would have turned on our enemy He now has to turn on us because our offense is worse than theirs.

So that should prove that it is our heart attitude that God is concerned about most. A right heart attitude will ultimately produce right actions, but people can discipline themselves to do good works yet have a wrong heart. God knows that if the heart is right, eventually other things will also become right.

That is really an awesome Scripture. All of us will have to admit that when someone has done us wrong, it takes a lot of "heart" work for us not to be at least a little bit happy to see that person get what is coming to him. We can act holy if we want to, but we all have a problem with that kind of despiteful attitude from time to time.

In Ezekiel 25:15-17 we read what the Lord has to say about this subject:

> *Thus says the Lord God: Because the Philistines have dealt revengefully and have taken vengeance contemptuously, with malice and spite in their hearts, to destroy in perpetual enmity,*

> *Therefore thus says the Lord God: Behold, I will stretch out My hand against the Philistines, and I will cut off the Cherethites [an immigration in Philistia] and destroy the remainder of the seacoast.*

> *And I will execute great vengeance upon them with wrathful rebukes and chastisements, and they shall know (understand and realize) that I am the Lord, when I lay My vengeance upon them.*

Basically, what God was saying in this passage is that He was going to take vengeance on the Philistines because they had taken vengeance on their enemies. If they had left the vengeance to Him, He would have taken it. But since they took it upon themselves to take vengeance, His anger was turned from their enemies to them.

When someone hurts us, besides being an act of wisdom to turn that situation over to God and let Him handle it, it is also a great act of trust on our part when we turn it over to Him and wait for Him to straighten the thing out.

15. A Heavy or Troubled Heart

> *Anxiety in a man's heart weighs it down, but an*
> *encouraging word makes it glad.*
>
> Proverbs 12:25

I believe every Christian should keep his heart light. The *King James Version* of Proverbs 12:25 says, *Heaviness in the heart of man maketh it stoop: but a good word maketh it glad.* We are not to go around with a heavy heart or with a spirit of heaviness on us because one of the things Jesus said He was sent to do was to lift the heaviness from God's people: *To grant [consolation and joy] to those who mourn in Zion — to give them an ornament (a garland or diadem) of beauty instead of ashes, the oil of joy instead of mourning, the garment [expressive] of praise instead of a heavy, burdened, and failing spirit . . . .*[1]

In John 14:1 Jesus told His disciples, *Do not let your hearts be troubled (distressed, agitated). . . .*

From these and other Scriptures, it seems clear that the Lord does not want us to have a heavy or troubled heart. The next time things aren't going right, remember that as leaders, it is vital that we keep our heart in a condition of lightness. We must not allow a heavy burden to rest upon us because leaders minister out of their hearts.

16. A Reasoning Heart

> *Trust in the LORD with all your heart,*
> *And lean not on your own understanding;*
>
> *In all your ways acknowledge Him,*
> *And He shall direct your paths.*
>
> Proverbs 3:5,6 NKJV

People who must reason out everything have a very hard time with faith because reasoning is not faith, and without faith it is impossible to please God.[2]

I can teach on reasoning because I used to be a class A, chief reasoner. I was the lady who had to have everything figured out. I had to have a plan. I had to know not only all about my own business but all about other people's business too — even God's. I was continually asking, "Why, God, why? When, God, when?" In that respect I had to reason everything out like the religious leaders of Jesus' day:

> *Now some of the scribes were sitting there, holding a dialogue with themselves as they questioned in their hearts,*
>
> *Why does this Man talk like this? He is blaspheming! Who can forgive sins [remove guilt, remit the penalty, and bestow righteousness instead] except God alone?*
>
> *And at once Jesus, becoming fully aware in His spirit that they thus debated within themselves, said to them, Why do you argue (debate, reason) about all this in your hearts?*

Mark 2:6-8

Do you ever hold a dialogue with yourself? The fact is, you probably talk to yourself more than you talk to anybody else. The question is, what are you saying to yourself?

These scribes were not saying those things in the above passage out loud but in their hearts. They were questioning within themselves about Jesus. Immediately, He became aware in His Spirit of their arguing, debating and reasoning and called it to their attention. He was able to pick up the condition of their hearts because He had a heart that was peaceful.

As leaders, we need to be aware of this problem of having a reasoning heart. It is a serious matter that we need to deal with, just as Jesus dealt with it in the hearts of those who followed Him.

DISCERNMENT COMES WHEN REASONING GOES

> *Now they had [completely] forgotten to bring bread, and they had only one loaf with them in the boat.*
>
> *And Jesus [repeatedly and expressly] charged and admonished them, saying, Look out; keep on your guard and beware of the leaven of the Pharisees and the leaven of Herod and the Herodians.*

And they discussed it and reasoned with one another, It is because we have no bread.

And being aware [of it], Jesus said to them, Why are you reasoning and saying it is because you have no bread? Do you not yet discern or understand? Are your hearts in [a settled state of] hardness?

Mark 8:14-17

In this passage, we see again the discernment of Jesus and how He was able to perceive the reasoning in the hearts of His disciples who were as dumb as we are sometimes. I'm not being insulting; that's just a fact.

For all their reasoning, they failed, as we often do, to understand what the Lord was saying to them. He was not talking about literal bread; He was talking about spiritual leaven, about the teachings and practices of the Pharisees. He was warning His disciples to be on guard against letting these legalistic tendencies get inside of them because He knew they would poison their whole lives. He was telling them, "Beware of the Pharisees' hypocritical attitude. They don't practice what they preach. They preach good things, but they don't do what they say."

Trying to get through to His disciples, Jesus reminded them of His miraculous feeding of the five thousand and the four thousand:

Having eyes, do you not see [with them], and having ears, do you not hear and perceive and understand the sense of what is said? And do you not remember?

When I broke the five loaves for the 5,000, how many [small hand] baskets full of broken pieces did you take up? They said to Him, Twelve.

And [when I broke] the seven loaves for the 4,000, how many [large provision] baskets full of broken pieces did you take up? And they said to Him, Seven.

And He kept repeating, Do you not yet understand?

Mark 8:18-21

In this passage Jesus was saying to them, "Don't worry about forgetting to bring bread. I can do a miracle to provide bread. I am not talking about the emptiness of your stomachs; I am talking about the condition of your hearts."

Notice that He said to them in verse 17, "Why are you reasoning? Do you not discern?"

That is what I used to do. I used to have a lot of problems with reasoning. I was always trying to figure things out. Then one day the Lord said something interesting to me in my heart. He said, "As long as you continue to reason, you will never have discernment."

Discernment starts in the heart and moves up and enlightens the mind. As long as my mind was so busy reasoning, God couldn't get through to me, just as Jesus couldn't get through to His disciples.

This is an important issue. Reasoning is such a huge problem because reasoning is not faith. *The Amplified Bible* translation of Romans 8:6 says that the mind of the flesh is sense and reason without the Holy Spirit. It goes on to say that those operating in the mind of the flesh will experience a miserable life. Those who flow in the mind of the Holy Spirit will have life and peace. Reasoning belongs to the mind of the flesh and does not produce good fruit. The "reasoning" I am referring to is the reasoning we do that is *contrary to the Truth*[3] in the Word of God. As I discussed before, God wants us to use common sense! He wants us to use our minds to reason, but He wants us to reason in a way that lines up with His Word.

One thing that caused me to continue to seek deliverance from reasoning was the fact that I felt confused so much of the time. I soon learned that I was not alone in that respect. In one of my meetings I asked, "How many of you are experiencing confusion in your life?" Out of 300 people in the audience, 298 lifted their hands. Only my husband and one other person did not raise their hands.

Yet Paul tells us in the Bible that God is not the author of confusion.[4] As children of God, we are not supposed to go around confused all the time because we can **discern** things. That is why the Lord told me in my heart, "Tell My people to stop trying to figure out everything, and they will not be confused."

I like what Mary did when the angel of the Lord appeared to her and told her she would become pregnant by the Holy Ghost. Instead of getting into reasoning, trying to figure out what she was being told, she simply said, "Lord, let it be done unto me according to Your Word."[5]

We are told in the Bible that Mary pondered things in her heart.[6] It is OK to ponder things. It is one of the right conditions of the heart that we will look at later on. But the minute we begin to feel confused, that is when we know we have crossed over from pondering into reasoning. Obviously, however, we cannot go through life never thinking or making plans.

Having a reasonable number of plans can make our lives simpler, but having too many plans can complicate them. Balance is the key to victory in our minds.

One of my daughters was a planner par excellence. To handle all the details she had to deal with, she had to have a plan. But she got out of balance with it. She was planning things to the point that it was driving her crazy. God had to deal with her about keeping her heart peaceful. He showed her that it was fine to have everything planned, as long as she did not allow herself to be controlled and manipulated by her plans. Today she has come a long way in overcoming her tendency to try to reason and figure out everything in life.

> IF WE TRY TO FIGURE OUT WHY EVERYTHING HAPPENS IN LIFE, WE WILL NOT HAVE PEACE OF MIND AND HEART.

You cannot have peace of mind and heart if you are reasoning all the time. If you are lacking peace in your life, it may be because you are trying to figure out too many things. Stop asking, "Why, God, why?" Just say, "Lord, You know, and I need to be satisfied with that. When You are ready to show me, do so. Until then, with Your help, I'm going to laugh and have a good time, trusting that You are in charge and that You will take care of everything that concerns me."[7]

17. An Envious and Striving Heart

For ye are yet carnal: for whereas there is among you envying, and strife, and divisions, are ye not carnal, and walk as men?

1 Corinthians 3:3 KJV

Envy and jealousy cause us to strive after things that God will give us in His timing, if it is His will that we have them. A jealous, envious heart in no way blesses God. We are not to covet what other people have — not even their ministry.

As leaders, we must not covet someone else's position in ministry. We must not covet someone else's church, staff, the size of their following or any other part of their ministry. That is not pleasing to God.

We need to be happy with what God has given us. We need to trust Him that if we are supposed to have more, He will give it to us when He knows we are able to handle it.

You may be thinking, **I believe the devil is keeping me from being blessed.**

I look at it this way. If I am doing what God wants me to do, and my heart is right before Him, no man on earth or devil in hell can keep me from having what God wants me to have.

I believe that many times blaming everything on the devil is just an excuse not to grow up. It is an excuse not to develop personal character and let God do the work on the inside of us that He wants to do.

I am not saying that the devil does not try to prevent us from fulfilling our ministry. He tried to prevent Jesus from fulfilling His ministry too, but he wasn't successful. He may come against us, but he will not prevent us.

There will be times when we have to press on in spite of opposition from the enemy, but if we are in the will of God, He will give us the strength to carry on until we achieve what He wants us to achieve. It is not the devil that prevents us from fulfilling our destiny, it is our uncircumcised flesh, which we haven't dealt with or crucified yet. We will talk about the uncircumcised heart later in this chapter.

Yes, the devil is alive and well, and, yes, he does come against people. But if we teach them that fact in an unbalanced, excessive way, they will blame Satan for everything. He likes that because it draws attention toward him and the problems he causes, and away from God and His promises. Instead of focusing on the works of the enemy, we need to keep our eyes on God and on letting Him have His way with us.

I used to have a problem with jealousy and envy, especially in the realm of ministry. Until I got over it, my ministry did not grow.

As we have seen, just because we have potential does not mean that we are going to fulfill our potential. To do that, we must cooperate with God.

The thing that finally set me free from jealousy and envy was realizing that God had an individual, tailor-made, personalized plan for me. I don't have to compare myself with anyone else. I don't have to get into competition with any other ministry. All I have to do is say, "Lord, I want Your will for my life. My times are in Your hands. Whatever You want me to do, that is what I want to do. What others do is none of my business. All I am supposed to do is what You want me to do."

There is nothing more frustrating than striving after things God has not given us, trying to make things happen that God has not anointed or trying to do something about something we can do nothing about.

The key to happiness and fulfillment is not in changing our situation or circumstances, but in trusting God to perform His good plan in our life until we see results.

> **The key to happiness and fulfillment is in trusting God to perform His good plan in our life until we see results.**

18. A Greedy, Lustful Heart

> *Then [Israel] believed His words [trusting in, relying on them];*
> *they sang His praise.*
>
> *But they hastily forgot His works; they did not [earnestly] wait for*
> *His plans [to develop] regarding them,*
>
> *But lusted exceedingly in the wilderness and tempted and tried*
> *to restrain God [with their insistent desires] in the desert.*
>
> *And He gave them their request, but sent leanness into their souls and*
> *[thinned their numbers by] disease and death.*
>
> Psalm 106:12-15

We need to be careful about a greedy, lustful heart that can never be satisfied.

Although God had led the Israelites out of bondage in Egypt and had destroyed Pharaoh and his army who were chasing after them, the Israelites were not satisfied. They continued to gripe and complain every step of the way. No matter how much He provided for them, they always wanted more. They were on the way to the Promised Land, but they were not enjoying the journey.

Many times that is our problem also.

When I was teaching twenty-five people every Tuesday evening in my living room, that was all I was mature enough to handle. I had a vision to do what I am doing now, so I grumbled, murmured, pleaded, prayed, fasted, rebuked devils — and never got out of my living room. All my efforts were a waste of time and energy. I could have been relaxing, praising God, laughing and enjoying my family, my husband, my children and my life. But no, I had to be miserable all the time because I wasn't getting my way.

I finally got an opportunity to teach another Bible study. I was happy with that for a little while, but not for long.

Then I went to work for a church in St. Louis where I was associate pastor for five years. After a while I wasn't satisfied there anymore.

Then I got my own ministry. It wasn't long until I was unhappy with that.

No matter what I was doing, I was always wanting something else.

If people are not careful, they can waste their entire lives by always wanting something else. They fall in love and can't wait to get married. Then once they are married, they can't be happy until they are not married.

They have kids and can't wait for them to grow up and start school. As soon as the kids are in school, they can't wait until they graduate. As soon as that happens, they can't wait until they get married and have kids of their own.

On and on it goes. No matter what their place in life, they are always wanting something else. They keep murmuring and grumbling to God about what they want. Then as soon as He gives it to them, they start in griping and complaining again because they want something else.

The moral of the story of the Israelites is that they got what they asked for, but they were not really ready to handle it. The Lord gave them what they wanted, but He also gave them leanness in their soul. What does "leanness in their soul" mean? It simply means that they were not happy.

Can you imagine how miserable I would be if I had this ministry but wasn't spiritually prepared for it? What if I had to handle the responsibility of the building we own, the bills we have to pay, the radio and television programs we put on, the books we write, the offices we have to run, the employees we have to manage and so on? Even though I want it, the weight of all that would crush me.

I thank God He didn't give all that to me when I first began to ask Him for it because if He had, I would have made a fool of myself, lost the ministry and probably died from the stress.

Beware of a greedy, lustful heart. Don't always be wanting something God is not ready to give you. Learn to settle down and be happy with what you have while the Lord is preparing you for something better.

Let God take time to lay a solid foundation in your life before you start begging Him to build a big building on it. We always want more, but only God knows when we are stable enough to be able to handle it.

> LEARN TO SETTLE DOWN AND BE HAPPY WITH WHAT YOU HAVE WHILE THE LORD IS PREPARING YOU FOR SOMETHING BETTER.

19. An Uncircumcised Heart

You stubborn and stiff-necked people, still heathen and uncircumcised in heart and ears, you are always actively resisting the Holy Spirit. As your forefathers [were], so you [are and so you do]!

Acts 7:51

God showed me what an uncircumcised heart is. To circumcise is to cut off. When a person has an uncircumcised heart and something wicked or evil comes into it, he doesn't cut it off. He lets it stay there. But a person who has a circumcised heart will immediately cut off any wrong attitude that comes into his mind, so he can live before God with a circumcised heart.

Remember, the devil is going to come at us with wrong heart attitudes at every opportunity, but taking his bait never helps us. It only hinders our growth and development. The Lord showed me that if I have a circumcised heart, when anger, hatred, jealousy, envy or any other kind of wrong emotion comes into my mind, I must get rid of it immediately. If I don't, if I let it stay there, I am not being what He has called me to be, as Paul tells us in Romans 2:28,29:

> For he is not a [real] Jew who is only one outwardly and publicly, nor is [true] circumcision something external and physical.

> But he is a Jew who is one inwardly, and [true] circumcision is of the heart, a spiritual and not a literal [matter]. His praise is not from men but from God.

A good leader maintains a circumcised heart by saying no to anything that will keep them from being a person whose heart is right before God.

20. A Condemned Heart

> For if our heart condemns us, God is greater than our heart, and knows all things.

> Beloved, if our heart does not condemn us, we have confidence toward God.

> And whatever we ask we receive from Him, because we keep His commandments and do those things that are pleasing in His sight.

> 1 John 3:20-22 NKJV

A condemned heart steals confidence.

Anyone who wants to be a leader must learn how to handle condemnation. When he sins, he had better know how to shake it off and go on because no one is perfect. He may have a perfect heart, a heart after God's Own, but he will still not be perfect in his every thought, word and deed.

I know how condemning it is to teach others about what is right and then foul up in that very area myself. When we do that, we feel a double dose of condemnation because the devil will say to us, "You of all people ought to know better." If we listen to him, he will make us feel that we are not worthy to be a leader of God's people.

We have got to be able to shake off the feeling of condemnation because if we don't, we will have no confidence before God. Without confidence, we will have no faith. And without faith, we cannot please God[8] or receive from Him the things He knows we need to do what He has called us to do.

That is why we are told to guard our heart with all diligence. As we have seen, it is out of the heart that flow the issues of life.

God convicts us of our wrongdoing; He does not condemn us. Conviction helps us to repent and be lifted out of the problem; condemnation only pushes us down and makes us feel bad about ourselves.

Romans 8:33,34 tells us that God justifies us; He does not bring charges against us. Jesus does not condemn us. He died for us. He sits at the Father's right hand actually pleading in intercession for us. I have learned from this Scripture that when I feel condemned, I am either doing it to myself or it is the devil doing it to me. Always submit to God's conviction, but resist Satan's condemnation.

CHAPTER 8

POSITIVE CONDITIONS OF THE HEART, PART 1

*. . . For the Lord sees not as man sees; for man looks on the
outward appearance, but the Lord looks on the heart.*

1 Samuel 16:7

God is the God of hearts. He does not look at the exterior of a person,
or even the things a person does, and judge the individual by that
criterion. Man judges after the flesh, but God judges by the heart.

It is possible to put up a good front and still have a lousy heart. It is
also possible to be dealing with problems on the outside and still have a
right heart on the inside. God is much more inclined to use a person
with a good heart and a few problems than He is to use a person who
seems to have it all together but who has a wicked heart.

It is very important that we get in touch with our inner life and our
heart attitude, the way we feel and think about things, what the Bible
calls the hidden man of the heart, as we saw, if we want to be used by
God as a leader in His kingdom or have any success as a Christian.

In the previous chapters, we looked at some of the negative
conditions of the heart that keep a person from being the leader God
wants them to be. Now we are going to consider some of the positive
conditions of the heart that God wants His leaders to have.

1. A Willing Heart

And the Lord said to Moses,

Speak to the Israelites, that they take for Me an offering. From

*every man who gives it willingly and ungrudgingly with his heart
you shall take My offering.*

Exodus 25:1,2

When we talk about a willing heart, we are basically talking about "want to." Without it, we will never do anything.

In the many years of my ministry I have had to press through a lot of negative things. Yes, there was a call on my life, but I had to have something in addition to a call. I had to have a lot of "want to."

By observing myself and other people, I have come to the conclusion that we end up doing what we want to do. If there is something we want to do strongly enough, somehow we will find a way to do it.

"Want to" is a powerful thing. With it we can lose weight, keep our house clean, save money, get out of debt or reach any other goal in life we may have set for ourselves. We don't really like to face the fact that our victory or defeat has a lot to do with our "want to." We like to blame everything on someone or something else. But I think we need to sit down and take a good old-fashioned inventory of our "want to." We need to be at least honest enough to say, "Lord, I didn't win the victory because I really didn't want to. I didn't pray or read the Bible because I didn't want to. I didn't spend time meditating on the Word and talking with You because I didn't want to. Instead, I sat around all night on the couch watching television — because I wanted to."

There is nothing wrong with rest and entertainment, but we need to keep our priorities straight. As I said, we are really good at laying the blame for our failures on someone or something else besides ourselves. We like to blame the devil, other people, the past and on and on, when the truth is that most of the time the bottom line is, we just don't have enough of the right kind of "want to."

If you and I are going to be in leadership, and we are going to serve God, we must have "want to." We must have a willing heart. As a matter of fact, God is not interested in our good works if we are not doing them with a willing heart.

Many years ago God had to deal with me because I was living under the Law. I was very legalistic and insecure because of a lot of wounds from my past. I was doing all the right things, but I was doing them for all the wrong reasons. I was doing them because I was afraid if I didn't do them, God would get angry at me or He would not be pleased with me.

So many times I prayed because I thought I had to. My heart really wasn't in it. I just did it out of a sense of obligation. I would religiously read the Word, covering so many chapters of the Bible every day, and put in my hour of daily prayer because then I would feel that I had fulfilled the Law.

I remember God speaking to me so clearly one day and saying, "Joyce, I don't want you to give Me anything or do anything for Me unless you want to."

A GOOD LEADER HAS A WILLING HEART — A "WANT-TO" ATTITUDE.

I remember thinking, **That can't be God.**

I am not saying that there are never times when we have to discipline ourselves. But even then, we should do so because we want to, not because we have to. We do have to discipline our flesh in order to do what is in our heart because the flesh wars against the Spirit. We don't always feel like doing what we want to do, but it is not necessary that we **feel** like doing it, only that we **want** to do it. The will should take the lead role — not feelings.

There are many times when I do not feel like traveling around the country holding conferences. But I continue to do that because deep down inside I want to. My flesh may not always want to do it, but my spirit does, so I do it anyway, in spite of my feelings, because I have a willing heart. That is what God wants His people to have, as we see in His Word:

Take from among you an offering to the Lord. Whoever is of a willing and generous heart, let him bring the Lord's offering. . . .

They came, both men and women, all who were willinghearted, and brought brooches, earrings or nose rings, signet rings, and armlets or necklaces, all jewels of gold, everyone bringing an offering of gold to the Lord.

The Israelites brought a freewill offering to the Lord, all men and women whose hearts made them willing and moved them to bring anything for any of the work which the Lord had commanded by Moses to be done.

Exodus 35:5,22,29

Do you know what a strong "want to" will do in the area of giving? It will cause us to give sacrificially. If we want to strongly enough, somehow, some way, we will find something to give.

I remember when Dave and I didn't have much money, so we would take pictures off the wall and bedspreads off the beds and give them away. It is amazing the sacrifices you will make if you really have a strong enough "want to."

In 1 Chronicles 29:6 we read, *Then the chiefs of the fathers and princes of the tribes of Israel and the captains of thousands and of hundreds, with the rulers of the king's work, offered willingly.* We are not going to work if we don't want to. But if we want to strongly enough, we will work. We will do whatever it takes to get the job done. Smart people realize that nothing worthwhile is ever accomplished without work.

BE WILLING TO BE WILLING

*Then the people rejoiced because these had given willingly, for with
a whole and blameless heart they had offered freely to the Lord.
King David also rejoiced greatly.*

1 Chronicles 29:9

Do you like it when people do something for you, but you know they don't really want to do it? I absolutely despise that. I believe that comes from my upbringing. It seemed to me that even when my father allowed me to do things, he really didn't want me to do them. So to this day if people don't really want to do something for me, I would rather they just forget it.

If we are like that, how much more is God like that? We human beings do a halfway decent job of hiding our true feelings from people, but we cannot hide our heart from God. We may as well start being honest about the way we feel and start doing things out of a willing heart, or at least start praying for God to give us a willing heart, so we can do them for the right reason.

Sometimes we may have to pray, "Lord, make me willing to be willing." And sometimes we may have to pray, "Lord, make me willing to be willing to be willing — because I don't want to be willing at all!"

God examines our heart attitude, and whatever we do for Him must be done willingly:

> *I know also, my God, that You try the heart and delight in*
> *uprightness. In the uprightness of my heart I have freely offered*
> *all these things. And now I have seen with joy Your people who*
> *are present here offer voluntarily and freely to You.*

1 Chronicles 29:17

God is not pleased with what we do out of obligation or under the Law:

> *Let each one [give] as he has made up his own mind and purposed in*
> *his heart, not reluctantly or sorrowfully or under compulsion, for God*
> *loves (He takes pleasure in, prizes above other things, and is unwilling*
> *to abandon or to do without) a cheerful (joyous, "prompt to do it")*
> *giver [whose heart is in his giving].*

2 Corinthians 9:7

I like *The Amplified Bible* version of this verse because it emphasizes that God really delights in those who give to Him willingly, joyfully and cheerfully, but not those who do it legalistically, under compulsion or because they have been made to do it or talked into doing it.

In 1 Peter 5:2, Peter mentions this when he says, *Tend (nurture, guard, guide, and fold) the flock of God that is [your responsibility], not by coercion or constraint, but willingly; not dishonorably motivated by the advantages and profits [belonging to the office], but eagerly and cheerfully.*

Obviously, in this verse Peter is speaking to pastors and elders, those in leadership, but I believe what he is saying applies to anyone who wants to be used by God. He says that, first of all, we must make sure that we are doing it for the right reason, not for what we might get out of it. Second, he says that we are to do it with a good attitude.

For example, if you are going to go make a hospital call, don't do it complaining about it. If you are going to baby-sit for a friend because you really feel that is what God wants you to do, don't murmur about it.

We need to realize that whatever we do for another person, we are not really doing for that person, we are doing it for the Lord.[1] There are many things that we do simply because we love God that we wouldn't do for any other reason. Whatever we do for others — especially when we don't really feel like doing it, but we do it anyway because we want to, and so we do it with a good attitude — that is pleasing to God.

The point is that whatever we do for God, He wants us to do it with a willing heart. If we are not going to do it that way, then we may as well not do it at all. I don't believe we receive any reward for doing things with a bad attitude.

I am convinced that the central part of a believer's life is his heart attitude. It is not the show we put on for others on the outside that matters; it is the truth inside us that we cannot hide from God.

BE GOD PLEASERS

Servants, obey in everything those who are your earthly masters, not only when their eyes are on you as pleasers of men, but in simplicity of purpose [with all your heart] because of your reverence for the Lord and as a sincere expression of your devotion to Him.

Colossians 3:22

Here we are told that we are to be good, faithful, loyal, profitable and hardworking employees. We are to do our jobs well and with a good attitude. We are not to be two-faced, showing our employers what we think they want to see and then showing something different when they are not around. We need to be real, sincere, honest and trustworthy.

I think it is a tragedy for those of us who have jobs to murmur and grumble about them when there are so many people who do not have jobs. We should be grateful for our work and thankful we are able to do it.

We are not to be men pleasers, but God pleasers. We are not to do right only when the boss is around and then do things like making personal telephone calls on company time when no one is looking. It is amazing how people scatter when the boss walks into the room. They all scurry back to their places and try to look busy because they know they have been slacking off.

These are the kinds of things God is interested in because we are supposed to be living epistles read of all men. We are not going to win the world with bumper stickers, tape recorders and Jesus pins, and no fruit in our lives. It is not coming to work with all our paraphernalia declaring that we are Christians that will draw men to Christ; it is our giving a full day's work for a full day's wage, submitting to those in authority over us with a good attitude and doing whatever we are asked to do without grumbling, griping or complaining that is going to make people look at us and want what we have.

In Colossians 3:23,24 Paul tells us, *Whatever may be your task, work at it heartily (from the soul), as [something done] for the Lord and not for men, knowing [with all certainty] that it is from the Lord [and not from men] that you will receive the inheritance which is your [real] reward. [The One Whom] you are actually serving [is] the Lord Christ (the Messiah).*

Do you know what happens when we do our work with all our heart and soul, and do it not unto men but unto God? We receive our reward from Him, not our boss. We can look to the Lord for the reward that we truly deserve.

2. A Stirred Heart

That is why I would remind you to stir up (rekindle the embers of, fan the flame of, and keep burning) the [gracious] gift of God, [the inner fire] that is in you by means of the laying on of my hands [with those of the elders at your ordination].

2 Timothy 1:6

God wants us to stay stirred up. He is not into deadness. The Bible says that the dead do not praise the Lord.[2] God gets no praise out of deadness. He is not looking for a dead church, but a living church.

I love what Jesus said when He raised Lazarus from the dead. First, He told Lazarus to come forth from the tomb. Then He told the onlookers to take the grave clothes off of him.[3]

There are a lot of born-again, Spirit-filled people who have never taken off their grave clothes. They just reek with deadness.

God doesn't want us to be dead; He wants us to be stirred up.

As we have already seen, in one of Paul's letters to his young disciple, Timothy, he told him to stir up the gift that was within him.[4]

Apparently, Timothy was getting fearful and weary and unsure of his call. His spirit was sinking, so Paul came in with a strong word to revive him. In 2 Timothy 1:5 Paul reminded him of his faith and how it had come to him. He told him in essence, "I remember your grandmother's faith. I remember your mother's faith. I remember when I laid my hands on you and we prayed for you and the gifts that are in you." Then he said, "Now stir up the gift within you."

> **KEEP YOUR GOD-GIVEN GIFT, THAT FIRE WITHIN YOU, STIRRED UP. WHEN YOU START TO GROW COLD, STIR UP THAT GIFT AGAIN.**

Nobody can stir up your gift, that fire within you, the way you can. Other people can stir you up, as I am trying to do in this book. But as soon as you are alone or as soon as you put down this book, you can grow cold again. That is when you have to stir up yourself.

Life is more exciting if we have a stirred-up heart. What's the sense in going around moaning and groaning and saying, "I really don't want to do what I have to do. I really wish I didn't have to do it. I'm so sick and tired of doing this"?

Half the church is sick and tired because all we do is go around saying we are sick and tired. Sooner or later we have to get sick and tired of saying we are sick and tired. That is when we will do something about it.

HOW DO WE GET STIRRED UP?

And they came, each one whose heart stirred him up and whose spirit made him willing, and brought the Lord's offering to be used for the [new] Tent of Meeting, for all its service, and the holy garments.

Exodus 35:21

Those who built the tabernacle of the Lord were those who had a willing heart, those who kept themselves stirred up about the things of God.

You may be thinking, **I wish I could be excited, but I just don't feel that way. I don't really know how to get myself stirred up.**

One way is to quit hanging around with a bunch of lifeless people all the time. If you wonder why you feel depressed, lazy, cold and half dead, it may be because you are associating with people who are that way. Spirits are transferable. What I mean by that is, if you stay around people who are excited and stirred up about the things of God, it won't be long until you get excited and stirred up too. If you stay around a visionary, you will soon get a vision. But if you stay around people who want to do nothing but sit on the couch, eat doughnuts and watch soap operas, pretty soon that is what you will be doing.

It doesn't do any good to say, "I wish I felt that way." You have to decide to do something about the way you feel. If you want to have victory over your feelings strongly enough, you will do whatever it takes to get it. If you don't want to have that victory, no one can make you want it strongly enough to do anything about it.

We have got to stop whining around and feeling sorry for ourselves and wishing: "I wish I had this" and "I wish I didn't have that. I wish my parents loved me more. I wish I had more money. I wish my back didn't hurt. I wish . . . I wish . . . I wish. . . ."

I used to do that. For years I went around wishing, until the Lord spoke to me and said, "You can be pitiful or you can be powerful, but you cannot be both. So take your pick."

Years later I read a statement that said, "A lot of people have a wishbone, but they don't have a backbone."

I thought, **That's the truth.**

Wishing won't get us anything. We have got to dig in and do whatever we have to do to get it.

In Romans 12:11 we are told, *Never lag in zeal and in earnest endeavor; be aglow and burning with the Spirit, serving the Lord.* In order to be always aglow and burning, we have to stay on fire.

How do we stay on fire? I have discovered that the Word of God coming out of my own mouth in the form of prayer, praise, preaching or confession is the best way that I can find to fan the fire. It stirs up the gift within, keeps the fire aflame and prevents my spirit from sinking within me.

The writer of Ecclesiastes tells us, *Whatever your hand finds to do, do it with all your might, for there is no work or device or knowledge or wisdom in*

Sheol (the place of the dead), where you are going.[5] There is no point in putting off starting things until later.

That is actually being passive, and it is one of the greatest tools that Satan uses against God's people.

Procrastination and laziness are the cousins of passivity, and they usually all attack in a group. A passive person waits to be moved by an outside force before they will take action. We are to be motivated and led by the Holy Spirit within us, not by outside forces. The best way to be on guard against the spirit of passivity is to do it now, and **do it with all your might.**

> BE MOTIVATED
> AND LED BY THE
> HOLY SPIRIT,
> NOT BY OUTSIDE
> FORCES.

Remember, everything we do is to be done unto the Lord and for His glory. We should do it through Him, to Him, for Him, by Him and with Him. And we should do it willingly, with our whole heart stirred up within us.

3. A Wise Heart

> *And thou shalt speak unto all that are wise hearted, whom I have filled with the spirit of wisdom. . . .*
>
> Exodus 28:3 KJV

It absolutely amazes me some of the stupid things we do. We wonder why we don't have the things in life we want, when all we have to do is watch how we act.

In the book of Haggai we see a group of people who did not like their circumstances at all. God's response to them was, *. . . consider your ways (your previous and present conduct) and how you have fared.*[6]

We may be gifted, but if we have gifts but no wisdom, those gifts will get us nowhere but in trouble. If we want to succeed in ministry, we have to have spiritual gifts and wisdom, but remember, we must also have a lot of common sense. That is really what wisdom is, just plain old common sense.

It really does not make any sense to put off something God says to do for eighteen years, and yet the Israelites did it and could not understand why they were not prospering. Yes, success in ministry requires more than gifts.

In Exodus 35:30-33, Moses talks to the Israelites about gifts, telling them:

> . . . *See, the Lord called by name Bezalel son of Uri, the son of Hur, of the tribe of Judah;*
>
> *And He has filled him with the Spirit of God, with ability and wisdom, with intelligence and understanding, and with knowledge and all craftsmanship,*
>
> *To devise artistic designs, to work in gold, silver, and bronze,*
>
> *In cutting of stones for setting, and in carving of wood, for work in every skilled craft.*

In this passage Moses is telling the people of God that the Lord has taken this man Bezalel and filled him with gifts.

According to the Bible, each of us has been given different gifts, all to be used for the benefit of the body of Christ.[7] Every person is gifted in some way. One of the things we need to do is exercise our gift and stop trying to have someone else's gift.

Some of us are so busy trying to do somebody else's thing that we never get around to doing our own thing. That usually happens because of insecurity, of not knowing who we are in Christ and not being satisfied with doing the part that has been given to us by the Lord.

If God has given you a part in the church that does not include standing in front of the people and ministering, then do that part because if you try to put yourself up in front of people, you will not be happy with it or successful at it.

God gifts everyone, but many people never get around to using their gifts because they don't use wisdom.

In Exodus 35:34,35 Moses continued to speak to the Israelites about gifts, saying, *And God has put in Bezalel's heart that he may teach, both he and Aholiab son of Ahisamach, of the tribe of Dan. He has filled them with wisdom of heart and ability to do all manner of craftsmanship, of the engraver, of the skillful workman, of the embroiderer in blue, purple, and scarlet [stuff] and in fine linen, and of the weaver, even of those who do or design any skilled work.*

When I first read that passage, I underlined the words **wisdom** and **ability**. God does not just give us ability; He gives us wisdom to go along with it.

Dave and I have watched so many people who struggle in ministry, and it is not because they are not gifted and talented, but because they don't use any wisdom.

We must use wisdom in anything we do in life, whether it is a ministry, a business or a marriage.

For example, a woman may be gifted with great beauty; she may be extremely talented; she may be able to cook, grow a garden and do all the things the Proverbs 31 lady does well. But she can still completely ruin her marriage if she doesn't use wisdom.

In Proverbs 24:3 we are told, *Through skillful and godly Wisdom is a house (a life, a home, a family) built, and by understanding it is established [on a sound and good foundation].*

Where does wisdom show up in our lives? It shows up in the way we talk, act, handle our money, meet our responsibilities, treat other people, keep our word and in a thousand other ways. There are all kinds of ways we have to walk in wisdom, and yet one of the greatest tragedies in this life is that so many of God's own people are just not operating in wisdom. They are totally stressed out because they are going in ninety-five different directions at once.

God once told me when I was murmuring and complaining about my schedule, "You know, Joyce, you are the one who made your schedule. I didn't make it, and I never told you to do all the things you are trying to do."

It is not wisdom to get overcommitted and then spend our time murmuring and grumbling about it.

WISDOM WILL GET YOU SOMEWHERE

And David went out wherever Saul sent him, and he prospered and behaved himself wisely; and Saul set him over the men of war. And it was satisfactory both to the people and to Saul's servants.

1 Samuel 18:5

I just happened to notice this verse one day and underlined it. David was a man who was anointed to be king,[8] yet he was put in the household of Saul for some training and some crucifixion of the flesh.

Anyone who is anointed for leadership has to get around a Saul somewhere in their life. God uses the Sauls in our life to get the Saul out of us. God always puts us around someone who is sandpaper to us to smooth off our rough edges.

Just because we are anointed for leadership does not mean that we get to move immediately into a position of leadership.

There is a work that has to be done in us, a testing that has to take place first. Later, we will look at some of the tests of the heart of a leader that we must go through before we get promoted.

After I had noticed and underlined this verse about David's serving under King Saul, my attention was drawn to verse 14 which says, *David acted wisely in all his ways and succeeded, and the Lord was with him.* Why did David succeed? Not just because he was anointed, but because he acted wisely.

Do you realize how many people fail simply because they do not use any wisdom? How many years did I get myself into trouble, even though I was gifted and anointed, because I was not using any wisdom?

I discovered that without wisdom, we are not going anywhere. That is why God wants us to have a wise heart.

4. A Perfect Heart

> *For the eyes of the Lord run to and fro throughout the whole earth*
> *to show Himself strong in behalf of those whose hearts are blameless*
> *toward Him. . . .*
>
> 2 Chronicles 16:9

The *King James Version* of this verse says that God looks for those *whose heart is perfect toward him.* What does it mean to have a perfect heart? It means to have a heartfelt desire to do right and to please God.

A person who has a perfect heart truly loves God, though he himself may not be perfect. He may still have things in the flesh to deal with. His mouth may still get him into trouble. He may make mistakes or lose his temper. But when he does, he is quick to repent and make it right with God again. If he has offended someone else, he will humble himself and apologize.

If we have a perfect heart toward God, He counts us as perfect and works with us while we are trying to manifest that perfection.

I am not a perfect person, but I do believe I have a perfect heart toward God. I am sure there are things in my heart which need to be exposed and rooted out that I don't know about, but I believe God only holds us responsible for those things we do know about. I don't have perfect performance. I still do things every day I wish I didn't do. But I love God with all my heart. There are many people with right hearts, and those are the ones God uses.

I used to read the verse above and misunderstand it. I thought it was saying that the eyes of God roam to and fro across the face of the earth looking for someone in whom He might show Himself strong. I would always think, **Boy, I had better straighten up.** Then I finally saw the rest of that verse about God's looking for someone whose heart is perfect toward Him.

When God looks for someone to use, He doesn't look for somebody with a perfect performance but a terrible heart attitude. He looks for someone who may not have a perfect performance but who has a right heart toward Him.

If that describes you, I believe that you are going to get a word from God through this book that is going to make a major difference in your life.

God has all kinds of positions open in His kingdom. To fill those positions, He is always bringing one person down and lifting another person up.[9] If we don't behave ourselves and keep a right attitude, we won't be in a position for God to use us in the way He wants to use us. He can promote us, but He can also demote us.

In our organization when we get ready to promote people, we don't look for those who are the most talented; we look for those who have a right heart attitude, those who are willing to do a little extra when called upon to do so.

That is the way God is. And one of the main things He looks for when He is ready to promote a person is a perfect heart.

5. A Tender Heart

> *And become useful and helpful and kind to one another, tenderhearted (compassionate, understanding, loving-hearted), forgiving one another [readily and freely], as God in Christ forgave you.*
>
> Ephesians 4:32

Having a tender heart is equivalent to having a tender conscience, and tenderness of conscience is vital to being used by God.

In 1 Timothy 4:1,2 Paul wrote, *But the [Holy] Spirit distinctly and expressly declares that in latter times some will turn away from the faith, giving attention to deluding and seducing spirits and doctrines that demons teach, through the hypocrisy and pretensions of liars whose consciences are seared (cauterized).*

It is dangerous to become hard-hearted and to develop a seared conscience so that we can't really tell if we are doing anything wrong or not. One way we develop a tender conscience is by being quick to repent, and when God convicts us of something, not making excuses.

When God shows us we did something wrong, just say, "You're right Lord, I'm wrong. There is no excuse, so please forgive me and help me not to do it again."

It is amazing how much that will help us have a tender conscience toward God. But as soon as we start trying to reason things out and make excuses for our wrongs, we start getting a little callus on our conscience. It becomes just a little bit harder for us to feel than it was the time before.

For example, if I mistreat someone without repenting of it, my conscience begins to get callused. The next time I do it, my conscience gets a little more callused. Soon, although I go around presenting myself as a person who loves God, He cannot use me anymore because I'm mistreating people and talking down to them and talking wrong to them. The worst thing is, I don't even realize that I'm doing it because I no longer have a tender heart and a tender conscience toward God.

We must remember that God does not care how gifted or talented we are; His primary concern is our heart attitude. If we have a willing heart, a stirred-up heart, a wise heart, a perfect heart and a tender conscience, the devil may as well get out of our way because nothing can stop us from being used by God.

Acts 23:1 describes the kind of conscience Paul had:

> Then Paul, gazing earnestly at the council (Sanhedrin), said, Brethren, I have lived before God, doing my duty with a perfectly good conscience until this very day [as a citizen, a true and loyal Jew].

How many of us can go to bed at night saying, "Well, Lord, I can go to sleep with a perfectly good conscience"?

In Acts 24:16, Paul describes what he did to keep his conscience tender:

> Therefore I always exercise and discipline myself [mortifying my body, deadening my carnal affections, bodily appetites, and worldly desires, endeavoring in all respects] to have a clear (unshaken, blameless) conscience, void of offense toward God and toward men.

Why did Paul strive to keep a clear conscience? Because he knew he could not minister out of a hard heart. He knew that if he wanted to help others, he had to keep a tender conscience toward God.

I believe all of us should pray on a regular basis, "Lord, help me to have a tender heart and a tender conscience toward You."

6. A Faithful Heart

> So then . . . consider Jesus. . . .
>
> [See how] faithful He was to Him Who appointed Him [Apostle and High Priest], as Moses was also faithful in the whole house [of God].
>
> Hebrews 3:1,2

In Hebrews 3 we are told that both Moses and Jesus were faithful. In the New Testament, the Greek word translated *faithful* means "to be trusted, reliable";[10] in other words, to be dependable.

Do you know what it means for us to be dependable? It means we have to keep our word. If we tell somebody we are going to do something, then we need to do it. If we say we are going to be somewhere at a certain time, we need to be there and on time.

It is amazing how many people are just not dependable. They can't be counted on to do what they say they will do or be where they say they will be when they say they will be there.

Again, it doesn't matter how gifted a person is; if he is not faithful, God cannot use him. And we must understand that God tests faithfulness. It is not enough to say, "Oh, yes, I'm faithful," because God will say, "Well, let's see."

Do you know how God tests our faithfulness? He assigns us to do something for a period of time that we don't want to do, something that is not fun or exciting, something that may require us to submit to someone else's authority for a while, and He'll tell us in our heart, "Just be faithful."

> **GOOD LEADERS SURROUND THEMSELVES WITH FAITHFUL, DEPENDABLE PEOPLE.**

For five years I worked in someone else's ministry. Out of that experience came Life In The Word Ministries. I had a strong call on my life, which meant that I had to be faithful. I went through a period of time in which I was faithful, but not with a right heart attitude. So God had to deal with me until I learned to be faithful with a good attitude.

Faithfulness is not just showing up day after day; it is showing up day after day with a good attitude. God will reward that kind of faithfulness. Luke 16:12 tells us that if we are faithful over what belongs to someone else, God will give us our own.

I love knowing that I have people around me who are faithful and dependable. That is a master key to being a good leader.

Can people count on you to be a little more faithful, a little more dependable, a little more reliable? That is a question we all need to ask ourselves from time to time.

Remember, if you will do that, if you will be faithful over a little, then God will make you ruler over much.[11]

7. A Fixed and Steadfast Heart

> *My heart is fixed, O God, my heart is steadfast. . . .*

> Psalm 57:7

What does it mean to have a fixed heart? It means to have our mind made up so that we are not going to change it.

If we are going to experience any kind of victory, we must be determined. If we are going to see the fulfillment of God's will, walk in or follow the leading of the Spirit or accomplish anything worthwhile in this life, we must dig in both heels and set our face like flint. We must have a lot of what I call "holy determination."

Now, it won't do us any good to be determined if we are not in the will of God. We know His will by reading His Word because His Word is His will. But it also won't do us any good to know the will of God if we are not determined to see it come to pass in our life. Why? Because the devil is waiting around every corner to steal that will from us.

We must understand that there will be opposition. The devil is not going to roll out a red carpet for us just because we decide to get saved and serve God. He is going to oppose us at every turn.

In Galatians 5:17 we are told that . . . *the desires of the flesh are opposed to the [Holy] Spirit, and the [desires of the] Spirit are opposed to the flesh (godless human nature); for these are antagonistic to each other [continually withstanding and in conflict with each other], so that you are not free but are prevented from doing what you desire to do.*

I don't see any hope of any of us making it if we have a wimpy spirit. We have got to make up our mind and not change it.

Some people make up their mind, but as soon as things become a little hard, they change it. It is amazing how many people want to be in the ministry, until they find out what it is all about.

I get really concerned when I see people who are changing all the time. Every time you turn around they have a new call and a new vision. They may start out being called to prison ministry. When they find out that is hard, they get called to evangelism. When they discover that is hard, they are suddenly called to music ministry.

The problem is that because of the mentality of our society, we are always looking for something easy. We think everything should be drive-through and push-button. If we can't microwave it, we don't mess with it. There are no microwave ministries. In fact, anything we want to do at microwave speed is not worth doing — except microwaving!

So many people can't seem to make up their mind about what they want to do. We need to know what we want to do, and we need to have a fixed and a steadfast heart and be totally determined that we are going to do it — "I'm determined that I'm going to serve God. I'm determined that I'm going to do His will. I'm determined that I'm going to fulfill His call on my life. I'm determined that I'm going to stay happy. I'm determined that I'm going to walk in peace."

We've got to be determined if we are going to have what God wants us to have. His will won't just happen in our life. We are partners with God. He will always do His part, but we must also do our part. Part of what we have to do is not give up. We must be filled with "holy determination" to press on until we see the fulfillment of God's plan for our life.

> PRESS ON WITH "HOLY DETERMINATION," AND GOD'S PLAN WILL BE FULFILLED IN YOUR LIFE.

8. A Confident Heart

My heart is fixed, O God, my heart is steadfast and confident! . . .

Psalm 57:7

Notice that this passage says that not only must our heart be fixed and steadfast, it must also be confident.

I have discovered that staying confident at all times is vital to successful ministry. I have found that even while I am busy ministering, even while I am up in front of an audience teaching, the devil will try to introduce thoughts into my head to make me lose confidence.

For example, if two or three people look at their watches, the devil whispers to me, "They're so bored they can't wait to get out of here." If a couple of people get up and leave to go to the restroom, the devil will say, "They're leaving because they don't like your preaching."

I know that when people are up singing, it is not uncommon for the devil to tell them, "Nobody likes this. You picked the wrong music. You should have chosen a different song. Your voice sounds lousy. You're singing off key." And on and on.

The mind is a battlefield, and the devil lies to everybody through wrong thinking. The one thing that he's trying to steal all the time is our confidence.

Whatever we do for the Lord, the devil will try to do something to cause us to lose confidence. He doesn't want us to have confidence in our prayers. He doesn't want us to believe we can hear from God. He doesn't want us to have any confidence concerning the call on our life. He doesn't want us to be confident that people like us, that we look nice, that we have any sense, that we know anything. He wants us to go around feeling like a failure. That is why we need to keep a confident heart within us all the time.

We shouldn't drag ourselves out of bed each day in fear or discouragement. Instead, we should get up every morning prepared to keep Satan under our feet. How do we do that? We do it by confidently declaring what the Word says about us such as, "I am more than a conqueror through Jesus.[12] I can do all things through Christ Who strengthens me.[13] I am triumphant in every situation because God always causes me to triumph."[14] As we will see, that not only causes the devil to leave us alone, but it also strengthens our confidence.

That's what David did in the Bible. We should have the attitude he had when he declared in Psalm 27:3, *Though a host encamp against me, my heart shall not fear; though war arise against me, [even then] in this will I be confident.* David was saying, "It doesn't matter how many demons come against me; I am keeping my confidence in the Lord."

Many times when the devil starts attacking us, our confidence begins to wane because we start thinking, **What have I done wrong? Why is my faith not working?** The minute we have trouble, the devil wants us to start asking, "What's wrong with me?" Nothing is wrong with us. It is the devil who has the problem.

That doesn't mean that we can't have problems, that there are not times when we open the door to the enemy. But even if we have done that, it does not mean that we have to give up our confidence that God loves us and that He is going to rescue us from the mess we have caused, set us right side up again, continue to bless us — and teach us something in the process.

The apostle Paul assures us of that in Philippians 1:6: . . . *I am convinced and sure of this very thing, that He Who began a good work in you will continue until the day of Jesus Christ [right up to the time of His return], developing [that good work] and perfecting and bringing it to full completion in you.*

The devil constantly attacks our confidence by trying to convince us that we will never change. He wants us to think we will never get control over our temper, never learn to be patient, never be able to stay awake while we are praying, never be able to remember what we read in the Bible, never get through a single day without screaming at our children, never bring our mouth under control and on and on. The devil is always trying to plant negative thoughts in our mind and heart. Everything he says is always "never, never, never": "You are **never** going to be any different. You are **never** going to change. Things are **never** going to work out for you. Your life is **never** going to improve. You will **never** be what God has called you to be."

That is when we need to get out our Bible and read the Word to the devil, saying, "Is that what you think, Satan? Well, just listen to this!"

We don't talk back to the devil enough.

BE CONFIDENT OF YOUR FUTURE

Some people have a problem with talking back to the devil, but Jesus did it. In Luke chapter 4, every time Satan would tempt Him, Jesus would answer back, "It is written . . . " and quote a Scripture to the devil. That was how He defeated him.

Sometimes I think we are just too lazy to do that. We go around letting the devil make us miserable when we could put a stop to the whole thing if we would just go to the Bible and say, "Devil, I am tired of your lies. I don't want to hear them anymore today. Just listen to this . . ." Then begin quoting the Word of God.

Remind Satan that he was defeated on the cross many years ago, that Jesus has the keys of death and hell and gave believers authority over Satan. Tell him that you know he is a liar and the father of lies and that the truth is not even in him. Say about yourself what God says, not what the devil says. Say that you are the head and not the tail, above and not beneath, that you are blessed by God and that He loves you very much.[15]

These are the kinds of things we need to do in the privacy of our own home if we want to have victory. It is great to go to meetings and get all excited and worked up, but the real victory has to be won on the home front. We have got to *fight the good fight of faith*[16] individually. Nobody is going to come and do it for us. We have to do it for ourselves. Other people can encourage us, love us and pray for us, but when it comes down to "where the rubber meets the road," each of us has to know who we are in Christ and be determined that we are not going to give up and quit.

Be confident about the call of God on your life. Be confident that you hear from Him, that He is pleased with you, that He is going to meet all your needs. Be confident that God loves you and has a great future planned for you, as He says in Jeremiah 29:11: *For I know the thoughts and plans that I have for you, says the Lord, thoughts and plans for welfare and peace and not for evil, to give you hope in your final outcome.*

Satan wants you to be condemned by your past, but God wants you to be confident of your future.

CHAPTER 9

POSITIVE CONDITIONS OF THE HEART, PART 2

You are on the road to developing the leadership qualities God has placed in you. God has given every one of us gifts and abilities for leadership. But we must take what He has given us, and with His help, develop it. That requires making an effort, and we don't always feel like doing that.

By now, you may have discovered that the condition of your heart is in a state of chaos from years of having a wrong heart attitude. If so, don't be discouraged. As I said earlier, each of us has some area of our heart we need to work on.

Come to grips with that fact, and as you read about more positive conditions of the heart in this chapter, I encourage you to do whatever you need to do to get your heart straightened out — and keep on doing it over and over until you get good results.

9. A Merry Heart

> A merry heart does good, like medicine, but a broken spirit dries
> the bones.
>
> Proverbs 17:22 NKJV

One way we can keep a merry heart is by listening to music. When we listen to it, we tend to find ourselves humming or singing along, even when we are not aware of it. When we have a merry heart, we can have joy in our heart even while going about our work.

We can also have more energy and vitality because the Bible tells us that the joy of the Lord is our strength.[1]

We have a choice. We can grumble our way through our troubles, or we can sing our way through our troubles. Either way, we have to go through troubles, so we may as well go through them happily.

I believe that we can understand from Proverbs 17:22, *A merry heart does good, like a medicine.* . . . (NKJV), that if we were happier, we would probably be healthier.

The Amplified Bible version of this verse says, *A happy heart is good medicine and a cheerful mind works healing.* . . . Proverbs 15:13 says, *A glad heart makes a cheerful countenance, but by sorrow of heart the spirit is broken.* The Bible uses the word "countenance" in many places, so I think we should pay attention to it. Our countenance is our face, the way we look. God is concerned about our face and how we look because either we are walking advertisements for Jesus or we are walking advertisements for Satan. That's why it is important that we learn how to have a cheerful countenance and a pleasant look on our face.

> **WHEN WE SMILE, IT PUTS OTHER PEOPLE AT EASE.**

My husband has a secretary who is always smiling. Everything he asks her to do, she does it with a smile. I think that is the way God wants all of us to be. When we smile, it puts other people at ease. It gives them freedom and liberty and a sense of confidence.

It is amazing how much more comfortable and secure we are when we smile at one another and how much discomfort and insecurity we cause one another when we go around with a sour look on our face.

Sometimes our problems are not caused by the devil — they are the result of the way we feel and act. We need to cheer up. When we relax and smile, it makes us and everyone around us feel better.

One of my favorite Scriptures is John 10:10 in which Jesus says, *The thief comes only in order to steal and kill and destroy. I came that they may have and enjoy life, and have it in abundance (to the full, till it overflows).* One reason I love this Scripture is that I spent many years of my life thinking it was wrong for me to enjoy myself. As a matter of fact, the Lord had to remind me just recently, "Joyce, I want you to enjoy life."

I am a worker. I can get so caught up in getting things done that I forget that it is OK just to relax and enjoy life. That is what my husband does. He gets out of bed in the morning humming and singing. If I am not careful, I will wake up and start trying to figure something out. If I don't have a problem to solve, I will try to solve someone else's. I seem to have to have something to be dealing with and seeking God for. It is hard for me to get it through my thick head that God might just want me to get out and smell the flowers, go to the zoo or just be glad to be alive. That is what He was telling me when He said, "Joyce, I want you to enjoy life."

God is life, and every good thing He created is part of that life. We get so caught up in doing and accomplishing, in working and keeping our commitments, in trying to keep up with everybody and get ahead in life, that if we are not careful, we will come to the end of our life and suddenly wake up and realize that we never really lived.

I don't believe God created the world and all the good things in it so we would do nothing but worry and struggle and be frustrated trying to solve problems all the time. He wants us to enjoy our life. That is what Jesus meant in John 10:10 when He said that He came that we might have and enjoy life, that we may have it in abundance, to the full, till it overflows.

When Jesus spoke of the enemy in that verse, He was not just talking about the devil. He was also talking about the religious system of His day.

If there is anything that sucks the joy of life out of us, it is dead, dry religion. The Bible doesn't talk about religion. It talks about a personal relationship with Jesus Christ. Religion is nothing but a set of rules and regulations that we are supposed to follow to keep God happy.

Religious people are afraid of liberty. They are afraid to do anything a little bit differently from what everyone else is doing because they might stray outside the guidelines that keep them safe and secure.

Sometimes I try to be different on purpose. Every now and then I get a little holy anger on me against the box that people try to put me in. I get a little feisty and break out into something new.

Jesus was very angry with the religious people of His day. He called them whitewashed tombs full of dead men's bones.[2] They had no real life in them, and their ministry to others put them into bondage instead of liberating them. I once read that by the time Jesus came, religious people had taken the Ten Commandments and turned them into two thousand rules and regulations that people were expected to follow. Can you imagine the bondage of that and the continual guilt they experienced due to their failure to keep the rules?

So many people are fighting discouragement because of an attack of the devil on their life. Jesus did not die for us to have to wage continual, unending warfare. He wants us to enjoy victory. But the problem is that we are just not determined enough to have what He died to give us.

For a great deal of my life I was not a "happy camper." I was saved, filled with the Spirit and engaged in ministry, but I really wasn't enjoying any of it. I was taking the responsibility and doing the work because that is my nature. I am a very responsible person. I not only take responsibility for my own life, I will also take responsibility for everybody else's if I don't watch it.

Dave handles things so differently. For example, when I used to have to correct our older son David about something, I couldn't seem to be able to settle down about it afterwards. Dave, of course, could say what he wanted to say to him and then go on about his business and never think about it again.

So I began to think, **What is my problem? Why can't I be relaxed like Dave instead of going around upset all the time?**

Dave finally told me, "Joyce, you take the responsibility for making David happy again. That is not your job. Your job is to correct him. It is between him and God how long it takes him to get happy again."

I grew up in a dysfunctional home in which nobody was ever happy, so I was always trying to make everybody happy. I was always playing the peacemaker between the people in my life. I was always asking, "What can I do to make you happy?" I was always trying to fix everybody else's life while never enjoying my own. So I have had to learn to lighten up and enjoy myself.

We have got to learn to enjoy what we do. Whatever your job is, enjoy it. Don't spend your life waiting for things to change before you can get happy. Learn to be happy now.

Don't go around talking about how you feel all the time. Learn to make some decisions. Do some things on purpose. Go ahead and make the devil mad by being happy even though you may not feel like it. That will really drive him crazy.

In John 15 Jesus talks about abiding in Him. And abiding in Christ means staying in a place of rest. In verse 11 of that chapter He says, *I have told you these things, that My joy and delight may be in you, and that your joy and gladness may be of full measure and complete and overflowing.*

> DON'T SPEND YOUR LIFE WAITING FOR THINGS TO CHANGE BEFORE YOU CAN BECOME HAPPY. LEARN TO BE HAPPY NOW.

It sounds to me like Jesus wants us to be happy. He says it here, and He also said it in John 10:10. In John 17:13 He prayed to the Father about His disciples, saying, *And now I am coming to You; I say these things while I am still in the world, so that My joy may be made full and complete and perfect in them [that they may experience My delight fulfilled in them, that My enjoyment may be perfected in their own souls, that they may have My gladness within them, filling their hearts].*

Jesus wants us to be glad. He wants us to have a merry heart. He wants us to put a smile on our face so everybody around us can feel happy and secure. But sometimes we are too selfish to care about how others feel. Yet we go to church and pat each other on the back and say, "I love you with the love of the Lord."

Our love life is seen in the little things we do for one another — or don't do because we don't feel like it. What a difference we could make in our household, in the church, in the world if we would start being a little more pleasant, just smile at each other and have a merry heart.

10. A New Heart

> *And I will give them one heart [a new heart] and I will put a new spirit within them; and I will take the stony [unnaturally hardened] heart out of their flesh, and will give them a heart of flesh [sensitive and responsive to the touch of their God].*
>
> Ezekiel 11:19

The Bible says that we have to have a new heart. In Ezekiel 11 God promises to give His people a new heart to replace the stony, hardened heart that is in them. This new heart will be sensitive and responsive to Him.

WHAT A DIFFERENCE WE COULD MAKE JUST BY BEING MORE PLEASANT, SMILING MORE AND HAVING A MERRY HEART.

This promise is repeated in Ezekiel 36:26 in which the Lord says, *A new heart will I give you and a new spirit will I put within you, and I will take away the stony heart out of your flesh and give you a heart of flesh.*

We are all familiar with being given a new heart at the time of the New Birth. The New Birth, or spiritual birth, occurs when we receive Jesus in our heart. It takes us out of the worldly way of living and places us "into Christ" and a new way of thinking, speaking and acting.[3] But even after that experience, we are told in Romans 12:2 that we must have our minds completely renewed. In Ephesians 4:23 we read that we are to be constantly renewed in the spirit of our mind, having a fresh mental and spiritual attitude. Attitudes begin in the mind. Our mind is renewed by the Word of God. Reading the Word daily renews our mind and changes our attitude.

If we are going to be leaders for God, serving Him properly and displaying the kind of mental and spiritual attitude He wants us to have, we must keep a fresh, new heart all the time.

We need an attitude adjustment every single day and often many times during the day because it is so easy to develop a wrong attitude. God doesn't want us to have a wrong heart; He wants to give us a new heart.

11. An Understanding Heart

My son, if you will receive my words and treasure up my commandments within you,

Making your ear attentive to skillful and godly Wisdom and inclining and directing your heart and mind to understanding [applying all your powers to the quest for it];

Yes, if you cry out for insight and raise your voice for understanding.

If you seek [Wisdom] as for silver and search for skillful and godly Wisdom as for hidden treasures,

*Then you will understand the reverent and worshipful fear of the Lord
and find the knowledge of [our omniscient] God.*

Proverbs 2:1-5

We need to seek understanding — to understand God's Word and
will, to understand ourselves and to understand other people. One
reason we don't understand other people is that they are not like us. We
think that if others are different from us, there must be something wrong
with them. We don't understand them at all.

That is why we need to ask God for an understanding heart because
an understanding heart is one of the heart conditions anybody must
have to minister to others. How can we possibly minister to others if we
don't have a clue to what they are going through?

One way we understand what people are going through is by going
through it ourselves. We don't have to go through exactly the same
thing they are going through, but I don't think anyone can understand
a hurting person without having been hurt or without having gone
through something similar.

It is amazing how caring and compassionate we are when we have
gone through a few problems of our own, and how flippant and
judgmental we can be if we have not had the same problem ourselves.
How easy our answers can be: "Well, now, Sister, you just need to
believe God." How different it is when we have been hurting for months
ourselves and somebody comes along with a problem. We throw our
arms around that person and say, "Oh, I **understand** how you feel."

We all want understanding. It is one of the things we cry out to God
for when we are going through rough times. We just want to be
understood. Jesus understands, as we see in Hebrews 4:15,16:

*For we do not have a High Priest Who is unable to understand and
sympathize and have a shared feeling with our weaknesses and
infirmities and liability to the assaults of temptation, but One Who
has been tempted in every respect as we are, yet without sinning.*

*Let us then fearlessly and confidently and boldly draw near to the
throne of grace (the throne of God's unmerited favor to us sinners),
that we may receive mercy [for our failures] and find grace to help in*

good time for every need [appropriate help and well-timed help,
coming just when we need it].

Jesus can help us because He knows what we are going through. We know that we can open up to Him because He understands. If we are afraid of judgment and rejection, we won't do that, and neither will others open up to us.

That is why we as leaders have to have an understanding heart. We have to seek to understand. And one of the ways we can do that is by taking the time to think about what it would be like to be in someone else's situation.

I honestly believe that in the church today we are too selfish and self-centered. All of our thoughts are about ourselves. If we would think — really think — about others, we would be more inclined to do things for them.

I am not sure that Jesus ever prayed for anybody until compassion was flowing. I recall an instance in the Bible in which a man came to Him asking for healing for his son who was possessed by a demon that caused him terrible suffering. Jesus asked the man, "How long has your son been like this?"[4] That made no difference to Jesus' healing him. I believe He asked it because He wanted to have even more compassion than He already had for that father and his boy.

We need to be concerned enough about people to ask them questions about their situation — "How long have you been like this? Where does it hurt and for how long?"

When some believers ask a person how they are doing and they say that they are having a rough time, we tend to answer, "Well, praise the Lord!" But when we are hurting or in trouble, that is not how we want others to respond to us. We want them to show us some real heartfelt understanding and compassion.

My aunt and uncle were wonderful Christians, but they did not come from the same kind of Christian background as many of our friends. When my uncle died, out of respect, some of the people in my ministry came to the funeral home. One of them saw my aunt crying and said to her, not really meaning any harm, "Well, praise the Lord."

My aunt was offended. It really bothered her for a long time. She would say, "Why in the world would somebody tell me to praise the Lord because my husband is dead?"

Well, obviously in situations like that, we should continue to praise the Lord anyway, but when someone is hurting, as my aunt was, that kind of response may not come across as a comfort.

In 1 Corinthians 9:20 Paul said that if he was with a Jew, he'd act like a Jew and if he was with a Greek, he'd act like a Greek, whatever it took to win them to Christ and not offend them. That is part of not being selfish.

Instead of being so selfish and self-centered, where we only think about ourselves, we need to be more sensitive and understanding to others. We become that way from seeking God. We seek Him by reading His Word, praying and talking with Him daily. Seeking Him will cause us to have an understanding heart.

12. A Purposed Heart

> *This is the [Lord's] purpose that is purposed upon the whole earth [regarded as conquered and put under tribute by Assyria]; and this is [His omnipotent] hand that is stretched out over all the nations.*
>
> *For the Lord of hosts has purposed, and who can annul it? And His hand is stretched out, and who can turn it back?*
>
> Isaiah 14:26,27

This passage tells us that God is a God of purpose, and that when He purposes something, it is going to come to pass.

Jesus knew His purpose. As we have seen, in John 10:10 He said that He came into the world that we might have life. In John 18:37 He told Pilate, . . . *This is why I was born, and for this I have come into the world, to bear witness to the Truth . . . John wrote of Jesus, . . . For this purpose the Son of God was manifested, that He might destroy the works of the devil.*[5]

I think we all need to know our purpose, but many people don't. They're frustrated because they feel purposeless. If we feel purposeless, we feel useless and worthless. But we must understand that we go through seasons in our lifetime.

Right now you may be in a time of transition from one season to the next. If so, don't be discouraged. God will show you what He has for you to do next. Sometimes you may have to step out and try a few things until you find what you are comfortable with. But you can be assured that whatever it may be, you do have a purpose, and you are never going to be fulfilled until you find it and start flowing in it.

God has a purpose for each one of us. He wants all of us to enjoy ourselves and to enjoy the life He has given us. But as far as our specific purpose, that varies from individual to individual and from one season of life to the next.

At the beginning our purpose may be to get married and raise children. That is a high calling. Once the children are raised, our purpose may be to lead people to God through worship and praise. Whatever it may be, we need to know what our purpose is and then do it on purpose.

I am a person of purpose, and I am not sorry I am because I think purposeful people accomplish a lot in life. A leader must know their purpose, and they must purpose to do their purpose on purpose. If they don't, it will never get done.

We even have to love on purpose. We don't love because we feel like it; we do it because we purpose to do it. Love is not a gooey feeling we get about people. It is a decision we make about people.

So is giving. We don't give because we just feel like giving. We give because we are convinced it is what God wants us to do. We give on purpose and for a purpose.

The same is true of being merciful, of being kind, of walking in the Spirit. We do those things, not because we always necessarily feel like it, but because it is what we are called to do. Love, joy, peace, patience, kindness, goodness and all the other fruit of the Spirit[6] are characteristics of the Holy Spirit that we have within us when we accept Jesus as our Savior. And we can release them if we do it on purpose.

Our flesh is not going to always agree with us to do these things. But we must choose to love on purpose, give on purpose, stay in peace on purpose. If we want to have peace, we must purpose to have peace because the devil will try to steal it a hundred times a day.

Everything we do for others we must do on purpose. We do it by being people of purpose, which comes from having a purposed heart.

13. A Pondering Heart

But Mary was keeping within herself all these things (sayings),
weighing and pondering them in her heart.

Luke 2:19

As we saw earlier, it is important to have a pondering heart and not a reasoning heart. God does not want us to have a reasoning heart. He doesn't want us trying to figure out everything in life. But He does want us to ponder.

We can tell when we have moved from pondering to reasoning by the confusion we experience. If we are confused, then we are not pondering in our heart; we are reasoning in our mind.

Mary had some pretty serious things happen in her life. She was just a sweet little girl who loved God when an angel of the Lord appeared to her and told her she was going to become the mother of the Son of God.

She had to have started thinking about Joseph, the man she was engaged to marry. She had to have started wondering about him and her parents, about how she was going to tell them and about how they were going to react. She had to have started wondering if anyone was going to believe her story.

But whatever Mary may have thought or felt, she controlled it because she said to the angel, "Let it be unto me according to the Word of God."[7]

Then when the birth actually took place and the angels appeared to the shepherds and told them to come to the stable and worship the Christ Child, the shepherds told Mary and Joseph and everyone else about what had happened. These things are what Mary kept in her heart and pondered, as we read in Luke 2:19.

I believe that when God speaks something to us, many times we need to keep it to ourselves. When God tells us something, He gives us the faith to believe what He has said to us. But when we try to tell it to others, they may think we have lost our mind.

You should have heard some of the things people said to me when I told them that God had spoken to me in my heart and called me into the ministry. Knowing my background and the condition I was in at the time, they were not encouraging at all.

That is one of the problems with sharing too much with others; we get discouraged instead of encouraged. Other people don't always have the faith to believe what God has told us.

Someone once said that Dave and I function under a gift of faith concerning the running of our ministry. I realize that is true. We do have a gift of faith for what we are doing.

WHEN GOD CALLS YOU TO DO SOMETHING, HE ALSO GIVES YOU THE FAITH TO DO IT.

When God calls you to do something, He also gives you the faith to do it. You don't have to go around afraid all the time that you are not able to do what He has given you to do.

I am not afraid of the crowds or what people think about me anymore. I am not afraid about the money we need to pay the bills for our ministry, and they are unbelievably high because we are on the radio and television so much. Media ministry is very expensive. But I don't have any fear about that. I used to at one time, but I don't anymore. Now when we have an opportunity to go on a new station or network that may cost us a lot of money, I just say, "Yes, sure, we can do that." It is a gift of faith.

When you have a gift of faith, things seem easy to you. But to someone else without that gift of faith, they may seem impossible.

When God spoke to Mary through the angel, there was a gift of faith that came with that word to her from the Lord so that she was able to say, "Let it be done unto me as You will." But she was also wise enough not to go around knocking on doors and saying, "I just had a visitation from an angel who told me I am going to give birth to the Son of God. I am going to get pregnant by the Holy Ghost, and the Child I am going to bear will be the Savior of the world." If she had done that, she would probably have been locked up somewhere. Mary knew how to keep her mouth shut and her heart open.

But when God speaks to us in His Word or in our heart, the first thing we want to do is run and tell everyone what He said to us. We should realize that if God has really told us something, it will surely come to pass just as He has said. Then everybody will see it, and we won't have to try to convince them that we really did hear from the Lord.

When God speaks to us and tells us things we don't really understand, things that seem to make no sense to us, things that we can't quite see, we need to do a little more pondering instead of going around asking everybody, "God said this to me. What do you think?" Usually, the ones we run to for advice don't even know what they're doing, let alone are qualified to tell us what to do.

Sometimes we talk too much, and as a result we just get ourselves more and more confused. When God speaks to us, we need to be quiet, zip our lip and ponder it in our heart, saying, "Lord, be it unto me according to Your will. Bring me clarity and understanding so I can know what I am to do in this situation."

Let's not have a reasoning heart; let's have a pondering heart, so we can stay in peace.

14. A Forgiving Heart

Then Peter came up to Him and said, Lord, how many times may my brother sin against me and I forgive him and let it go? [As many as] up to seven times?

Jesus answered him, I tell you, not up to seven times, but seventy times seven!

Matthew 18:21,22

As leaders, we are never going to get anywhere unless we are ready to forgive people. It is something that we are going to have to do frequently. The Lord tells us plainly in the Bible that if we will not forgive other people their trespasses or wrong things they've done against us, then God will not forgive us our trespasses against Him.[8]

What kind of condition would we be in if God refused to forgive us? We couldn't have a relationship with Him. Everything in our life would be stopped up. We like to think that we can stay angry at other people and yet go to God and receive forgiveness for our sins. But the Lord tells us in the Bible that is not so.

Jesus taught us to pray, "Forgive us our trespasses as we forgive those who trespass against us."[9] God is a God of mercy, but this issue of forgiveness is very important to Him. In His Word He tells us repeatedly that if we want mercy, we have to give mercy.

In Matthew 18:21,22 Peter asked Jesus how many times he had to forgive his brother, seven times? Jesus said not seven times but seventy times that many.

I don't know about you, but I am glad that God does not put a limit on how many times He will forgive us. How many of us have done the same wrong thing at least seventy times seven, and God has still forgiven us for it? We are willing to keep taking and taking forgiveness from God, but it is amazing how little we want to give forgiveness to others. We freely accept mercy, yet it is surprising how rigid, legalistic and merciless we can be toward others, especially if they have wronged us in some way. Yet the Bible says that the debt we owe God is much greater than any debt anyone may owe us.

In Matthew 18:23-35 Jesus told a story about a servant who owed a tremendous amount of money to his master and was forgiven of it. But then the servant went out and began to choke another servant who owed him only a small sum of money, threatening to have him thrown in prison if he didn't pay up immediately. The other servant begged him for more time to come up with the money, so he had the man thrown in prison. When the other servants heard about it, they told the master who called in the merciless servant and said to him, "How dare you leave my presence after receiving my forgiveness for such a huge amount and go directly out and be unforgiving with someone else for such a paltry amount!"

We are taught in the Word that there is a retribution for that kind of behavior. I think that a lot of the problems we have in our life are the result of our unforgiving attitude toward other people.

One of my daughters has said, "It is not easy to get a job at Life In The Word Ministries, but it is also hard to lose a job there once you get it." That is true. We check out our applicants very carefully. They have to pass a close inspection before they are invited to become part of our team. But once they are on the team, we will work with them, deal with them and correct them over and over again.

Many times I don't really have the time to spend on all that. But the Lord always reminds me of how long He has done that for me throughout the years of my ministry, especially at the beginning when I had so many problems. He didn't just push me out because I didn't make it the first time. He believed in me, chose me, worked with me, counseled with me and took me around the same mountains again and again.

That is what we do with our employees. As long as a person is correctable, we will work with him. The only ones we cannot work with are those who are so full of pride they can't be told anything. The one thing we will not put up with in our organization is strife because it destroys the anointing. Dave and I have worked too hard to have a strong anointing on this ministry to allow someone to come in and destroy it through strife.

The bottom line is, if we are going to get along with people, we are going to have to do a lot of forgiving.

FORGIVENESS RELEASES ANOINTING

In verse 34 of Matthew 18, Jesus said that the master turned the unforgiving servant over to the torturers, or the jailers, until he paid his debt in full. I believe that when we refuse to forgive other people, we are the ones who end up in a prison of emotional torment. We hurt ourselves much more than we hurt anyone else because when we harbor bitterness, resentment and unforgiveness toward a person, we are miserable.

At the end of that story, Jesus warned His audience, *So also My heavenly Father will deal with every one of you if you do not freely forgive your brother from your heart his offenses.*

If you want to be used by God in ministry, you must learn to be forgiving because this is one area in which Satan will attack you constantly. He wants you to get all bound up in bitterness, resentment and unforgiveness because he knows the strife and disagreement it produces will totally shut down your ministry.

We are told in the Bible that where there is unity there is anointing.[10] We have already seen that the anointing is God's power; it is His ability resting on us to help us do things easily that would otherwise be hard. It is impossible to minister without anointing. There can be hype without anointing, but there cannot be true ministry without anointing. If the anointing is not on a ministry, people will not come to it. Even if they do come, they will not stay because most people can tell the difference between hype and anointing.

> GOD'S ABILITY HELPS US DO THINGS EASILY THAT WOULD OTHERWISE BE HARD.

I have to have the anointing on my ministry because I don't have much else. I have a gift of communication, and that's it. All I know to do is stand in front of an audience and try to be obedient to God. I don't do anything fancy. I just step out in faith and prayer, believing that God is going to work — and He has always been faithful to do so.

I have discovered that I cannot be unforgiving and still have the anointing. I cannot have strife in my ministry, in my marriage, in my home or in my relationships with other people and still have the anointing upon me.

If you want to have the anointing, you must learn to be a sweetheart, easy to get along with and quick to forgive.

CHAPTER 10

POSITIVE CONDITIONS OF THE HEART, PART 3

In this chapter we will look at several more positive heart conditions through which God will help us develop into successful leaders.

As you begin to put them into practice in your life, I believe they will help you get from where you are to where God wants you to be in leadership.

15. An Open Heart

One of those who listened to us was a woman named Lydia, from the city of Thyatira, a dealer in fabrics dyed in purple. She was [already] a worshiper of God, and the Lord opened her heart to pay attention to what was said by Paul.

Acts 16:14

In the city of Philippi, to which God had directed Paul and those traveling with him, there was a group of women who gathered together on the bank of a river for prayer. Paul began to speak to these women, telling them some things they had never heard before. They were used to living under the Jewish Law, and Paul was delivering a message of grace. One of the women named Lydia had an open heart to receive what Paul had to say.[1]

The reason an open heart is so important is that without it, we won't listen to anything new or different. It is amazing the things in the Bible we will refuse to believe because they are not part of what we have been taught in the past. Why can't our believing be progressive? Why can't we accept that there may be a few things we don't know? That doesn't mean that we should be so open that we believe anything the devil wants to dump on us, but it does mean that we should not be so narrow-minded that nobody can teach us anything new. We should not be afraid to listen to what is being said and check it out for ourselves by reading the Bible and talking to God about it to see if it is really true.

We are supposed to be single-minded, not narrow-minded. I get concerned about people who think there is only one way to do things, and it is their way. It is hard to work with people like that.

We must have an open heart. It will tell us when what we are hearing is true. Our mind may be closed, but our heart must be open to God to allow Him to do new things in our life — not weird, off-the-wall things, but new things.

A GOOD LEADER'S HEART IS OPEN TO THE TRUTH.

Some leaders have so much pride they won't listen to anything that anybody tells them. A good leader's heart is open to the truth.

WILLING TO LEARN NEW THINGS

The next day Jesus desired and decided to go into Galilee; and He found Philip and said to him, Join Me as My attendant and follow Me.

Now Philip was from Bethsaida, of the same city as Andrew and Peter.

Philip sought and found Nathanael and told him, We have found (discovered) the One Moses in the Law and also the Prophets wrote about — Jesus from Nazareth, the [legal] son of Joseph!

Nathanael answered him, [Nazareth!] Can anything good come out of Nazareth? Philip replied, Come and see!

Jesus saw Nathanael coming toward Him and said concerning him, See! Here is an Israelite indeed [a true descendant of Jacob], in whom there is no guile nor deceit nor falsehood nor duplicity!

John 1:43-47

I used to wonder about those verses. It seemed that Nathanael was making a negative statement when he said, "Can anything good come out of Nazareth?" Yet in the next verse Jesus seemed to be complimenting him by saying, "Here is a true Israelite, in whom there is no guile, falsehood or duplicity."

Then one day I saw it. Nathanael had a negative opinion of Nazareth because it was the prevailing sentiment of the day that nothing good ever happened in Nazareth.[2] So when he heard that Jesus was from Nazareth, Nathanael was initially closed to the idea that He was the true Messiah simply because of where He came from.

So often we are like Nathanael. We decide that a person cannot be any good because of where he lives or where he comes from. We are so biased and opinionated, often without even realizing it. We have prejudices that have been placed in us by others through the things they have said to us. That's why we have to carefully examine our heart to see if it is truly open.

The thing Jesus seemed to like about Nathanael was that although he had a strong opinion that nothing good could come out of Nazareth, he was willing to go and check it out. Even though he may have had a strong opinion, he had an open heart. Philip said to him, *Come and see*, and he did. As a result, he found himself in a strong relationship with Jesus:

> *Nathanael said to Jesus, How do You know me? [How is it that You know these things about me?] Jesus answered him, Before [ever] Philip called you, when you were still under the fig tree, I saw you.*
>
> *Nathanael answered, Teacher, You are the Son of God! You are the King of Israel!*
>
> John 1:48,49

In James 3:17 in *The Amplified Bible* we find some key aspects of what true godly wisdom is. One of the things this verse says about wisdom is that it is willing to yield to reason (reason that is in line with the Truth of God's Word, as discussed previously).

If we refuse to listen to reason, then we have no wisdom because wisdom listens. People who have wisdom know they don't know everything. They have humility, and humility has an open heart; it is always willing to learn something new.

16. An Obedient Heart

But thank God, though you were once slaves of sin, you have become obedient with all your heart to the standard of teaching in which you were instructed and to which you were committed.

Romans 6:17

> PEOPLE WHO HAVE WISDOM KNOW THEY DON'T KNOW EVERYTHING. THEY ARE ALWAYS WILLING TO LEARN SOMETHING NEW.

If you are not obedient, you may as well forget about being a leader in the body of Christ. It is not possible.

In this verse, Paul wrote that the believers in Rome were obedient with all their heart. God has revealed to me that people can be obedient with their behavior and not be obedient with their heart.

He showed me this concerning my being submissive to my husband at a time when I was trying to get beyond the rebellious attitude and was coming into a relationship with the Lord in which I wanted to be submissive. I felt that was what the Lord was demanding of me and that I could not do anything else in our ministry until that issue was taken care of.

I wanted to be obedient to God, but I didn't want to be obedient to Dave. I wanted to be submissive to God, but I didn't want to be submissive to Dave. There were times when Dave wanted me to do something, and I didn't want to do it. I knew that God was pressing me to be submissive, so I would do what Dave asked me to do, but then God had to take me a step further by saying, "You are doing the act, but you are still not submissive because your heart is still wrong."

With God, the attitude of the heart is everything. We can do what our boss tells us to do while murmuring and grumbling behind their back. If we do that, we are not the kind of employee the Bible tells us to be. We may seem to get away with it, but we will not get our reward.[3]

There are rewards for obedience. According to the Bible, the obedient lifestyle brings rewards with it.[4]

I have found out that if I will do what God asks me to do, the blessings of God will chase me down and overtake me, but only if I have done it with the right heart attitude. It is not just a matter of putting on a show, but a matter of having the right attitude of heart.

Sometimes I do what Dave wants me to do, but I still don't want to. Really, I may be angry inside or want to rebel. So although I do what I am supposed to do, I have to repent of my wrong attitude, and God forgives me.

> **A LIFESTYLE OF OBEDIENCE TO GOD BRINGS REWARDS WITH IT.**

Sometimes I have to pray, "Lord, You know the truth. You know I really don't want to do this. I don't think it is right. I think it is unfair. But because I love You, I am going to do it. I ask You to give me the grace to do it with a right heart attitude." We all go through these types of experiences.

Jesus set the example for obedience, as we see in Philippians 2:5-8:

> *Let this same attitude and purpose and [humble] mind be in you which was in Christ Jesus: [Let Him be your example in humility:]*

> *Who, although being essentially one with God and in the form of God [possessing the fullness of the attributes which make God God], did not think this equality with God was a thing to be eagerly grasped or retained,*

> *But stripped Himself [of all privileges and rightful dignity], so as to assume the guise of a servant (slave), in that He became like men and was born a human being.*

> *And after He had appeared in human form, He abased and humbled Himself [still further] and carried His obedience to the extreme of death, even the death of the cross!*

I want to encourage you to come up higher in your obedience. Be quick to obey, prompt to obey, radical in your obedience, extreme in your obedience. Don't be the kind of person God has to deal with for three or four weeks just to get you to do the simplest little thing. If there is something between you and someone else, and God is pressing you to make it right, just do it. If you own something that God is telling you to give away, then give it away. Six months down the road don't still be saying, "Now, God if this is **really** You. . . ."

We get into situations like that because we hope that it is not God Who is telling us to do something we really don't want to do. Just because our flesh doesn't want to let go of something does not mean that we can't be obedient to God.

Once I had a rhinestone bracelet for a brief period of time. It was an antique that someone had sent me. I love sparkly things, and I thought it was a very beautiful bracelet.

The first time I ever wore it, a girl who sings in our meetings walked by me, and the Lord said to me, "Give her that bracelet."

I didn't want to do that. But I have enough reverential fear and awe of the Lord that I know when He says to do something, it is for a good reason and that I just need to trust Him whether I want to or not. Now I don't mean fear in a negative sense here; I'm talking about showing reverent trust, love and obedience toward Him.[5]

Afterwards, every time I saw that girl wearing that bracelet my flesh still moaned a little bit. But you must understand the nature of the flesh. If you wait until you feel like doing what is right, you will never get around to doing it.

We must be obedient to God whether we feel like it or not, and we must do it with a good attitude. We must not go around in mourning after we have been obedient.

It is time for us to take off our sackcloth and ashes. Too often we obey God and then get depressed about it afterwards. We get downright discouraged and feel sorry for ourselves. We think, **Every time I get something, God asks me to give it away.** But we must remember, rewards come with obedience.

God never tries to take anything away from us. He is always trying to get us to sow the seed that is necessary to bring another blessing into our lives. We cannot outgive God; it is impossible.

17. A Believing Heart

> *But without faith it is impossible to please and be satisfactory to Him.*
> *For whoever would come near to God must [necessarily] believe. . . .*

Hebrews 11:6

A believing heart is one of the heart attitudes that is absolutely vital to have if we want to be used by God.

That may sound funny since we are called believers. Don't we all have a believing heart? No, we don't. The church is full of "unbelieving believers."

Every now and then we need to ask ourselves, "How easy is it for me to believe?" For example, when we see someone ministering healing to others, do we really believe that healing is taking place?

In my own Christian life, I had some unbelief in that area at one time. Several years ago in the early days of the outpouring of the gifts of the Spirit, when they were being openly displayed by some parts of the church more than others, I saw a lot of people trying to make things happen that were not happening. I got so turned off by it that for a long period of time I had a hard time believing that any of it was real. I had to repent, ask God to forgive me, and go back and start all over again at square one.

As I became hungry to see God do miracles in my ministry so I could help people in a more profound way, especially those who were sick and in pain, He had to show me that I did not have a believing heart in this area. I had become hard-hearted and doubtful from seeing people falsify or misuse the gifts of the Spirit. These gifts include healing and miracles.

We need to keep a believing heart. We need to become like little children and just believe, as Jesus tells us in Matthew 18:3: . . . *Truly I say to you, unless you repent (change, turn about) and become like little children [trusting, lowly, loving, forgiving], you can never enter the kingdom of heaven [at all].*

So many things in the Bible are connected to believing.

Romans 10:9,10 says that in order to be saved, a person must believe in his heart and confess with his mouth. So salvation is a twofold thing. In order to receive it from God, we first believe in our heart, and then we must confess with our mouth. What we believe, we end up saying. We know that because we are told that *out of the abundance of the heart the mouth speaks.*[6]

Closet Christians concern me. I am bothered by people who want to be saved but don't want anybody to know it, people who say they believe but who claim that "religion is a private thing."

Religion is not a private thing. The first thing people did who were saved in the Bible was go out and tell somebody. It is impossible for a person to be full of Jesus and keep his mouth shut about it.

I believe Romans 10:9,10 can be a pattern for our lives. The way we receive anything from God is by believing with our heart and confessing with our mouth.

In Luke 24:25 Jesus chastised those who were slow of heart to believe. As leaders, we must be quick to believe.

In Matthew 8:13, a powerful Scripture, Jesus says, . . . *it shall be done for you as you have believed.* . . . It is amazing how much we can do if we believe we can do it. It is also amazing how little we can do if we believe we can't do it. We need to get up and start every day by saying over and over, "I believe I can; I believe I can."

In Matthew 9:28 Jesus asked, . . . *Do you believe that I am able to do this?* . . . Later, in Mark 5:36 TEV, He said, . . . *"Don't be afraid, only believe."*

There have been many times in my life when I have been discouraged and not known what to do, or felt that nothing was working and that everybody was against me. Whether it was about unfilled financial needs or unrelenting pain in my body, I would say to God, "What do You want me to do?" The thing I have heard over and over again is, "Only believe."

Hebrews 4:3 tells us that believing brings us into the rest of God. Once we enter that rest, it is wonderful because although we may still have a problem, we are not frustrated by it anymore.

In Mark 11:24 Jesus said, "Whatever you ask for in prayer, believe that you receive it, and you will get it." In John 8:45 He said, "I am speaking the truth, but you don't believe Me."

In Acts 16:31 we are told, "Believe in the Lord Jesus Christ, and you will be saved." Hebrews 11:6 tells us that those who come to God must believe that He exists and that He rewards those who seek Him.

Can you see from these Scriptures how important it is to believe? If you and I want to receive anything from God, we must first believe that He is, and then we must believe that He is good.

BELIEVING IS A WIN-WIN SITUATION

Romans 15:13 is one of my favorite Scriptures. It says that joy and peace are found in believing.

I remember when I was going through a period of time in which I had lost my joy and my peace. I didn't know what was wrong with me, but I knew something was wrong.

One night I was pretty desperate, so I went over to the little Promise Box and began flipping through it. I pulled out one of the little cards in it, and immediately the Lord spoke to me through it. It simply said, "Romans 15:13: Joy and peace are found in belief."

As soon as I got back to believing, my joy and peace came back. And the same is true for you. As soon as you start doubting, you lose your joy and peace, but as soon as you start believing again, your joy and peace come back to you.

God has given us a tool to keep ourselves radically happy and peaceful. All we have to do is believe.

Of course, as soon as we start believing, the devil starts screaming in our ears, "That's stupid! What if you believe and you don't get what you are believing?" That's when we have to answer back, "No, it's not stupid. What if I believe and get what I am believing? But even if I never get it, I am still happier and more peaceful by believing than I am by doubting."

So it is a win-win situation. There is no way to lose when we believe because if we believe, we are liable to get what we are believing for. But even if we don't, we will stay happy and peaceful. So it is vital that we keep a believing heart.

Jesus said that we must be like little children. Little kids believe whatever they are told. It is amazing how suspicious we get the older we get. After we have been through a few hard times and been hurt or disappointed a few times, it gets harder for us to be like little children and just go on believing. But even as full-grown adults we can come back to that childlike faith. We can have a believing heart if we want to, and we have to if we want God to be able to use us.

Moses was a mighty man of God. But, remember, after he had wandered through the wilderness for forty years leading the Israelites and getting blamed for their stupidity and stubbornness, there came a time in his later life when he became slow of heart to believe. So in order to fulfill His plan and mission for the nation of Israel, God had to remove Moses and put Joshua in his place. Joshua had a fresh, new spirit of faith.

There are times when we all need a fresh, new spirit in us, the heart of Joshua and Caleb that says, "Let's go and take it because we are well able to do so."[7]

We need to have the kind of believing heart that says, "What do You want me to do, Lord? Whatever it is, I'll do it!" We shouldn't have to have three confirmations, two angels, three trumpet blasts and four prophecies before we act. We just need to have the confirmation in our heart of what God is saying to us.

In 1 John 4:16 we are told that we need to believe in the love that God has for us. And in 1 Corinthians 13:7 KJV we are told that love believes all things. In other words, love has a believing heart.

18. An Enlarged Heart

Our mouth is open to you, Corinthians [we are hiding nothing, keeping nothing back], and our heart is expanded wide [for you]!

There is no lack of room for you in [our hearts], but you lack room in your own affections [for us].

2 Corinthians 6:11,12

The *King James Version* of verse 11 says that our heart is enlarged. That is what we need to have, an enlarged heart.

Sometimes we don't have room in our heart for everyone. We have such a small heart that we can take in only those who are just like us, those who think and act the way we do. But the Lord wants us to have room enough in our heart to take in everyone, even those who are not like us, those who do not think and act the way we do, those we don't like and who don't like us, people who have opinions of their own.

19. A Pure Heart

Blessed are the pure in heart: for they shall see God.

Matthew 5:8 KJV

God is seeking leaders who are pure in heart. A leader who has a pure heart, who is wholeheartedly serving God, is a truly powerful leader. In Psalm 51:6, David tells us that having a pure heart means having truth in our inner being, which is the real person. It's all about paying attention to our thought life because out of it come our words, our emotions, our attitudes and our motives.

It took me a long time to realize that God will not bless actions done out of wrong motives.

Purity of heart is not a natural trait. It is something that must be worked on in most of us. In 1 John 3:3 we see that we should desire and work toward purity of heart because it is God's will. This is a challenge that every leader should be excited about accepting. But we don't have to take the challenge on alone.

We are created by God to be dependent upon Him, to bring Him our challenges and to allow Him to help us with them. No one but God and the individual know what is in our heart. But our God is an expert at removing worthless things out of us while retaining the valuable.

> **GOD IS AN EXPERT AT REMOVING WORTHLESS THINGS OUT OF US WHILE RETAINING THE VALUABLE.**

There is a price to pay to have a pure heart, but there is also a reward. We don't have to be afraid to make the commitment to allow God to do a deep work in us. We may not always feel comfortable about the truths He will bring to us, but if we will take care of our part — facing it, accepting it and allowing it to change us — God will take care of making sure that we are blessed.

20. The Heart of a Father

After all, though you should have ten thousand teachers (guides to direct you) in Christ, yet you do not have many fathers. For I became your father in Christ Jesus through the glad tidings (the Gospel).

1 Corinthians 4:15

Paul had a father's heart toward the believers in the church in Corinth.

A father's heart is that tender, nurturing, training, teaching, stick-to-it kind of attitude that doesn't give up on people just because they don't learn right away.

A father delights in teaching his children how to walk or to play ball. He doesn't get mad at them because they don't master the steps the first time. He keeps working and working with them until they learn how to do it.

Paul said that the church is full of instructors, full of teachers, full of people who can preach a sermon and tell others what to do. But he also said there are not enough fathers in the church.

If you want to be a leader in the body of Christ, especially if you want to be a pastor, you must have the heart of a father. Whatever your calling, it's not enough to outwardly say and do all the right things — inwardly you've got to have the right heart attitude.

Many times we have a lot of fancy ideas about ourselves, which, sad to say, are not always true. It is fine to learn about all these positive conditions of the heart and say, "Yes, amen." But the fact is that once we know these things, before we can move into leadership, God has to test us to see what kind of heart we have. Why? Because our true character shows during times of testing.

As we will see next, there are things in us that we would never believe were there unless God did something to force them to the surface where they can be dealt with. Tests show us our problem areas so we can cooperate with the Holy Spirit and work with Him to change them. Through the testing, God shows us what kind of heart we have to make us into the leader He designed us to be.

PART 3

TESTING
THE HEART OF A LEADER

CHAPTER 11

TESTS OF LEADERSHIP, PART 1

*Oh, let the wickedness of the wicked come to an end, but establish the
[uncompromisingly] righteous [those upright and in harmony with
You]; for You, Who try the hearts and emotions and thinking powers,
are a righteous God.*

Psalm 7:9

In this passage the psalmist tells us that God tests our heart, emotions
and thinking powers. In Jeremiah 11:20, the prophet Jeremiah says that
God tests the heart and mind.

How do we test anything? We put pressure on it to see if it will do
what it says it will do, if it will hold up under stress. God does the same
thing with us. When we pray, asking Him to use us and to put us into a
position of leadership, His answer is, "Let Me try you out first. Let Me
put you to the test."

It is very sad to me how many people never make it past the trying
point. They don't ever pass the test. They spend their whole life going
around and around the same proverbial mountains. But in God's school
we don't flunk. We just get to keep taking the test over and over until we
pass it.

One of the ways God tests us is by requiring us to manifest what we
say we know. Head knowledge alone is not enough. It doesn't mean
anything if we can't produce the goods.

Webster's 1828 dictionary defines the word *test* as "that with which
any thing is compared for proof of its genuineness; a standard."[1] It also

says that *to test* is "to compare with a standard; to try; to prove the truth or genuineness of any thing by experiment. . . ."[2]

In Deuteronomy 8:2, the Bible says that God led the Israelites in the wilderness for forty years to humble them, to prove them and to see if they would keep His commandments. Tests come in hard times, not in good times because not everything God asks us to do is going to be easy. That is why He tests us to see if we are ready and able before He promotes us to a higher level of responsibility.

There are so many things that come our way every day that are just nothing more than a test. For example, sometimes when we have to wait to be seated at a table in a restaurant and then we get a bad meal, it's a test. Sometimes when we are going to pull into a parking space and someone zooms in behind us and takes it, it's a test. Sometimes when our boss tells us to do something we don't want to do, it's a test.

James 1:2-4 says that tests bring out what is in us. It is in times of trial that we become best acquainted with ourselves and what we are capable of doing. Peter didn't think he would ever deny Jesus, but when he was put to the test, that is exactly what he did.[3] God is not impressed with what we say we will do; He is impressed with what we prove we will do under pressure. We don't get promoted in ministry because we have our Bible underlined in two colors, but because we have been tested and tried and it was hard, but we dug in and we passed the tests.

If you are frustrated today about the call of God on your life, I can tell you that you are in the testing ground. What God does with you later fully depends on how you pass your tests now.

Let's look at some Scriptures that talk about tests and what they do for us.

James wrote, *Blessed (happy, to be envied) is the man who is patient under trial and stands up under temptation, for when he has stood the test and been approved, he will receive [the victor's] crown of life which God has promised to those who love Him.*[4]

David prayed in Psalm 26:2, *Examine me, O Lord, and prove me; test my heart and my mind.* Not many of us pray for tests, but that won't keep us from getting them.

In 1 Peter 1:6,7, Peter tells us, *[You should] be exceedingly glad on this account, though now for a little while you may be distressed by trials and suffer temptations, So that [the genuineness] of your faith may be tested, [your faith] which is infinitely more precious than the perishable gold which is tested and purified by fire. [This proving of your faith is intended] to redound to [your] praise and glory and honor when Jesus Christ (the Messiah, the Anointed One) is revealed.*

In 1 Peter 4:12, he also tells us not to be surprised or dismayed by the tests that we have to endure because by them God is testing our "quality," or our character. Peter was writing to the church here and saying, "When you go through these things and you have these tests, don't act like it is something from outer space. We all go through this. You don't have to be confused about what is going on. God is testing your quality. He's testing your character. He's testing you to see what manner of person you are. He's testing your heart."

Every time God gives us a test, we can tell how far we've come and how far we still have to go by how we react in that test. Attitudes of the heart that we didn't even know we had can come out when we are in tests and trials.

Then in verse 13 Peter says that we should rejoice with triumph in our suffering so that Christ's glory may be revealed through us.

In 1 Timothy 3:10 Paul tells us that leaders should be tested before given responsibility. In other words, leaders become leaders after they have paid their dues.

In God's economy, leaders are not promoted because of what they know or think they know, by their education or by how polished or charismatic they are, but by what they do during testing times.

The testing times that God permits in our life are actually for our benefit, but when we're going through them, we don't always feel like they are going to be for our good.

IT'S ALL FOR OUR GOOD

We are assured and know that [God being a partner in their labor] all things work together and are [fitting into a plan] for good to and for those who love God and are called according to [His] design and purpose.

Romans 8:28

This is one of my favorite Scriptures in the Bible. I learned a long time ago that just because I don't understand what is going on does not mean God does not have a purpose for it, or that just because I don't feel good about something does not mean it is not going to work out for the best.

Many people are trying to lead who have never been through the training process. I don't think such people will last in leadership very long or will ever be the kind of leaders God wants them to be because God always tests the heart of a leader.

In this chapter I would like to share with you a list of some of the tests that a person must pass before God promotes them to a leadership position.

1. The Trust Test

But He knows the way that I take [He has concern for it, appreciates, and pays attention to it]. When He has tried me, I shall come forth as refined gold [pure and luminous].

Job 23:10

> WE MUST LEARN TO TRUST GOD WHEN WE DON'T UNDERSTAND WHAT IS GOING ON IN OUR LIFE.

One of the tests we can expect to encounter in our journey with God is the trust test. We must learn to trust God when we don't understand what is going on in our life.

How many times do we say to God, "What is going on in my life? What are You doing? What is happening? I don't understand this at all."

Sometimes the things happening in us seem to be taking us in the exact opposite direction of what we feel that God has revealed to us.

A good example is our older son, David, who is now director of world outreach for our ministry. He travels all over the world and has a major responsibility to help us find the right places to invest our money and to make sure it is being used properly.

Some time ago he met and married a young woman, who had thought for a long time that she was going to be a missionary, so she went to Puerto Rico to attend Bible college and learn the language. Then when she and David met, they fell in love and got married. Afterwards, he also went to Puerto Rico and began to learn the language.

We could see that they had a call on their lives, but we kept feeling inclined to ask them to come to St. Louis and work for us in the ministry here. That really didn't make any sense to us, since they were supposed to be missionaries. They felt led to come back to work for us, but that didn't make any sense to them either.

Sometimes that is the way God leads us, and we must learn to follow His leading; otherwise, we are going to be led by our head and miss the will of God for our life.

> SOMETIMES GOD LEADS US IN WHAT APPEARS TO BE THE EXACT OPPOSITE DIRECTION OF WHAT WE FEEL HE HAS REVEALED TO US.

So although it was confusing to them, our son and his wife came back to the States for a period of time, asking, "Lord, if we are supposed to come back here, why did we have to go to language school? Why did we go over there and get settled on the mission field?"

Part of the answer is what we will discuss later as the **time test.** Just because God tells us to do something does not mean that we are supposed to run out and do that thing tomorrow or next year or even five years from now. He wants us to wait on Him and move in His perfect timing. Why? Because all the things we will do in between will be part of what we are ultimately going to do, although each piece by itself may not make much sense to us at the time.

Although we and others were sensing a missionary call on our son's life, we were not taking into account the fact that there were some things that desperately needed to be done in his life before he could handle that call. David was a wonderful young man, but he needed a lot of work done on his character. He had a very strong personality, a very quick temper. If he had not gone through a crucifixion of the flesh, he would not have been fit or prepared to hold the position he now holds.

Yes, there was a missionary call on David's life, but God had an opening in His kingdom called Director of World Outreach for Life In The Word Ministries in St. Louis, Missouri. There were a lot of things that David had to go through before he could fulfill the call of the Lord. He had to go through many tests, and one of them was the trust test. He had to learn to trust God even though what was happening in his life made no sense to him at the time.

This is where many people give up and fail, where they get confused and fall by the wayside and go back to something that will be quicker and easier for them.

If you are in a place right now where nothing in your life makes any sense, trust God anyway. Say to yourself, "This must be a test."

One of the things I have learned through the years is this: **There is no such thing as trusting God without unanswered questions.** If we have all the answers to all the questions, there is no need to trust because we already know everything.

As long as God is training us to trust, there are always going to be things in our life we just don't understand. That is why we have to learn to say, "God, I don't understand, but I trust You."

We must learn to trust in God when we don't understand, when heaven is silent.

Don't you just love it when God is not saying anything?

Dave and I talk about God speaking to us and leading us, but to be honest, we don't have a running conversation with Him all the time in which He is giving us minute-by-minute directions for our lives.

Sometimes I will go for as long as two years without having any direct, specific instruction from God about the overall plan He has for my life and ministry. I hear from Him about what to preach, how to handle a certain situation, what decision to make, and things like that, but no fresh word from Him involving life-changing direction.

Sometimes I start to get frustrated and feel like saying, "Tell me something, Lord." But I have learned that if He is not telling me anything, I need to stay busy doing the last thing He told me to do, whatever it was, and just keep trusting Him. It may be five years before He gives me another direction. If He speaks something different to me, then I will do it. But until He does, I will just go on doing what He has already told me to do.

Without trusting God, life is miserable. So we must learn to trust God when we don't understand, when heaven is silent, when we don't see tomorrow's provision.

You and I are always feeling that we need an answer for tomorrow. But have you learned yet that tomorrow's answers usually don't come until tomorrow gets here? In that sense, it is like the story of the manna recorded in Exodus 16.

When God rained down that manna from heaven, He forbade the Israelites to gather more of it than what they needed for one day at a time. I believe that was a trust test.

> **Tomorrow's answers from God usually don't come until tomorrow gets here.**

Just think about it. We are out in the middle of nowhere with no food, and God rains down food upon us. There is plenty there, all around us. We could collect enough for a week, but God says, "No, don't do that. Just gather what you need for today and let the rest lie there; don't touch it."

Our little minds immediately go to work, reasoning, **But if I don't gather it up and use it, it will just go to waste. God is not a God of waste, so that word surely can't be from Him. If I gather only enough for today, what is going to happen if there is none tomorrow? I'm going to get awfully hungry. I'd better gather just a little bit extra in case God doesn't come through.**

But we also remember what happened when the Israelites did gather more than enough for just one day. It rotted and began to stink.

I think the reason a lot of us have so many rotting, stinking messes in our lives is that we stay so busy trying to gather tomorrow's provision today. We would be much happier, and enjoy much better provision, if we would just learn to trust God.

2. The Security Test

> . . . *put no confidence or dependence [on what we are] in the flesh and on outward privileges and physical advantages and external appearances.*

> Philippians 3:3

We are not to put confidence in the flesh, not ours or anybody else's. Where does God want our confidence to be placed? In Him alone.

In John 15:5 Jesus said, *I am the Vine; you are the branches. Whoever lives in Me and I in him bears much (abundant) fruit. However, apart from Me [cut off from vital union with Me] you can do nothing.*

God despises independence. He wants us to be totally dependent and reliant upon Him. He wants us to be as dependent upon Him as a branch is on a vine — it will wither quickly if it gets off the vine. He wants us to lean on Him for everything in our life.

How then does God test us in this area of being secure in Him?

Sometimes we think we are very secure in our confidence in the Lord until somebody rejects us, and suddenly we don't understand what is happening to us or why. (If you don't think God permits such things to happen, you are wrong because He does.) They may hurt us at the time, but eventually they help us get our trust where it belongs and away from where it does not belong.

The sad truth is that people are just not always reliable. If you are in a circle of people and are placing your faith in them, I can promise you that sooner or later one or more of them is going to let you down. Somebody is going to disappoint you by doing what you didn't expect them to do or not doing what you did expect them to do. That is just part of human nature.

When that happens to us, God is trying to save us a lot of agony by saying, "Why didn't you put your confidence in Me to start with?"

TESTS CAUSE THE IMPURITIES IN OUR LIVES TO RISE TO THE TOP WHERE THEY CAN BE DEALT WITH.

Yes, we can have relationships with people. We can trust people to a certain degree. But when we put trust in people that should be put in God alone, He is obligated to show up their weaknesses, so we can know we have our trust in the wrong place.

How does God make a leader? He gives us test after test after test because tests cause the impurities in our lives to rise to the top where they can be dealt with. Nothing shows the real us like a test.

My daughter once shared how far she had come in the area of staying peaceful and not getting all upset about little things that go wrong. The next day she dropped some cream cheese onto the kitchen floor that should have gone on her toast. She picked it up and slammed it into the trashcan. She saw by that test where she really was in her attempt to live peacefully. True, she didn't throw it across the floor as she would have done a year earlier. But she also didn't react in the calm, quiet way she knew she should have in that situation.

God keeps giving us little tests like that and keeps making us go through them again and again until we learn. The tests don't change, but we change. Wouldn't it be wonderful if we could get to the point where none of those irritating little things in life bother us at all?

I got so hungry for peace that I finally decided I would make any adjustments necessary in my life to have it because I was no longer willing to go around being upset all the time. I discovered that it was not my circumstances that needed to be changed; it was me.

To be honest, some people spend their whole lives trying to make everybody and everything else change — trying to control other people, trying to control the devil, trying to control their circumstances — without ever realizing the real source of their misery and unhappiness. They go around saying, "God, I'm not happy. The devil is aggravating me. Other people are failing me and disappointing me. I need certain things to make me happy, and You're not giving them to me." They never get around to changing because they always expect everyone and everything else to change.

God wants to use all those people and things we don't like, to change us. Then once we are changed, either they will go away or else they won't bother us; so either way it won't make us any difference.

WHAT ARE YOU LEANING ON?

Cease to trust in [weak, frail, and dying] man, whose breath is in his nostrils [for so short a time]; in what sense can he be counted as having intrinsic worth?

Isaiah 2:22

Here God is asking us, "Why are you putting your trust in weak, frail and mortal people who are only alive for so short a time? In what sense can they be counted as having intrinsic worth? Instead, put your trust in Me."

Then in the next verse, in Isaiah 3:1, we read, *For behold, the Lord, the Lord of hosts, is taking away from Jerusalem and from Judah the stay and the staff [every kind of prop], the whole stay of bread and the whole stay of water.* Here the Lord is saying that He is taking away from His people all their props.

What happens to us when our props are pulled out from under us? We discover what we are really leaning on, what we are really rooted and grounded in. Let me give you an example.

My husband, Dave, and I play golf frequently. Out on the golf course there are often little twigs planted that will one day grow into trees. Those little plants are so tiny and weak that they usually have sticks set on either side of them as props to hold them up because they have no strength or roots. Without those sticks to hold them up, when the wind and rain came, they would be destroyed.

That is the way we are as new believers. When we begin our walk with God we need a prop system, something to help us stand up straight and strong. We need a group of people around us to keep us studying the Bible, praying and seeking the Lord. If we don't have that support system, when the storms of life come against us, they will blow us over.

Our support system may take many forms, but whatever it is, sooner or later God is going to start taking it away by removing the props from under us. At first, this is pretty scary because we don't understand it, and we don't like it. We start saying things like, "Oh, Lord, do You really want me to quit going to that prayer meeting? I don't know if I can make it through the week without it. Do You really want me to stop going for counseling and, instead, just come to You? Do You really want me to stop getting in the prayer line and just trust You for my healing? Oh, I don't know if I can make it without these things."

The props God starts removing from under us may be things that we derive a lot of pleasure and satisfaction from, things like singing or playing an instrument or being part of the worship team. Then suddenly, for whatever reason, we lose that position, or God requires us to give it up. It is then that we discover how much of our sense of value and worth depends on the things we are doing.

I once had a job as associate pastor in a church in St. Louis. I worked there five years. I liked that job. I had my own little group of friends there. Everybody knew me. I had a seat on the front row and a parking place outside with my name on it. I thought I was really important.

Since I came from a dysfunctional background in which I did not receive the kind of love and nurturing I needed so that I knew who I was in Christ, I was not aware that I was deriving my sense of value and worth from what I did. Even though it was what I was called to do, and God wanted me to **do** it, He did not want me **to be dependent** upon it. He wanted me to be able to separate what I was doing **for** Him from who I was **in** Him so that even if I was no longer doing it, my sense of value and worth would still be intact. He didn't want me thinking that if I was no longer a teacher and a preacher, then I was nothing.

> GOD WANTS US TO BE ABLE TO SEPARATE WHAT WE ARE DOING FOR HIM FROM WHO WE ARE IN HIM.

Just because we transfer from worldly works to Christian works when we accept Jesus as our Savior, it doesn't mean that we don't bring some of the worldly baggage and garbage with us, that we don't still play the same worldly games only now under "Christianese." We still try to manipulate ourselves into positions. We still try to associate ourselves with the right people, making sure we are part of the right group that will get us what we want.

We need to learn to stop trying to promote ourselves and let God place us where He wants us to be. I have discovered that God does not have to keep me where He did not put me. If I put myself some place, then I have to keep myself there. And that is hard to do.

In my life, God has had to knock a lot of props out from under me. He called me out of the job I had at that church in St. Louis. I soon discovered that when I went to church on Sunday morning, I no longer had my private seat in church or my reserved space in the parking lot. After a while, people would even come up to me in church, introduce themselves and ask, "Are you new here?" I felt upset and irritated. I wanted to say, "I have been here since there were only thirty people here! I used to be associate pastor at this church! Don't you know who I am?"

I was like that tree that had its props knocked away. I had a group of about twelve lady friends in that church, and I had put a lot of dependence on them. During my time there, some of them had turned against me and said some things they should not have said. They had started accusing me of things I had not done. I was so hurt and disappointed. I just couldn't believe it.

God has to strip away everything we put our security in but Him. He is a God of restoration. He restores our mind, our emotions, our soul, our health. When we start to restore a beautiful, expensive piece of antique furniture, we have to first strip away the old paint or varnish on it before we apply a new finish. If you feel that stripping going on in your life, don't be upset. Cooperate with the Lord while He does His work.

Don't be like that little twig blowing in the wind because its props have been taken away. Instead, put down some roots so that one day you can stand tall and steady and be a tree of righteousness.[5]

3. The Rejection Test

> *Remember that I told you, A servant is not greater than his master [is not superior to him]. If they persecuted Me, they will also persecute you. . . .*
>
> John 15:20

People will reject us just as they rejected Jesus and Paul and the other apostles and disciples. We will be rejected because Jesus said that the servant is no greater than his master, and that just as He was rejected, so will we be also.

It is especially hard when we are rejected by people who are wrong and who are saying and doing wrong things.

Psalm 118:22 says, *The stone which the builders rejected has become the chief cornerstone.* This passage is talking about David, who was rejected by the Jewish rulers, but later on was chosen by the Lord to be the ruler of Israel.[6] In Matthew 21:42 Jesus quoted this verse to the chief priests and the Pharisees, referring to His rejection by them as the Son of God; He also referred to Himself as the Chief Cornerstone of the church.

Even though people may reject us, if we will hold steady and continue to do what God is telling us to do with a good attitude, eventually we may become the chief cornerstone wherever He places us. God can promote us and make us a leader even though everybody else may think we are nothing. God can lift us up and place us where no man can put us.

When I first started preaching, I was so insecure. If a few people got up and walked out of the service, the devil would tell me they were leaving because they didn't like women preaching. That did happen a few times in churches whose pastors had warned me ahead of time that they had never had a woman in their pulpit and were not sure how their congregations were going to react. When it did happen, I would always be embarrassed and feel bad.

Then God gave me this Scripture in Luke 10:16: *He who hears and heeds you [disciples] hears and heeds Me; and he who slights and rejects you slights and rejects Me; and he who slights and rejects Me slights and rejects Him who sent Me.*

The Lord simply told me, "I am the One Who called you. Don't worry about what people think. If you do, you are going to be worrying all your life because the devil will never stop finding people who will think something unkind about you."

In Matthew 10:14 when Jesus sent His disciples out into the towns and villages to preach, He told them what to do if people rejected them. He didn't tell them to stand around and cry and be wounded, hurt, bleeding and embarrassed. He said, *And whoever will not receive and accept and welcome you nor listen to your message, as you leave that house or town, shake the dust [of it] from your feet.* In verse 23 He said, *When they persecute you in one town [that is, pursue you in a manner that would injure you and cause you to suffer because of your belief], flee to another town; for truly I tell you, you will not have gone through all the towns of Israel before the Son of Man comes.*

So if there is a call on your life, and one person or group of people rejects you, there will be others who will accept you. Just shake the rejection off and move on.

You and I have got to learn to shake off our troubles and problems, our disappointments and rejections.

In Acts 28:1-5 we read a story about Paul and his traveling companions who were shipwrecked on the island of Malta. While Paul was gathering sticks to lay on a fire they had built to warm and dry themselves, a snake crawled out of the fire and fastened itself to his hand. Seeing this, the natives of the island were convinced that Paul was a murderer because, although he had been saved from the sea, this deadly snake had bitten him and their avenging goddess of justice would not allow him to live.

In verse 5 we read, *Then [Paul simply] shook off the small creature into the fire and suffered no evil effects.*

There is an entire message in that verse. When the devil "bites" us and tries to fasten himself to some area of our life, whether it is with fear, rejection, discouragement, disappointment, betrayal, loneliness or whatever, the Bible tells us what to do — simply **shake it off and go on.**

Often this rejection is from people who are very close to us. Jesus' own family, his own brothers, rejected Him and His ministry.[7] The same thing may happen to any of us.

If we are going to follow the Lord and do things that are different from what everyone else is doing, they are going to find fault with us and reject us. That is the only way they can feel that what they are doing or not doing is OK. When that happens, just shake it off and keep pressing on toward fulfilling what God has called you to do.

4. The Judas-Kiss Test

But Jesus said to him, Judas! Would you betray and deliver up the Son of Man with a kiss?

Luke 22:48

Another test we may encounter is what I call the Judas-kiss test, that is, the test of being betrayed by friends.

Some time ago I talked with a person who had just gone through something that was emotionally hard because it involved rejection and betrayal by some people this individual considered close and trusted friends. I told this person the same thing I am going to share with you right now in this book.

There were certain things that Jesus did for us that we should not have to go through. For example, He bore our sins so we do not have to bear them.[8] But there are other things that Jesus went through that He endured as an example for us, things we will have to follow in His footsteps and go through.[9] One of those things is rejection, as we have just seen. Another is loneliness, which we will discuss later. Another is being obedient, doing the will or God when we don't want to. Another is betrayal.

To be honest with you, I don't know very many key leaders, people who have been in positions of leadership for very long, who have not at one time or another in their lives been betrayed by someone they really loved, respected and trusted.

How many pastors have had an associate pastor who took part of the congregation and broke away to start a new church? That happens so often it is almost commonplace.

God may call someone out of a church to begin a new work, but there is a right and a wrong way to do that new work. It is never wise to leave anywhere in strife. Always remember: How you leave the old work is also how you enter the new work — you take the attitude with you that you left with.

> **HOW YOU LEAVE THE OLD WORK IS ALSO HOW YOU ENTER THE NEW WORK — YOU TAKE THE ATTITUDE WITH YOU THAT YOU LEFT WITH.**

I was once part of a church whose leadership felt it was wrong for me to be teaching instead of my husband. They openly came against us, embarrassing us and hurting us. We wanted to storm out of that place and just go somewhere else, but God kept putting it on our hearts not to leave in strife. We waited for a long time and literally were persecuted during the wait. As we waited, the church began to die. The attendance was rapidly dropping, the Spirit of God was no longer moving, and it was evident there were serious problems.

The leaders tried to exercise control over members of the congregation instead of true leadership. They always became hurt and angry when anyone wanted to leave and do something else. They acted as if they "owned" the people, which is a wrong attitude to have.

In 2 Corinthians 1:24 the apostle Paul told the church at Corinth that he was not trying to be a dictator of their faith, but a promoter of their joy, and that is what leaders should be.

The leaders of this church treated many others the way they had treated us. God will not bless anyone who mistreats other people. As we waited, God took care of the situation. As His Word says, He is our Vindicator.[10]

Had I taken matters into my own hands and not followed the leading of the Holy Spirit, I would have left angry, hurt and bitter. By waiting, I was able to leave with a right heart attitude and be blessed in the next thing I put my hand to. Dave and I might not have the ministry we do today if we had not obeyed God at that time.

Satan loves betrayal because often when we are hurt by it, we feel we can't trust anybody. We want to give up, quit and go some place to "be the Lone Ranger" and "do our own thing," so we never have to experience that hurt again. Betrayal is something else we must learn to shake off and not let bother us. Jesus didn't let it get to Him, and we must not let it get to us either.

In Matthew 24:10 Jesus warns us that in the last days, things like betrayal are going to increase. He described these trying times in that passage, saying:

> And then many will be offended and repelled and will begin to distrust
> and desert [Him Whom they ought to trust and obey] and will
> stumble and fall away and betray one another and pursue
> one another with hatred.
>
> And many false prophets will rise up and deceive and lead
> many into error.
>
> And the love of the great body of people will grow cold because of
> the multiplied lawlessness and iniquity,
>
> But he who endures to the end will be saved.
>
> Matthew 24:10-13

If we believe we are in the last days, then we had better be aware of some of the signs of the end times. Mark 13:7,8 describes some of the signs as wars and rumors of wars, famines and earthquakes in different places, but it's more than that. One of those signs is an increase in betrayal, which is what we are seeing today.

But Jesus says that those who endure all these things to the end will be saved. So there are some things we are going to have to endure, some trials and tribulations we are going to have to go through. But when we go through them, as believers we know that with God's help, we will make it to the other side. And we have a choice on how we respond to them. So we might as well choose to let them make us better, not bitter.

It is not what happens to us that ruins us. It is our wrong response to what happens to us that ruins us. But we do not have to make a wrong response; we can choose to make a right response. As an example, let's look at the Judas-Jesus scenario, for which this test is named.

MAKE THE RIGHT CHOICE

Now the Festival of Unleavened Bread was drawing near,
which is called the Passover.

And the chief priests and the scribes were seeking how to do away
with [Jesus], for they feared the people.

But [then] Satan entered into Judas, called Iscariot, who was
one of the Twelve [apostles].

And he went away and discussed with the chief priests and captains
*how he might **betray** Him and deliver Him up to them.*

Luke 22:1-4

Judas was one of the twelve disciples of Jesus, yet we read that Satan entered into him. We must understand that Satan can work through anyone, even those who are close to us. That is why it is dangerous to expect too much of the people around us. As soon as we set ourselves up to expect them never to hurt us, we have set ourselves up for severe disappointment.

That does not mean that we should adopt a sour, bitter, cynical attitude toward everyone, saying, "Well, you just can't trust anybody these days."

That is not what I am saying. I like people, and I trust people. I don't go through life being suspicious of everyone I meet. But I also don't go through life expecting never to be hurt by anyone because I know they are flesh and blood just as I am, which means that they are going to fail just as I fail. Therefore, I put my trust not in people but in the Friend Who sticks closer than a brother.[11] I know what He will do, but I don't know for sure what people will do. They can love you one week and hate you the next.

People can change pretty quickly, just as Judas changed his opinion of Jesus, which is why he began to seek out how he might betray Him. Jesus knew everything. He already knew that Judas was going to betray Him. Why, then, didn't He do something about it?

One of the things I have learned about God is that although He knows what we are going to do, He still gives us an opportunity to choose.

Many times Dave and I will work with certain people, trying to bring them through some situation or give them opportunity to serve in ministry, and everything will just blow up in our faces and turn out to be a huge mess.

At such times I am tempted to say, "Well, we must have missed God." But Dave has told me again and again, "No, just because this happened does not mean that we missed God. God gives people opportunity. What they do with that opportunity is up to them."

So Jesus knew Judas' capability to do wrong, but He gave him opportunity to choose so He could see if he would change and make the right choice.

SATAN PLAYS ON OUR WEAKNESS

So six days before the Passover Feast, Jesus came to Bethany, where Lazarus was, who had died and whom He had raised from the dead.

So they made Him a supper; and Martha served, but Lazarus was one of those at the table with Him.

Mary took a pound of ointment of pure liquid nard [a rare perfume] that was very expensive, and she poured it on Jesus' feet and wiped them with her hair. And the whole house was filled with the fragrance of the perfume.

But Judas Iscariot, the one of His disciples who was about to betray Him, said,

Why was this perfume not sold for 300 denarii [a year's wages for an ordinary workman] and that [money] given to the poor (the destitute)?

Now he did not say this because he cared for the poor but because he was
a thief; and having the bag (the money box, the purse of the Twelve), he
took for himself what was put into it [pilfering the collections].

John 12:1-6

Judas was money hungry. That's why he was about to betray Jesus.
He had a problem with greed.

What does Satan do when he wants to get to a leader? He finds
someone close to the leader who has a weakness and then tries to use it
to destroy the leader.

I have seen this happen in my own life. Even my own children, who
love me very much, have weaknesses in their personality that can really
aggravate me.

It is a challenge to have your own children working for you in your
ministry. We are their parents, their pastors and their employers. And they
are all our best friends. So we have to be able to change hats really quickly
and say to them, "Now we are acting as your parents. Now we are acting
as your pastors. Now we are acting as your bosses. Now we are acting as
your friends." So Satan tries to take advantage of the situation and use it
to cause problems between us, just as he did with Judas and Jesus.

He even tries to bring discord and disharmony between Dave and
me. Like any married couple, Dave and I get along fine most of the time,
but there are certain things we do that can aggravate each other.

Dave may go months and months without doing anything that gets
on my nerves, but then all of a sudden the devil will really try to get to
me through him. Although that area is supposed to be dead and buried, it
is as though it suddenly has a resurrection and starts irritating me again.

One of the things about Dave that bugs me, and he knows it, is that
he is really big on details, while I just want to tell the meat and potatoes
of something. So every time I start to tell a story, he stops me and
corrects me. When I am talking, I don't like to be interrupted. I want
people to listen to what I have to say. Once I get started, I like to go
with the flow. I will be doing that, and Dave will say, "No, it wasn't like
that." So he will go back and start trying to fill in all the details about
little things that don't matter at all to the story as far as I am concerned.

I could tell four stories while he is still hung up on the details of the first half of the first story.

Am I right or is Dave right? Actually neither of us is right or wrong; we are just different. We all have individual strengths and weaknesses, and Satan plays on those weaknesses to cause trouble for us and for others.

In this story in John chapter 12, we see that it is getting close to the time when Jesus is going to die on the cross for our sins. All of a sudden Satan begins to work on Judas' weakness for money to try to use him to hurt Jesus.[12]

We must realize that when God gets ready to promote us, there are going to be times when Satan will step in to try to stop us. It is almost always when our greatest blessing lies right around the corner. He will try to cause us to manifest a bad attitude or to display a bad reaction so God will say, "I guess you're not ready yet, so one more trip around the mountain."

What should we do when that happens to us?

Shake it off.

We can weep and wail because we have been betrayed, but that is not going to help; in fact, it is just going to make matters worse. Instead, we should be determined that we are not going to let it stop us, that we are going to go on with God.

In the actual betrayal scene, Judas found Jesus in the Garden of Gethsemane and betrayed Him to His enemies with a kiss.[13]

But Jesus is not the only one in the Bible to have been betrayed by a close friend or relative. King David's own son Absalom betrayed him by leading a rebellion against him and trying to overthrow him.[14] Joseph was betrayed by his brothers, who sold him into slavery in Egypt where he was thrown into prison for a crime he did not commit.[15] Moses' sister Miriam and his brother Aaron turned against him and betrayed him in an unsuccessful attempt to take over his rightful place as God's spokesperson to the Israelites.[16]

Such betrayals lead us to the next test.

CHAPTER 12

TESTS OF LEADERSHIP, PART 2

In this section of the book we have been talking about the different tests God uses to bring impurities of the heart to the surface in our life. If we will face those impurities or problems we have, then God can work with us to remove them and to bring us up into a higher level personally.

God always brings us into a higher level personally before we can be brought into a higher level of promotion.

You may not have experienced every one of these tests we are talking about, but probably the ones you haven't experienced, you will before you get to where God wants you to be.

Remember, God doesn't test us to harm us but to make us into a better person, and in the long run, to make us into a better leader.

5. The Forgiveness Test

> *And the Lord turned the captivity of Job and restored his fortunes,*
> *when he prayed for his friends; also the Lord gave Job twice as much*
> *as he had before.*

Job 42:10

When we have been betrayed or otherwise done wrong, we must pass the test of forgiveness.

I am not going to say much here about this test because we have already talked about forgiveness in other parts of this book. We see many heroes in the Bible who had to forgive others — Moses, Paul, Joseph, Stephen, Jesus and on and on. But I will point out that in Job 42:7-10 we read that Job prayed for his friends, who did not stand with him in his pain and suffering when he lost everything, but who judged and criticized him. As a result of his prayer for them and his forgiveness of them, he received a double blessing from the Lord.

I am going to make that statement into a new slogan: **"If you do things God's way, He will give you double for your trouble."**

6. The Loving-the-Unlovely Test

For if you love those who love you, what reward can you have? Do not even the tax collectors do that?

Matthew 5:46

We all have a few people in our life who are like sandpaper to us. Some are like an entire package of sandpaper. It seems that when they are around, we are surrounded by sandpaper on all sides. The more sandpaper we have around us, the more rough edges we must have.

When God first called me to preach, I had so many problems — I was a mess. When I started teaching the Bible, I would sit on my living room floor dressed in short shorts, blowing cigarette smoke in everybody's faces while I was teaching them the Word.

> **GOD SEES WHERE WE ARE AND WHERE WE WILL BE AFTER HE FINISHES WORKING WITH US FOR A WHILE.**

You see, God sees not only where we are but also where we can be after He gets through working with us for a while.

Now keep in mind that while I was like that, God did not loose me on the world. He kept me on my living room floor with just twenty-five people.

To give you an idea of what I was like, let me share with you some of the problems I had. I didn't know anything about character, integrity, maturity, excellence, fruit of the Spirit. All of those kinds of things were like a foreign language to me. So one of the things that God did was surround me with people who just irritated the daylights out of me.

The three people I spent most of my time with just drove me crazy. One of them was Dave, one was a girl who lived next door and another was a close friend.

That's right. Dave's personality just about drove me nuts. I was always out ahead, and Dave was always hanging back. It seemed Dave had a ministry of waiting on God. I never waited on God for anything. I would decide where we were going and say, "Come on, God." I would run on ahead, and God could just catch up, as far as I was concerned.

Actually, neither Dave nor I was right. I was way out ahead of God, and Dave was way behind God. The Lord had to work on both of us to bring us into an area of balance.

You may be married to a person who drives you nuts, too. That doesn't mean you are married to the wrong person.

If God had not given me Dave for a husband, I would never have made it because nobody else would have put up with me. He just loved me unconditionally, and sometimes the worse I got, the more he loved me. He would actually laugh at me. Every once in a while I will get feisty, and he will say, "Yeah, that's that old fire in her eyes." Some time ago he told me, "One thing's for sure, honey — I can never say that I have ever been bored being married to you."

But I felt as though I was being crushed. I was married to a man who was not doing things the way I wanted them done. God was telling me that I had to submit to him, but we never had the same ideas about anything. My reaction was, "Lord, if I have to submit to him, I'll never get my way about anything!"

I had a friend who was a perfectionist, and I had a choleric personality, and to people who have a choleric personality, perfectionists are irritating. Then there would be someone else in my life who was really vague about things they wanted to do, and I was really goal-oriented and definite about everything I wanted to do. It just seemed that everywhere I turned I was being rubbed by sandpaper.

I thought everybody else had a problem. I was going around resisting all the things I now know God had placed in my life. Then I finally figured out that God puts irritating people in our lives so we can't get away from them. If we try to run from one, we find two more like them just around the corner.

I would go around singing, "I surrender all." Then the first time someone came along who wasn't very nice, I would become upset and want to get away from that individual.

We have got to learn how to love the unlovely. The next time you are around someone who is irritating to you, just say to yourself, "Don't panic, flesh. This is only a test." Just shake it off and go on.

In Galatians 6:1,2 we are told:

> Brethren, if any person is overtaken in misconduct or sin of any sort, you who are spiritual [who are responsive to and controlled by the Spirit] should set him right and restore and reinstate him, without any sense of superiority and with all gentleness, keeping an attentive eye on yourself, lest you should be tempted also.
>
> Bear (endure, carry) one another's burdens and troublesome moral faults, and in this way fulfill and observe perfectly the law of Christ (the Messiah) and complete what is lacking [in your obedience to it].

What is Paul saying to us in this passage? He is saying that we are going to have to learn to get along with each other. We are going to have to learn to put up with some things we don't like. Not everybody is going to think and speak and act the way we want them to. But forgiving them is part of what we must do as members of the body of Christ. Not everybody is going to be or do what we want, but we can forgive them and love them anyway.

7. The Time Test

> Nevertheless, do not let this one fact escape you, beloved, that with the Lord one day is as a thousand years and a thousand years as one day.

2 Peter 3:8

God does not move in our timing. He is never late, but He is usually not early either. He is often the God of the midnight hour. He sometimes waits until the last second before He gives us what we need. It is as though we are a drowning man going down for the last time, and God comes through to rescue us at the last moment.

We must learn to trust God's timing. But before we can do that, we must come to the place where we are broken before Him. What I mean is that our self-will and our spirit of independence must be broken before God is free to work His will in our life and circumstances.

Before He intervenes on our behalf, He has to be sure that we are not going to take matters into our own hands and do something out of His perfect timing.

Galatians 6:9 KJV says, *And let us not be weary in well doing: for in due season we shall reap, if we faint not.* The interesting thing about that Scripture is that it always seems to encourage people. Yet really in that verse God has not told us anything, at least nothing about when it is going to happen because "due season" doesn't mean anything specific. If we start checking out timing in the Bible, all we will find are descriptions like, "at the appointed time, in due season, in due time." Many times when I am waiting on God about a situation and I get discouraged about the time it's taking for Him to answer, someone gives me one of those kinds of Scriptures. It encourages me, but I still don't know anything because due time is really just the time that God knows is right.

> GOD MOVES IN HIS TIMING, NOT OURS. AND HE IS RIGHT ON TIME — NOT LATE, BUT USUALLY NOT EARLY EITHER.

The psalmist David wrote a power passage in Psalm 31:14,15: *But I trusted in, relied on, and was confident in You, O Lord; I said, You are my God. My times are in Your hands; deliver me from the hands of my foes and those who pursue me and persecute me.* Like the writer of this psalm, we must learn to put our confidence in the Lord, trusting Him to deliver us out of our circumstances in His perfect timing.

The psalmist also tells us in Psalm 34:19 KJV, *Many are the afflictions of the righteous: but the LORD delivereth him out of them all.* But it does not say exactly **when** God delivers the righteous, nor does it say **why** sometimes there is a waiting period before He delivers us.

I think one reason we sometimes have to wait for God to deliver us is that He is building compassion in us for those to whom we will be ministering later on.

Some years ago I got really sick for a period of time. I remember lying across the bed, praying and crying out to God. I didn't understand why He was not delivering me from my affliction. I was afraid of how the sickness was going to progress and what it might lead to.

Suddenly God spoke to me clearly and said, "This sickness is not unto death but unto life."[1] Although I did not know in the natural what He meant, by His Spirit within me I knew that He meant it was working more life in me, more trust in Him and a greater closeness to Him. I knew I didn't have to be afraid of it killing me because God would deliver me at the right time. And He did. He always does.

The bottom line is that we need to trust God's timing, believing that while we are waiting for our breakthrough He is doing a work in us for His purpose.

Growing in Faith

In 2 Corinthians 12:7-9 KJV Paul spoke about *a thorn in the flesh* that had been given to him and which he asked God three times to remove from him. We have come up with all kinds of ideas about what that thorn might have been, why it had been given to him and why God refused to remove it. I think we have missed the whole point because Paul specifically answered these questions himself:

> *And lest I should be exalted above measure through the abundance of the revelations, there was given to me a thorn in the flesh, the messenger of Satan to buffet me, lest I should be exalted above measure.*
>
> *For this thing I besought the Lord thrice, that it might depart from me.*
>
> *And he said unto me, My grace is sufficient for thee: for my strength is made perfect in weakness. Most gladly therefore will I rather glory in my infirmities, that the power of Christ may rest upon me.*

In *The Amplified Bible* translation of verse 9 God says to Paul, "My grace is enough for you to bear the trouble manfully." So while God is not yet giving us our breakthrough, He is giving us the grace, strength and ability to endure what we are going through and still walk in the fruit of the Spirit, acting the way we should act.

I believe there are different levels of faith. One level of faith gets us delivered **from** trials, but another level of faith takes us **through** trials. Some people may think that the delivering kind of faith is the greatest. Personally, I don't agree. I don't think it takes nearly as much faith to pray and get delivered from something as it does to continue to walk in belief in God's delivering power when it is not being manifested. It is in those testing times that we grow in faith.

There are times Dave and I will pray for something and receive our breakthrough right away. There are other times when we have to walk in faith for a certain period before we actually receive our breakthrough. In those times we have to believe the Word of God rather than our experience. That is one of the tests of leadership, and part of the preparation for it.

When Dave and I first received a call into ministry, I had a full-time job making as much money as Dave. I was in a position of leadership in a large wholesale food company. When I quit my job to devote full time to the ministry, our income was cut in half. We needed a financial miracle every month just to pay our bills.

I thought that because we had made the great sacrifice of letting go of my job, God would immediately take care of all our financial needs. But for six years we had to live on monthly miracles. It got so bad I had to believe God for household items like skillets, dishrags and the kids' tennis shoes. I was not accustomed to believing God for such things because I had always been able to provide them for us out of my paycheck.

It did not seem fair to me — we were tithing and actually giving more than we had given in our entire lives. Why wasn't God blessing us? Actually He was. He was not giving us everything we wanted, but He was taking care of us. We had to depend on Him like never before, literally trusting Him every month to do a miracle for us even to be able to pay our bills. This was a very hard lesson for me to learn, and I did not receive it without a fight.

I went around rebuking demons, fasting, praying and getting people to agree with me about our finances, but nothing happened to change our situation at all. I didn't understand what was going on. Month after month it was the same thing — for six long years. Finally, there came a time when we got a breakthrough, and things started looking up. We began to prosper more, and gradually God began to pour out more financial blessings upon us.

As I look back upon that time now, I know exactly why we had to go through it. How could I believe for what I need now to carry on an international ministry if I didn't have the faith to believe God for little personal household items? The reason I had never had to believe God for those things before was that I could always go out and buy them myself. So to teach me real faith, God had to make me totally dependent on Him.

While all this was happening, I didn't understand because it was a time test. I spent the first ten years of my Spirit-filled walk with God at the foot of His throne "whying" and "whening." Then I finally started doing some believing.

If you are going through a hard time right now, you may be in a time test. If so, determine to remain faithful, trusting that God will deliver you — in His perfect timing.

8. The Misunderstanding Test

No one understands [no one intelligently discerns or comprehends];
no one seeks out God.

Romans 3:11

There are times when we are misunderstood by people we expect to understand and comfort us. I believe there will always be people who don't understand us, our personality or the call on our life.

I remember when people would say to me, "Why do you act the way you do?" That was before I knew what I was called to do. I have always been a little strange. What I mean by that is, I didn't always like what other people liked or say or do things other people thought I ought to. I have always been really serious, and some people didn't understand me or my personality type.

GOD POLISHES THE EQUIPMENT, THE POTENTIAL ALREADY IN US, AND GETS IT IN GOOD WORKING ORDER.

I look back now and realize that all the equipment I needed to do the work of this ministry was already in me. God just had to polish it and get it in good working order.

When you don't know what God is going to use you for, sometimes you feel out of place. You feel that you don't fit into the regular regimen of what is going on around you. So when you are already feeling strange yourself, it is really confusing and disturbing when other people say things like, "What's wrong with you? Why do you act the way you do?"

They don't understand. But people didn't understand Jesus either. Nobody really understood Him or the call on His life.

Misunderstanding is another test you will have to go through in order to be a leader. You have to make up your mind that you are going to stand with God and do what He says even if nobody understands you, agrees with you or supports you. Jesus understands you, and that is enough.

When we are misunderstood, it is a good opportunity to practice forgiveness and keep a good attitude.

9. The Servant Test

So when He had finished washing their feet and had put on His garments and had sat down again, He said to them, Do you understand what I have done to you?

You call Me the Teacher (Master) and the Lord, and you are right in doing so, for that is what I am.

If I then, your Lord and Teacher (Master), have washed your feet, you ought [it is your duty, you are under obligation, you owe it] to wash one another's feet.

For I have given you this as an example, so that you should do [in your turn] what I have done to you.

John 13:12-15

God will give us opportunity to be a servant, and then He will check our attitude to see if we think we are too good for that.

Even Jesus gave us an example of servanthood by washing the feet of His disciples and then telling us, "You should do to others as I have done to you."

Some people cannot be servants because they don't know who they are in Christ. They have to be doing something important; otherwise, they don't feel they are worth anything.

I don't think we can begin to appreciate how valuable people are who will do whatever they are called upon to do for the sake of the ministry, regardless of how ordinary or mundane it may seem. There are too many prima donnas in the body of Christ, people who will do only what they think they are anointed to do.

We need to be willing to do whatever God wants us to do, to be used in whatever way He wants to use us. Those who have that kind of attitude are the ones who will reach the highest level of what God has for them in their lives.

The attitude of a servant is very important, but it must be an attitude that is displayed in every area of life and not just in ministry.

Some people are more willing to be a servant in the church than they are in their own home. If they were asked to do at home what they are perfectly willing to do at church, they would say, "Do you think I'm a slave around here?" Yet they think it is exciting to serve their church family. The fact is, what we are willing to do at church we should be even more willing to do at home because that is where our real ministry begins. Some of us need to learn to wash some feet at home (serve others there) before we even start trying to wash them at church.

A good example of the real nature and price of servanthood is found in Matthew 20:20-22:

> *Then the mother of Zebedee's children came up to Him with her sons and, kneeling, worshiped Him and asked a favor of Him.*

> *And He asked her, What do you wish? She answered Him, Give orders that these two sons of mine may sit, one at Your right hand and one at Your left in Your kingdom.*

> *But Jesus replied, You do not realize what you are asking. Are you able to drink the cup that I am about to drink and to be baptized with the baptism with which I am baptized? They answered, We are able.*

These two men were no more able to do what Jesus asked them than they were able to fly, and they had no business asking for it. That's why Jesus told them, "You don't have the slightest idea what you're asking for." They wanted the position, but they had no idea what would be required to get them ready for that position. When Jesus asked them, "Are you able to drink the cup that I must drink and go through the baptism that I must go through?" in their ignorance and arrogance they answered, "Oh, yes, yes, amen, we're up to it." But they weren't. Not at all.

Then Jesus said to them:

> . . . *You will drink My cup, but seats at My right hand and at My left are not Mine to give, but they are for those for whom they have been ordained and prepared by My Father.*
>
> *But when the ten [other disciples] heard this, they were indignant at the two brothers.*
>
> *And Jesus called them to Him and said, You know that the rulers of the Gentiles lord it over them, and their great men hold them in subjection [tyrannizing over them].*
>
> *Not so shall it be among you; but whoever wishes to be great among you must be your servant,*
>
> *And whoever desires to be first among you must be your slave.*
>
> Matthew 20:23-27

There is not much that needs to be said about these verses. In them Jesus makes it pretty clear what it takes to be a great leader.

I believe that every day we have opportunity to be a blessing to other people. Even between Dave and me there are many times when we have an opportunity to do something for one another. Sometimes I may take advantage of one of those opportunities and do something nice for Dave, but then I may grumble about doing it. Occasionally, he will ask me to do something for him, and if I refuse or even hesitate because I don't want to get up and do it right at that moment, he will tease me by saying, "Well, Joyce, you just missed your blessing."

> A LEADER WITH A SERVANT'S HEART RESPONDS TO THE OPPORTUNITIES GOD GIVES EVERY DAY TO BE A BLESSING TO OTHERS.

At other times when I don't want to do something my family asks me to do, they will say, "You'd better practice what you preach!" They are right. Since I preach to others what to do, I have to be careful that I do the same thing myself.

So the servant test is simply how we respond to the opportunities God gives us to be a blessing to others. It reveals whether we really and truly want to help people or whether we just want to be in the public eye.

When God anoints a person, He is not necessarily anointing that person to be famous. But He is anointing that person to be a servant, like His Son Jesus.

10. The Discouragement Test

And Saul said to David, You are not able to go
to fight against this Philistine. You are only an adolescent, and he has
been a warrior from his youth.

1 Samuel 17:33

The story of David's battle with Goliath is probably one of the best examples of this test found in the Bible.

When David volunteered to go out and fight the giant, nobody encouraged him. Everyone told him, "You're too young. You don't have the right armor. He's much bigger and more experienced than you are," and on and on.

Even King Saul questioned David's ability to overcome the boastful Philistine. But David encouraged himself by recounting the victories God had given him in the past:

And David said to Saul, Your servant kept his father's sheep.
And when there came a lion or again a bear and took
a lamb out of the flock,

I went out after it and smote it and delivered the lamb out of its
mouth; and when it arose against me, I caught it by its
beard and smote it and killed it.

Your servant killed both the lion and the bear; and this uncircumcised
Philistine shall be like one of them, for he has defied the
armies of the living God!

David said, The Lord Who delivered me out of the paw of the lion and
out of the paw of the bear, He will deliver me out of the hand of this
Philistine. And Saul said to David, Go, and the Lord be with you!

1 Samuel 17:34-37

If you want to be a leader and do something for God, you must understand that there will be hundreds, maybe thousands, of times when Satan will come against you to discourage you. Why does he do that? Because he knows you must have courage to overcome the attacks he launches against us to keep us from fulfilling God's good plan for our lives. When you become discouraged, you become weak and lose the courage you need to go forward. What must you do in times of discouragement?

Shake it off!

PITIFUL OR POWERFUL

In 1 Kings 18 and 19 we read the story of the prophet Elijah who became discouraged. After defeating 450 pagan prophets of Baal in a contest on Mount Carmel to prove who was the true God, Jehovah or Baal, Elijah received word from Queen Jezebel that she was going to have him killed. He was so shaken up by that news that he ran away and hid in the desert.

Why would a man of God who had just climbed to the top of a mountain, built an altar to God there, killed and cut up a bull and laid it out in pieces on the altar where God sent down fire to consume it, and then had single-handedly slain 450 prophets of Baal with the sword suddenly get scared and run from a single, solitary woman?

If you read that story, you will see that Elijah was just plain worn out. Exhausted by all his efforts, he needed a good night's rest and a good meal or two, which is exactly what God gave him.

As he was running away and came to a place to lie down and rest, an angel of the Lord woke him up and fed him. After he had napped a while longer, the angel woke him up again and had him eat some more before going on his way.

The problem with Elijah was simply discouragement brought on by fatigue. As a result, he went out by himself and had a pity party. He was so low he was ready to give up and die. So God had to minister to him and get him back on his feet again both physically and spiritually, which shows that even the great men and women of God get discouraged.

In the beginning of my ministry I got discouraged a lot. I don't get that way nearly as often now, but every once in a while I do have to fight against discouragement, just like anybody else.

When you have to wait a long time for something or when it seems that everything and everybody is against you, and you end up tired and worn out, sometimes you are just not ready to face the discouragement that comes with all these things.

I have learned that when those times come, I need to pray. I say to God, "Lord, You'd better help me. I can feel myself sinking." Then I get up and go on.

Don't wait until you are three days into a pity party so that it will take a truckload of Christians to come and scrape you up off the floor. When you first start to feel yourself sinking into discouragement, get someone to pray with you or for you, or just pray for yourself. It is not going to help at all to get discouraged. It is not going to change anything. It is not going to do anything to make you feel better. Instead, when you do get back up, you will just feel worse because you let yourself get into that miserable condition. Just learn to face discouragement and say, "I've been around this mountain before, but I'm not going to waste God's time going around it again. Despite how things look at the moment and how I feel right now, I'm going to get up and go on with the Lord."

The interesting thing about the Elijah story is that when God finally did speak to him, do you know what He said to him? "What are you doing here, Elijah?" Twice He said that.

That tells me that we need to stay away from discouragement. When we do get discouraged from time to time, God will help us. But He will not feel sorry for us. God is not into pity. As I mentioned earlier, He once told me, "Joyce, you can be pitiful or you can be powerful, but you cannot be both."

CHAPTER 13

TESTS OF LEADERSHIP, PART 3

Have you recognized any of the tests that we've talked about so far? You may have been going through some of these things without having a clue as to what's been happening in your life. Now that you've learned about some of them, isn't it wonderful to know what's been going on?

Every person who wants to be a leader has to go through tests if we want God to use us. They prepare us for the promotion into leadership that He has in mind for us.

I believe that learning about them is going to make a major difference in your life.

11. The Frustration Test.

> *I do not frustrate the grace of God. . . .*
>
> Galatians 2:21 KJV

We all get many opportunities to get frustrated. We get frustrated because the things we want to see manifested are taking too long or because what we have been given to do is too hard or because no one will help us. We get frustrated because the money we need is not coming in, and the aches and pains and burdens we have prayed to be removed from us keep going on and on and on.

I know what frustration is like because I spent a lot of years frustrated. I knew nothing of the grace of God. I have since discovered that when I get frustrated, it is almost always because I am trying to make something happen instead of waiting on the Lord to make it happen. If I am frustrated, it is a sign that I am acting independently.

In order to pass the frustration test, we have to let go and trust God to do what only He can do.

We have to let God be God.

IF YOU ARE FRUSTRATED WITH AN AREA OF YOUR LIFE, YOU MAY BE TRYING TO CHANGE YOURSELF RATHER THAN TRUSTING GOD TO CHANGE YOU.

Are you frustrated with your spiritual growth? Do you feel that you have been the way you are now forever? Does it seem that the more you pray and seek God, the worse you get? Are you wrestling with some area of your personality that is causing you problems, or is there some specific bondage in your life that you are dealing with? If so, the reason you are getting so frustrated may be that you are trying to change yourself rather than trusting God to change you. The minute you say, "Lord, I can't do this, so I let it go," if you are sincere, you can almost feel the frustration lift right off of you.

Frustration comes from trying to do something about something you cannot do anything about. God is the only One Who can make things happen for you in your life. He is the only One Who can bring the things you want and desire into your life. He is the only One Who can open doors of ministry for you. It is not going to do you any good to try to knock them down. The more you try to make your own way, the tighter the doors will stay closed. But when you do things God's way, suddenly He can open major doors for you and do it so fast it will make your head swim. You can end up running, trying to keep up with God and all the good opportunities He is giving you.

I waited years, teaching small Bible studies and little meetings of sixty, seventy-five or a hundred people. If I got three hundred people in a meeting, I thought I had hit pay dirt. I would fast, pray, believe and advertise, and still have just a tiny crowd. No matter what I did, nothing happened. Everything stayed the same. It was boring to me because I wanted progress.

Then all of a sudden one morning, my husband was getting ready to go to work, and I was getting ready for an appointment. We were on quite a few radio stations then and holding meetings around the country with three, four or five hundred people in attendance.

As we were each getting dressed, Dave had a literal visitation from God. The Lord spoke to him and said, "I've prepared you all this time to go on television, and now is the time. If you don't take this opportunity, it won't pass your way again. You have got to move now."

It was a good thing God spoke to Dave instead of to me because Dave is in charge of the finances. Not only that, Dave would be more inclined to hold back and say, "Let's wait and see." So I know exactly why God spoke to Dave — because of the money involved and because he had to be sure that it was something God wanted before he would move on it.

So Dave came to me and said, "I need to talk to you."

"I don't have time," I said. "I have an appointment."

Then he said, "I need to talk to you **now.**"

I could see that something major was happening because he was sobbing. I have seen Dave do that maybe three times in thirty-three years. He said, "God just opened up my heart to see the condition that people are in throughout the world."

Then he said, "Joyce, we've got the answer they need. We have the Word. God just told me He has prepared you all this time to go on television, and He wants you to do it now."

So in one little bathroom visitation from God, our whole life was turned around radically.

There I was, hidden away in St. Louis, Missouri. I could preach as well then as I can now. So why didn't God let me go on television back then to preach to all the millions that I am reaching now? He didn't let me do that because I wasn't ready. I did not have the character developed in me that I needed to go out and do what I am doing now. I would have gotten into one of my discouragement fits and given up.

Before you can move on with God, you have got to learn to trust His timing and not become frustrated.

12. The Self-Will Test

How have you fallen from heaven, O light-bringer and daystar, son of the morning! How you have been cut down to the ground, you who

*weakened and laid low the nations [O blasphemous, satanic
king of Babylon!]*

*And you said in your heart, I will ascend to heaven; I will exalt
my throne above the stars of God; I will sit upon the mount of
assembly in the uttermost north.*

*I will ascend above the heights of the clouds; I will make myself
like the Most High.*

Isaiah 14:12-14

It was self-will that destroyed Lucifer. In exalting himself, he said "I
will" five times. God had an answer for him: . . . *you shall be brought down
to Sheol (Hades), to the innermost recesses of the pit (the region of the dead).*[1]
In other words, "You will be cast down to hell."

When God asks us to do something contrary to our will, we must
always remember what Jesus said, . . . *My Father, if it is possible, let this cup
pass away from Me; nevertheless, not what I will [not what I desire], but as
You will and desire.*[2]

This is perhaps the hardest test to pass and pass quickly. Not getting
our own way is one of the most painful things we ever go through in life.
When we want something, we want it, and we don't give up easily. It
takes a lot of work and a lot of brokenness to bring us to the place where
we are pliable and moldable in the hands of God, to the point where we
can say, "Well, God, I'd rather You do this, but I'm willing to do whatever
You want."

In my own life, there are many times when I want to deal with an
employee a certain way, and God will tell me not to do it. So I have to
say, "Yes, Lord, if You want me to keep working with this person, I will."

Sometimes we want to give up on people before God wants us to
give up on them. Then there are other times when we want to keep in
relationship with people because we keep trying to convince ourselves
they will change. But if we really listen to our heart, God is telling us,
"Get away from them."

The bottom line is that we must be willing to do whatever God says,
and not what we feel or want. He may want us to give away things we
don't want to part with. He may want us to go places we don't want to

go, do things we don't want to do and deal with people we don't want to deal with. He may want us to keep our mouths shut when we want to say plenty. He may want us to turn off a television program or movie in the middle of it due to its ungodly content when we want to see how it turns out.

Whatever it may be that God wants us to do, to lead well we must be willing to put God's will ahead of our own.

13. The Wilderness Test

O God, You are my God, earnestly will I seek You; my inner self thirsts for You, my flesh longs and is faint for You, in a dry and weary land where no water is.

Psalm 63:1

Another one of the ways God tests us is by allowing us to go through dry times, times when it seems that everything in our life is dried up, times when nothing seems to minister to us or water our soul. We go to church, and we feel no different when we leave than we did when we came. We read the latest book or listen to the latest song, and it does us no good at all.

I have had those times in my life and ministry. I have gone through mountaintop times, and I have been through valley times. I have had dry times in my prayer life and in my praise and worship. I have had times in which I would go into a meeting or conference and be able to feel the anointing, and I have had times when I would go and feel absolutely nothing. There have been times when I would hear from God so clearly and would know that I had heard "a word in season" for me. There have been other times when I have not heard anything at all.

Looking back on my spiritual life, I realize that I have gone up and down, up and down. When I was up I felt like I was saved, and when I was down I felt like I was lost. I felt like I was called when I was up and not called when I was down. When dry times came upon me, I let them affect me. At the time I didn't know what was happening to me or why. Now I realize that God was working all the emotional stuff out of me and getting me to the point where I did not base my faith on how I felt.

I will be honest with you. I don't ever go through those times now. I mean, I just love God, and that's it. I worship Him, and that's it. I pray, I believe He hears me, and that's it. I know I'm called and I go out and do what I'm called to do, and I don't have all the ups and downs I used to go through. Why? Because I have learned to stop basing everything on my emotions. I don't let how I feel determine whether I believe God is with me or not. I just choose to believe He is.

There may be a long period of time when I don't feel the anointing, which I love to feel when I pray for people and lay hands on them. Sometimes I do feel that anointing, but at other times I don't. I just have to believe that whether I feel it or not, the anointing is still upon me.

I believe God has to hold back a lot of emotional experiences from us because we are so feeling-oriented. If I get to feeling the power of God too much, I may start thinking more highly of myself than I should. Therefore, God protects me from it so He can continue using me.

We must learn to trust that God knows what He is doing. If we feel something, that is fine. If we don't feel anything, that is fine too. We must remember that we are in this for the long haul — not just for those times when we feel good, and we get all excited about it, but also for those times when we don't feel anything at all.

The psalmist David went through dry times, as we see in Psalm 63:1: *O God, You are my God, earnestly will I seek You; my inner self thirsts for You, my flesh longs and is faint for You, in a dry and weary land where no water is.* We all experience such wilderness times: times when our prayers seem dry and the heavens are brass, times when we can't hear or feel anything from God. There may be times in our life's journey when God has begun using us, and then suddenly He seems to put us on a shelf. For some reason we don't know or understand, He lets us sit there doing nothing for weeks, months or even years. These are also testing times. They test whether we really believe we have a call and a vision.

In the beginning of my ministry, I taught home Bible studies for five years. Then God said, "I want you to quit teaching these Bible studies. Behold, I am doing a new thing." The "new thing" God had for me was to do nothing for an entire year! That was a very difficult, confusing time for me. That year-long dry time tested and purified the call of God on my life and revealed whether I really believed that I was called of the Lord.

A dry time may be a period in which a leader seems not to get anything they want. They become weary of sacrificing and desperately desire some kind of manifestation of something in their life. But everything is dry: their faith, their prayer, their praise and worship, their giving. Even their friends cannot comfort them.

It is in those times that the word of the Lord found in Isaiah 43:18,19 sounds really good: *Do not [earnestly] remember the former things; neither consider the things of old. Behold, I am doing a new thing! Now it springs forth; do you not perceive and know it and will you not give heed to it? I will even make a way in the wilderness and rivers in the desert.*

To the thirsty person who hears that Scripture, it is like a big drink of cold, refreshing water, so that he says within himself, **Yes, there is hope for me!**

14. The Loneliness Test

Then He directed the disciples to get into the boat and go before Him to the other side, while He sent away the crowds.

And after He had dismissed the multitudes, He went up into the hills by Himself to pray. When it was evening, He was still there alone.

Matthew 14:22,23

I believe every leader is going to have times in his life in which he feels lonely. I don't know what you think about the top, but let me share a little secret with you: Sometimes it can get pretty lonely up there.

In the kind of position I fill, almost everyone I associate with on a daily basis works for me. The relationship between an employer and his employees is different from the relationship between an employer and those who don't work for him. Sometimes employees don't realize that fact and think their employer separates himself from them somewhat because he thinks he is better than they are.

The cold, hard fact is that usually if I try to be chummy with the people who work for me, they develop a spirit of familiarity that causes them to take liberties with me they shouldn't take and to assume things about our relationship they shouldn't assume. Through years of experience

I have learned that I simply cannot become close buddies with most of my employees because it inevitably causes problems.

When you are in a position of leadership, people tend to look up to you. They may even develop expectations of you that are not realistic. They know you are only human, as they are, but they really don't want to see your human flaws and weaknesses. For example, they don't want to ever see you lose your temper or say anything negative about anything or anybody. The first time something like that happens, the devil whispers in their ear, "How can you receive ministry from someone who acts like that?"

Whatever position of leadership you may fill, realize that you must depend upon God to bring what I call "divine connections" into your life. By that I mean people who are right for you, people to whom you can get close, people who understand your call and how they should relate to you and your ministry.

God has given me several "divine connections." Some of the people He has brought into my life do work for me, but they have to have been prepared by God for that specific position. Those people are always endowed with wisdom and seem instinctively to know how to handle themselves at all times and in every type of situation when they are with me.

One of the things about leadership you need to understand is that if you really want to be a key leader, then you are going to have to experience some loneliness. You simply cannot be everybody's buddy and also be their leader.

Occasionally, you can go to lunch or parties or other social engagements with people over whom you have a position of authority. You can love them, care about them and even share to a degree in their lives. But in order to win and keep their respect as their leader, you must show reserve and restraint. Keep a certain distance between you and them. That is what Jesus did, and He is our example.

Many leaders don't understand that and it gets them into trouble. It also causes the people under them to judge things they don't understand.

I have gone through many lonely times, especially after I left my job at the church in St. Louis. One day during that time, God spoke something to me in my spirit that really helped me. He said, "Birds fly in groups and flocks, but eagles fly alone." What that boils down to is, if you want to be an eagle for God, then you are going to have to get used to doing a few things by yourself and not always be involved in every group that comes around.

15. The Faithfulness Test

> *And let them also be tried and investigated and proved first; then,*
> *if they turn out to be above reproach, let them serve. . . .*

1 Timothy 3:10

We are all going to be tested. There are no exceptions — everybody goes through different tests at times in our life. We will not be promoted until we pass our tests, but they are all open-book tests; the answers are found in the Book. No matter what we are going through, we can open the Bible and receive the revelation that God has placed there for us. He is never going to run out of great things to teach us.

Many of the requirements for a leader are found in the Bible. For example, in 1 Timothy 3:2-7 we learn that leaders must be above reproach, circumspect, temperate, self-controlled, sensible, well behaved, dignified. They must lead an orderly life and be hospitable, gentle and considerate, not quarrelsome but forbearing and peaceable. They must not be a lover of money. They must keep their own home in order before they can hope to keep order in the church. They must not be a new convert because of the danger of falling into pride. And finally, they must have a good reputation.

All of these requirements point to one overall qualification as a leader: We must be faithful. Just as God tested the Israelites in the wilderness, we must learn how to be faithful in the wilderness, faithful in the hard times. We must be faithful to keep on doing what is right, even when the right thing has not happened to us yet.

I believe that when our results take longer, it is because God is trying to do a deep, deep work in us, and He is preparing us for something later on that we don't even know about yet.

So we must be faithful, and we also must gird up our mind and be prepared for the opposition and adversity that always come with opportunity.[3] Such times of testing are part of the preparation for us by God. If we want God to use us, He is going to do a work in us first. That means we are going to have to go through a preparation time. But God tells us in His Word not to faint in our minds or give up while He deals with us to remove the impurities from us.[4]

Satan wants us to faint in our minds. In fact, he attacks us in our minds, telling us things such as, "This is not working. This is not doing you any good now and it's never going to do you any good. You might as well just give it up and go do something else."

So many people quit and give up on God right before their break-through. During the time of testing, we really need to be faithful because we never know when our breakthrough is going to come.

We must also be prepared for self-sacrifice and for some hard-learned lessons because we do not come equipped with knowledge.

I used to think that preparation was just going to be studying the Word and learning all I could in the Word. But much of my preparation came through my experiences as well as through studying the Word.

FAITHFUL FOR THE LONG HAUL

> GOD WORKS THROUGH AND BLESSES FAITHFUL PEOPLE, THOSE WHO ARE FAITHFUL IN THE WILDERNESS AS WELL AS IN THE PROMISED LAND.

God works through and blesses faithful people, those who are faithful in the wilderness as well as in the Promised Land. Being faithful is being devoted, supportive and loyal. Faithful people are worthy of trust or belief; they are reliable, consistent, constant, steady and steadfast, meaning that they will stay wherever God places them and be true to those God has given them to work with. There is a reward for such people.

If we want to exercise authority, we must come under authority. We must learn to be faithful and stay wherever God has placed us until He moves us. We must respect and be obedient to those in authority over us. We must do the right thing simply because it is right, even though we may never understand why — which is a real test of our faithfulness and obedience. We must be faithful to stay under that authority even when it does not seem right because eventually that is where our blessing will come from.

David remained loyal and faithful to King Saul, recognizing and respecting God's anointing on him, even though Saul was out to kill him.[5] In his training for leadership, David learned to stay under the protective hand of God. He didn't rise up against Saul; he waited for God to deliver him.

Job was faithful to the Lord in spite of all the tests and trials he had to go through in his darkest days. The hardest part of the ordeal must have been the fact that Job didn't know or understand why he had to suffer.[6]

Moses was faithful over God's people during the forty years they wandered in the wilderness. He too was put to the faithfulness test many times. Before God put him in charge of the Hebrew people, he had already had his years of preparation. Moses had spent forty years on the backside of the desert learning how to be faithful. We don't know what went on out there, but it was what prepared him to lead all those people out of bondage.

John the Baptist was tested and remained faithful to his calling as Jesus' forerunner, even though it eventually cost him his life.[7]

Such examples encourage us to be faithful, even when nobody knows us or seems to care what we are doing or going through. Despite the hardships, we must stay where we are and continue to do what we have been given to do because God is doing a deep, deep work in us. He is building character in us, equipping us for the long haul.

> **NEVER LEAVE ANYTHING GOD HAS ASSIGNED YOU TO DO UNLESS HE HIMSELF RELEASES YOU FROM IT.**

Never, never leave anything God has assigned you to do unless He Himself releases you from it.

BE FAITHFUL IN THE SILENT YEARS

In Hebrews 3:1,2 we are told: *So then, brethren, consecrated and set apart for God, who share in the heavenly calling, [thoughtfully and attentively] consider Jesus, the Apostle and High Priest Whom we confessed [as ours when we embraced the Christian faith]. [See how] faithful He was to Him Who appointed Him [Apostle and High Priest], as Moses was also faithful in the whole house [of God].*

In His earthly life, Jesus was faithful to the One Who appointed Him. Yet Jesus went through some silent years in His life. After His marvelous birth and prophetic baptism, we hear nothing about Him again until age twelve, when He was found debating with the teachers in the temple.[8] All we are told about these silent years is that . . . *the Child grew and became strong in spirit, filled with wisdom; and the grace (favor and spiritual blessing) of God was upon Him.*[9]

After that experience in the temple at age twelve, once again the Bible tells us nothing about what transpired in the life of Jesus except that He . . . *increased in wisdom (in broad and full understanding) and in stature and years, and in favor with God and man.*[10]

Jesus spent thirty years[11] in preparation for a three-year ministry, during which time He was faithful and obedient to His earthly parents as well as to His heavenly Father.[12] It was during those silent years that He grew in strength, wisdom and knowledge.

The instant society that we live in today is ruining people because we have everything so instant and so easy, we think everything coming from God should be instant and easy. But godly strength, wisdom and knowledge, spiritual maturity and character are developed in us as we go through tests, and we continue to do what we know is right, even when it doesn't feel right or doesn't feel good to us. If we want to grow up in God and do what He has called us to do, we have to just settle down and be faithful.

There is no "microwave maturity." Character is prepared in the crockpots of life, in the slow cookers, the ones that seem to take forever to get anything done.

PART 4

THE REQUIREMENTS
OF LEADERSHIP

CHARACTER DEVELOPMENT

*For those whom He foreknew [of whom He was aware and loved
beforehand], He also destined from the beginning [foreordaining them]
to be molded into the image of His Son [and share inwardly His
likeness], that He might become the firstborn among many brethren.*

Romans 8:29

In Part 3 we considered the tests that build the character of a leader.
"What is so important about character?" you may ask.

Character is important because it determines the image that is
presented to others.

Paul tells us in the Bible (in the Scripture quoted above) that we are
to be transformed into the image or likeness of Jesus Christ, the Son of
God. In Galatians 4:19 Paul wrote, *My little children, for whom I am again
suffering birth pangs until Christ is completely and permanently formed
(molded) within you.* That means we are to be transformed into Christ's
character. We are to have the same character that Jesus had. Then we can
project His image and likeness.

BE CHRISTLIKE

*God said, Let Us [Father, Son, and Holy Spirit] make mankind in
Our image, after Our likeness. . . .*

Genesis 1:26

When God said, "Let Us make man in Our image," this image does not refer to physical likeness, but to character likeness. He did not mean that we were going to look like Him physically. He meant that we were going to take on His nature, His character, as reflected in His Son Jesus.[1]

In Colossians 1:15 Paul tells us that Jesus is . . .*the exact likeness of the unseen God [the visible representation of the invisible]; He is the Firstborn of all creation.* As believers, we are to be transformed into His image and likeness. As we have seen, we are to follow in His footsteps.

The greatest goal of every believer, and certainly those of us who want to be used by God in positions of leadership, should be Christlikeness. We should want to handle situations the way Jesus would handle them and treat people the way Jesus would treat them. We should want to do things the way He would do them. That should be our goal.

Jesus is to be our example. In John 13:15 He said to His disciples, after washing their feet like a servant, *For I have given you this as an example, so that you should do [in your turn] what I have done to you.* And Peter tells us in 1 Peter 2:21: *For even to this were you called [it is inseparable from your vocation]. For Christ also suffered for you, leaving you [His personal] example, so that you should follow in His footsteps.*

The vocation, the high calling of every believer, is to be transformed into the image of Jesus Christ. God is going to keep working with each of us until we get to the place that we act the way Jesus would act in every situation of life, until we manifest the same kind of fruit of the Spirit that He manifested.

MOLDED INTO HIS IMAGE

And all of us, as with unveiled face, [because we] continued to behold [in the Word of God] as in a mirror the glory of the Lord, are constantly being transfigured into His very own image in ever increasing splendor and from one degree of glory to another; [for this comes] from the Lord [Who is] the Spirit.

2 Corinthians 3:18

The *King James Version* of this verse says that we . . . *are changed into the same image from glory to glory, even as by the Spirit of the Lord.* But exactly how does that transfiguring take place?

In Romans 8:29 we are told that those whom God foreknew and loved beforehand He destined and foreordained to be molded. God doesn't want us to be moldy; He wants us to be molded. Molded into what? Molded into the image of His Son. Why? So that we can . . . [. . . *share inwardly His likeness], that He might become the firstborn among many brethren.*

According to the Bible, God is the Potter, and we are the clay.[2] We are like a hard, cold lump of clay that is not very pliable or easy to work with. But God puts us on His potter's wheel and begins to refashion and remake us because He doesn't like what we have become.

Sometimes that process of refashioning and remaking is very painful to us. The reason it hurts so much is that we do not fit the mold into which God is trying to fit us. So God has to prune away portions of us — a piece here, an entire section there.

"But, Lord, I like that part of me!" we cry out. "I've had it for years, and I want to keep it."

"What are You doing to me?" we ask. "That hurts — stop it!"

God keeps working and working on us, trimming away this little bad attitude and that wrong mindset, remolding and reshaping us until gradually we are transformed into His image — from glory to glory.

BE PATIENT WITH YOURSELF

And I am convinced and sure of this very thing, that He Who began a good work in you will continue until the day of Jesus Christ [right up to the time of His return], developing [that good work] and perfecting and bringing it to full completion in you.

Philippians 1:6

Don't be discouraged with yourself just because you have not yet arrived. The Lord would not be angry with you if He came back today and found you just as you are, **if** you had the attitude of pressing on. As long as you get up every single day and do your best to try to cooperate with God, He is pleased with you.

Remember, God will still be dealing with us and working on us right up until the very day that Jesus returns to the earth.

I have been a teacher of the Word of God for more than twenty years. During those years I have spent lots and lots of time in the Word. I have been in more church services than I could even begin to number. I have spent untold hours studying and writing. In doing this I have changed very much, but I still need to change more.

I am concerned about the things in my life that still need to change because I want them to change. But I know that change comes about by degrees as I go from glory to glory.

Most people are so busy trying to move on to the next level of glory that they don't enjoy the level they are in at the moment.

Enjoy where you are right now on the way to where you are going. Be patient with yourself as you are being transformed into God's image.

CHARACTER IS DEVELOPED BY HABITS

> BASICALLY, OUR CHARACTER IS WHAT WE DO OVER AND OVER.

God wants to restore all of our godly character. Habit is actually character.

Habits are formed by discipline or the lack of discipline. Our character is basically what we do over and over. It is what other people have come to expect of us, like being on time, for example. If we are always on time for everything, people naturally come to expect that of us. They know they can count on us in this area. So punctuality becomes one of the traits of our character. In the same way, if we are always late, a lack of punctuality becomes part of our character.

Punctuality is one area of my character in which I still need to come up higher. There are situations in which I am on time, but there are other situations in which I am not. There are also situations that I can do nothing about, as when I get stuck in traffic.

We should not get legalistic about these character issues, but we do need to make an effort to develop character in those areas in which we know we have problems. We must remember that character is developed by habits, and changes in character come about by developing new habits. If we know that we have a habit of being late for everything, then we need to develop character in that area by learning to keep our word and being on time — every time.

What disturbs me is that many Christians today don't seem to think that things like punctuality have anything to do with spirituality. They think spirituality is just floating around on a cloud somewhere singing the "Hallelujah Chorus"[3] and owning every Christian book and tape album.

The development of godly character has much to do with discipline and the habits we form. For example, just as we can develop the habit of being on time, I believe we can develop the habit of listening or giving to other people. What is interesting is the fact that if we will listen to people, they will always tell us what they want or need.

If we are truly listeners and givers, we will try to help others receive what they need and be a blessing to them. But often our problem is that we spend far too much time trying to bless ourselves and not nearly enough time trying to bless someone else.

Godly character is especially important in the world in which we live today because we are finding more satanic and demonic traits in people today than godly character traits.

Interestingly enough, a hundred years ago or so, the whole world, even those who were not aggressively serving God, had enough moral values that they still had fairly decent character. But today that is not the case.

We read in Isaiah 60:1,2 KJV that in the last days the darkness will become gross darkness. But God says, "My glory shall arise upon My people."

We are to go out and be a light in a dark place. In order to do that, we have to be people of integrity, people of character.

As you will see next, character is not the same as charisma.

CHARISMA IS NOT CHARACTER

According to Webster, one definition of *charisma* is "b. Great personal magnetism: CHARM,"[4] but *character* is "3. Moral or ethical strength: INTEGRITY."[5] There are a lot of people who have charisma, but no character.

You and I may have a gift that can take us places that our character cannot keep us. Our character is seen in how much strength we have to do the right thing even when we don't feel like doing it or don't want to do it.

OUR CHARACTER IS SEEN IN HOW MUCH STRENGTH WE HAVE TO DO THE RIGHT THING EVEN WHEN WE DON'T WANT TO DO IT.

Character is revealed by what we do when nobody is watching.

That was a key issue in my life.

Many people are men pleasers but not God pleasers.[6] They will do the right thing when somebody is watching them, but they won't do the right thing when nobody sees but God.

As Christians, our commitment should be, "I am going to do the right thing simply because it is right."

Character is also seen when we do the right thing to others even though the right thing is not yet happening to us.

One test of our character is, will we treat somebody right who is not treating us right? Will we bless someone who is not blessing us — or someone who is even cursing us?

That is what Jesus did, as we read in 1 Peter 2:22,23: *He was guilty of no sin, neither was deceit (guile) ever found on His lips. When He was reviled and insulted, He did not revile or offer insult in return; [when] He was abused and suffered, He made no threats [of vengeance]; but He trusted [Himself and everything] to Him Who judges fairly.*

We must be people of character because good character is so very important in our world today.

CHARACTER COUNTS!

In the meanwhile, when so many thousands of the people had gathered that they were trampling on one another, Jesus commenced by saying primarily to His disciples, Be on your guard against the leaven (ferment) of the Pharisees, which is hypocrisy [producing unrest and violent agitation].

Nothing is [so closely] covered up that it will not be revealed, or hidden that it will not be known.

*Whatever you have spoken in the darkness shall be heard and listened
to in the light, and what you have whispered in [people's] ears and
behind closed doors will be proclaimed upon the housetops.*

Luke 12:1-3

It is very important what goes on behind closed doors.

A person who has not developed character will act one way when
in church with Christian friends and another way when at home with
the family.

We must be on our guard because there are so many people who act
"goody-goody" when they are trying to impress others, but as soon as
they are put to the test they get ornery really quickly.

It is easy to recognize those who have character and those who don't.
In the final pages of this chapter, I would like to share with you a list of
areas in which leaders must have character.

THE CHARACTER OF A LEADER

1. Spiritual Life

A person who wants to be a leader must have good character in their
spiritual life. That means they must have a deep personal relationship
with God, which includes putting God first in every area of their life.

We must all beware of working for God but
spending no time with Him.

> **WE MUST ALL BEWARE OF WORKING FOR GOD BUT SPENDING NO TIME WITH HIM.**

Just because I spend my life ministering to others
does not mean that I don't have to get up every
morning and spend time with the Lord. I cannot say,
"Well, since I have put in so many hours working for
You, Father, I'm just going to take a two-week vacation
starting tomorrow."

Of course, I do take vacations from the ministry from time to time.
But when I do, I don't take a vacation from God. I can't afford to do that.

Some time ago I visited with a man named Don Clowers who has
been in the ministry for many, many years. Although he is now pastor of
a church in Dallas, Texas, he used to be a healing evangelist who held

meetings in a huge tent. He was a close friend of A. A. Allen and knew many of the great healing evangelists back in the forties and fifties. I like to get with him sometimes and ask him questions about those days. He tells me about how things were back then and teaches me a lot about ministry.

One time we were discussing what causes some people to get promoted and what causes some other people to fall. In the course of our conversation, I asked him what people can do to maintain a position in which God places them.

The reason I asked that question is that Dave and I are in the ministry for the long haul. We don't want to be just shooting stars, to be on top of the mountain for a while and then suddenly disappear so that nobody knows whatever happened to us.

God brought Dave and me up very, very slowly. In fact, it took twenty-two years to get us fully established so that we were on radio and television and known around the world with all kinds of great engagements and opportunities afforded us. We both want to stay in that position. If we live to be ninety-five, we both want to be doing something great for God.

> ONCE YOU ARRIVE AT THE TOP, YOU STILL NEED TO KEEP DOING THE THINGS THAT GOT YOU THERE IN THE FIRST PLACE!

So I asked Don Clowers how we can maintain the position of prominence to which God has raised us. He said to me, "You know, Joyce, one of the biggest mistakes I have seen people make is thinking that once they have arrived at the top, they don't have to do the very things that got them there in the first place."

He went on to explain that those who rose to great heights in the ministry were those who had reverential fear and awe of the Lord, those who spent a lot of time with Him, treated other people right and really walked in the fruit of the Spirit. The things that God saw in their character was what released Him to promote them.

But once they got to that place of promotion, all of a sudden they began to think they were so important, they didn't have to do all those things anymore, so they eventually fell.

We must remember that what goes up can come down. God lifts up, and God brings down.[7] So if we are to be leaders in His kingdom, we must have and keep character in our spiritual life. We must maintain a good prayer life and stay in close fellowship and relationship with God.

2. Personal Life

A person who wants to be a leader must have good character in their personal life.

What goes on when a leader is not in the pulpit will determine what comes forth from the pulpit. That holds true for whatever area of leadership a person is in — what goes on in their personal life will determine what comes forth in their professional life.

For example, the anointing that Dave and I have upon us when we go out to minister in the name of the Lord will depend upon what we have been doing behind the scenes. If we have a lot of junk going on in our private lives, then we will not be able to minister effectively to others in our meetings.

We may still have charisma and be able to produce hype, but without character we will not be able to operate with an anointing.

What happens in private always has an effect upon what happens in public.

3. Social Life

A person who wants to be a leader must have good character in their social life.

What a leader chooses for entertainment — what they read, what they do for fun and relaxation, what they talk about with friends and family, what they watch on the movie, TV or computer screen — shows their character. These things are all important, just as surely as how much faith they have, how many hours they spend praying or how many Scriptures they have memorized. None of these "spiritual" things will mean anything if the leader cancels them out by their wrong thoughts, words and activities.

An excessive need for entertainment reveals a lack of character. Our society today is entertainment crazy. If we don't keep ourselves continually entertained in some way, shape or form, we get really depressed. We need to go back and read what God says in Exodus 20:9,10: *Six days you shall labor and do all your work, But the seventh day is a Sabbath to the Lord your God; in it you shall not do any work. . . .*

It is not that God doesn't want us to rest, relax and have a good time, but work is supposed to outweigh entertainment.

The Western world is addicted to entertainment. We have to be careful what we take into our temple. Jesus told His followers, "Be careful how you hear."[8] We also need to be careful what we read — even family newspapers and magazines can have articles, advertisements and photos in them that are suggestive or even indecent. We must also be careful of the TV shows and movies we watch in order to avoid poisoning ourselves and ruining our witness.

I have collected a lot of the old classic movies on video. I have about seven hundred of them. My kids don't go to Blockbusters; they get their movie videos at what they call "Joycebusters."

When I want to watch a good, clean movie, which I like to do to get my mind off everything that is going on around me, I don't have any trouble finding one that is not full of junk I don't want or need to see.

I have read that by the time the average child has reached the age of eighteen, they have seen thousands of violent acts. Even the cartoons today are filled with violence. And then we wonder why people in our society act the way they do.

Am I saying that we Christians should not watch television or movies? No, I am saying that we must be selective in what we watch. We must remember the computer phrase GIGO: **garbage in, garbage out.** If we take garbage into our system, then one way or another that garbage is going to come out of our system. I don't know about you, but I would rather sit around and be bored all evening, if necessary, than to poison my personal system and ruin my spiritual life.

4. Marital and Family Life

A person who wants to be a leader must have good character in their marital and family life. They must treat their spouse right, take care of their family responsibilities, spend time with their children, get their priorities straight, assure that their sex life is healthy and keep their home in order.

You may think this is crazy, but I think a leader ought to keep their lawn mowed and their house looking neat inside and outside.

As we saw in 1 Timothy 3:1-5, they should also keep their children under control and live a disciplined life. They should have their life in order and be well thought of by those in the world.

5. Financial Life

A person who wants to be a leader must have good character in their financial life.

Do you know how many lending agencies will not lend money to churches because they have found that a majority of them don't pay their bills? Of course, not all churches are like that. There are some wonderful churches and church leaders who have tremendously godly character. But there are also some who do not, and these are the ones Satan uses to make the rest of us look bad.

Those in positions of spiritual leadership should pay their bills on time. They should not be in debt. This does not mean they can never purchase anything that requires payments, but it does mean that they should not live on plastic and spend more than they make.

The devil is making it easier and easier to get into debt — "Buy now and make no payments until next year." Then when the payments do come around, we don't even remember what we did with whatever it was we bought!

So often we go around grumbling and murmuring, "I just hate all this debt. I rebuke you, Satan." Yet it was not the devil who got us into that debt; it was we ourselves because of our own ignorance and stupidity.

A spiritual leader must be a tither and a giver beyond the tithe. He must be generous and willing to meet needs as God gives him the opportunity.

It blesses me to see our children moving in the area of giving. Every one of them is doing that. It is very exciting to see them really becoming radical, outrageous givers. I am thrilled to see them being a blessing wherever they go. As a result of their giving, I am seeing the blessings of God chase them down and overtake them, just as He promised they would.[9]

What a person is willing to give away shows a lot about their character. A leader is a giver, but they are a wise giver. They use wisdom with their finances. They know what is going on with their money.

6. Speech

A person who wants to be a leader must have character in their speech; they must speak the truth.

This is an important area. Character is missing in those who embellish stories so much they are no longer truthful, just to make them sound good.

There have been times when we have been invited to hold meetings in churches whose pastors assured us that there was room for two thousand people to attend. We would get there and find that the building would only hold nine hundred at most. Or we would get there and find that the building would hold two thousand but that there were only enough parking spaces for forty cars. At times the police have had to come and make people move their cars because they were parked illegally.

That kind of thing is not a positive witness to the world of our character.

Sometimes we stretch the truth to get what we want or we neglect to tell the whole truth because we don't want to look bad.

It is a challenge to tell the absolute truth in every situation. Some insecure leaders tell people whatever they want to hear because they are afraid of losing their popularity if they speak the truth.

7. Integrity

A person who wants to be a leader must have character in their dealings with others. They must keep their word. They must be a person of integrity.

In Matthew 21 we read about an incident in the life of Jesus: *In the early dawn the next morning, as He was coming back to the city, He was hungry* (v. 18). *And as He saw one single leafy fig tree above the roadside, He went to it but He found nothing but leaves on it [seeing that in the fig tree the fruit appears at the same time as the leaves]. And He said to it, Never again shall fruit grow on you! And the fig tree withered up at once* (v. 19).

I used to feel sorry for that fig tree. I didn't understand this story at all. I thought, **It wasn't the fig tree's fault that it didn't have any figs on it. Why did Jesus curse it?**

Some time later God showed me the reason. As this verse in *The Amplified Bible* notes, on a fig tree the fruit appears at the same time as the leaves. So when Jesus from a distance saw the fig tree with leaves on it, He went to it expecting to find fruit on it. When there was none on it, He cursed it. Why? Because it was a phony; it had leaves but no fruit.

In the body of Christ, we must be very careful that we don't have just leaves and no fruit. We are not going to win the world with only a bumper sticker on our car, a Jesus pin on our lapel, a tape recorder slung over our shoulder and a big Bible and a stack of teaching tapes under our arm. We must have fruit because Jesus has said that it is by our fruit that we will be known.[10]

CHAPTER 15

THE IMPORTANCE OF A BALANCED LIFE

*Be well balanced (temperate, sober of mind), be vigilant and
cautious at all times; for that enemy of yours, the devil, roams
around like a lion roaring [in fierce hunger], seeking someone
to seize upon and devour.*

1 Peter 5:8

I believe we live in a world that is out of balance. I also believe that
most of the people in it are out of balance.

One of the easiest things to do is to get out of balance. Yet one of the
things that we hear very little teaching about is the importance of being
in balance.

The apostle Peter had several things to say about this subject. He
tells us to be well balanced and sober of mind, which really means to be
disciplined and serious. He also tells us to be vigilant and cautious
because we have an enemy, Satan, who is out to seize upon us and
devour us.

In Ephesians 4:27 Paul emphasizes this same point when he tells us
to control our anger, warning us, *Leave no [such] room or foothold for the
devil [give no opportunity to him].*

Many times when the enemy gets into areas of our life and causes us
trouble, we try to rebuke him, but we never bother to find out how he
got in to start with and then make the adjustments we need to make to
keep him from coming right back in through that same door.

This verse is one of those "close the door in the devil's face" Scriptures.
It warns us that the devil is looking for someone who is lopsided or out

of balance, someone who is paying too much attention to one area of their life and letting the other areas of their life go to pot, so to speak, someone whose priorities are all out of line. When the devil finds that kind of person, he knows he can come in and do his dirty work.

The devil is always going to give us trouble, but he would not have nearly as much success at it if we would learn how to keep the door closed to him. Sometimes that door is not some big spiritual issue that we have to seek out. Many times it is some simple, practical area of our life that we have become almost too spiritual to pay any attention to.

CAN PEOPLE BE TOO SPIRITUAL?

I honestly think that sometimes people who are born again and Spirit filled get so radical they become almost too spiritual.

"How can anyone be too spiritual?" you may ask.

> **THE SOURCE OF A PROBLEM IS OFTEN NOT A BIG SPIRITUAL ISSUE, BUT A SIMPLE, PRACTICAL AREA THAT NEEDS OUR ATTENTION.**

Let me explain what I mean. We have a practical, natural side to our lives that we have to take care of. If we don't, it will end up hurting our spiritual side. For example, if we don't take care of our physical body, we will get sick. When we are physically sick, it affects us spiritually. When we are sick, we don't feel like praying, releasing our faith, believing the Lord or fulfilling the call of God on our lives. So the devil looks for ways to get us sick, so he can stop us from doing what God has called us to do.

When we have a problem, it is not always a spiritual area that is out of line. Many times it is a natural area that we are not paying attention to because we have become so spiritually minded we are no earthly good.

What is needed is balance.

STAY IN BALANCE

One of the many dictionary definitions of *balance* is "a harmonious or satisfying arrangement of parts or elements."[1] The verb form of the word *balance* is defined by Webster as "to regulate different powers, so as to keep them in a state of just proportion."[2]

So we stay in balance by regulating the different areas of our life to keep them in proper proportion to each other.

We have all been given powers or abilities. But we have to keep them regulated. If we have too much work and not enough rest we get out of balance. We become workaholics and end up burned out.

I get a lot of satisfaction out of work and accomplishments. Because I am a very serious-minded person, I don't like a lot of what I consider silliness or wasted time in my life. But because of my nature I tend to get out of balance in this area. I have to make sure that I not only work but also rest. But it is possible to go to the extreme and have too much rest and not enough work.

The *King James Version* of Ecclesiastes 10:18 says, *By much slothfulness the building decayeth; and through idleness of the hands the house droppeth through. The Amplified Bible* version reads, *Through indolence the rafters [of state affairs] decay and the roof sinks in, and through idleness of the hands the house leaks.*

In other words, people who rest too much tend to end up in trouble. Their houses, cars, clothes, bodies and everything else in their life become a mess because they don't do the work necessary to keep things clean and cared for. They fail to regulate the powers at their disposal. They are out of balance.

BALANCE TAKES WISDOM

People have the power to spend money or to save money. Some people try to save all their money. They won't spend any on themselves or their family. Either they are greedy or they are fearful about the future, thinking they have to save all they can to protect themselves from some unforeseen calamity. So they get out of balance.

Others will spend money on their family but not on themselves. Eventually, they will have to wake up and realize that if they don't do some things for themselves, they will get resentful and begin to feel like a martyr. A martyr is a person who does for others, but with an attitude that they're being taken advantage of. People with this kind of attitude are also out of balance.

Still others get out of balance with money by spending it all. When that happens, they start using credit cards and running them up to the maximum allowed. Then they try to get out of debt by rebuking "the devils of debt." They want a miracle to correct their lack of discipline.

Too often that is our problem. We get ourselves into a mess and then try to get ourselves out by some miraculous method. Then we make another mess and try to do the same thing again. We go from one mess to another, never wanting to take responsibility for our own mistakes. What we need to do is to get some balance and start exercising self-discipline.

We cannot walk in stupidity and spend our whole life ignoring the consequences. God has given us wisdom, and He expects us to use it.

I believe in resisting the devil as James 4:7 tells us to do, but I also believe in submitting to God as the same Scripture instructs. We cannot disobey God, get unwanted consequences and then resist the devil, thinking that will make all of the results go away that we don't like or enjoy.

It took me a long time to learn this lesson. As a new believer I was taught about my authority over Satan and told that I should exercise that authority and not allow Satan to bring bad things into my life. I was excited about this new information and immediately began trying to be authoritative against the devil. I realized I was getting no real results and finally learned that I could not open a door for the enemy and then simply resist the circumstances that I had brought upon myself. I had to learn to submit myself to God. Then, and only then, would I have authority to resist the devil.

This is a valuable lesson for all of us. If we behave unwisely and reap circumstances that we don't like, we must take responsibility for our wrong behavior and take whatever steps are necessary to undo the wrong we have done.

For example, if people do not manage their finances well and end up in financial trouble, they must pay off their debts. This will probably require a great deal of discipline and perhaps a period of time of not buying anything except real necessities. This is not a time to feel sorry for oneself or to get discouraged. Overspending causes the trouble, and only underspending will correct it.

It takes time to get into debt, and it takes time to get out of debt. We take years to make our messes and then get impatient with God if He does not deliver us miraculously in a few weeks.

God is merciful. There are times when He will get us out of the messes we have made. But there are other times when He will not deliver us from them because if He does, we will never learn not to get into them in the first place.

BALANCE MUST BE MAINTAINED

Balance is something that must be kept and maintained. It is not something we get into one time and stay there forever. We can be in balance on Monday and out of balance by Wednesday.

> EACH AREA OF OUR LIVES BROUGHT INTO BALANCE MUST BE KEPT IN BALANCE THROUGH REGULAR MAINTENANCE AND PROPER CARE.

Nor is balance achieved over everything at once. There are thousands of areas of our life, and each one of them has to be brought into balance and then kept that way through regular maintenance and proper care.

A car cannot continue to operate correctly without regular maintenance and proper care. The tires will get out of balance and wear unevenly. The timing will get off and cause the engine to run ragged. The oil will get low and dirty and cause friction and wear on the motor parts. The wiper fluid will run dry and cause the windshield to get dirty, which could lead to an accident. The air in the tires will get low, causing a rough, uneven ride. Eventually, the entire vehicle will wear out and have to be replaced.

MAKE ADJUSTMENTS

I do not consider, brethren, that I have captured and made it my own [yet]; but one thing I do [it is my one aspiration]: forgetting what lies behind and straining forward to what lies ahead,

I press on toward the goal. . . .

Philippians 3:13,14

If we desire to live a balanced life, we must regularly examine and regulate various areas to keep them in balance. Balance is kept through making adjustments in our life. That means change.

Sometimes it is hard for us to adjust to doing things differently. We see areas in our lives that need to be changed, but when God tries to change them, we get really nervous.

The fact is, in order to go on, we have got to learn to let go.

Nothing in life is so unchanging as change. There will always be changes that have to be made, and we don't like that. We want to go on to what lies ahead, but we really don't want to let go of what lies behind because we are comfortable with things as they are. We are secure with the way we have always done things, even if our way of doing things has been hurting us. If that is the case, it is time for change!

When we become willing to give up our way of doing things and accept God's way of doing things, we are on the road to becoming all that God wants us to be.

You Are Not Invincible

Moses' father-in-law said to him, The thing that you are doing is not good.

You will surely wear out both yourself and this people with you, for the thing is too heavy for you; you are not able to perform it all by yourself.

Exodus 18:17,18

It would not surprise me at all to learn that God is saying that same thing to you and me.

Sometimes we like to think that we are invincible. We don't like for anybody to tell us that something is too much for us to handle.

When God told Moses through his father-in-law that the work of dealing with all the Israelites was too heavy for him, that is exactly what He was saying: "This is too much for you; you can't handle it alone."

I was always the kind of person who thought I could do anything I set my mind to. I was thoroughly convinced that I could do all things through Christ Who strengthens me.[3] If someone tried to tell me differently, it just made me more determined to do it.

Now it is true that we Christians have to have a lot of determination if we are ever going to do anything for God because Satan will always come along to oppose us and try to stop us any way he can. But if we have the attitude that we can do **anything,** no matter what it is, we are out of balance, and sooner or later God will have to prove it to us: "No, you cannot do just anything. You can only do the part that I have anointed you to do."

> GOD CALLS AND ANOINTS A LEADER TO DO A CERTAIN WORK, BUT HE ALSO PLACES PEOPLE ANOINTED TO DO PART OF THAT WORK AROUND THAT LEADER.

When God calls a leader, He not only anoints that person to do a certain work, but He also places around him people who are anointed to do **part** of that work. That's what He meant when He told Moses through his father-in-law, "You are not able to perform it all by yourself."

For many years I did everything in my ministry but the worship because I can't sing well enough to do that. But I did everything else by myself. I taught in all the sessions, had prayer lines after the meetings and stayed and laid hands on each person even if it was a thousand or fifteen hundred people, as it sometimes was. Between sessions I would go out and greet people at the tape table, sign books and do just about anything they asked me to do because I tried to give them everything they wanted. I finally realized that if I kept doing that it would physically kill me.

One of the ways we get out of balance is by being men pleasers rather than God pleasers. Like Moses, I had to learn that I couldn't do it all — that I wasn't even supposed to try — because God had anointed others to help me.

ASK FOR HELP

When Moses' father-in-law saw all that he was doing for the people, he said, What is this that you do for the people? Why do you sit alone, and all the people stand around you from morning till evening?

Exodus 18:14

When God spoke to Moses through his father-in-law, He asked him, "Why do you sit alone?"

So many people sit alone in their position of leadership, trying to do everything themselves. If God has called us into some kind of ministry, He will also give us the help we need to carry it on.

Now they may not do it just the way we would like it to be done. They may not do the perfect job we think we would do if we did it ourselves.

In my own ministry, even my family and my husband, who love me very much, would say to me, "You need to advertise the tapes because no one can do that like you." So I would do it. Then they felt that I needed to receive the offerings, so I did that too.

Do you know what happened? With all the things I was doing alone, I began to have some health problems. Out of desperation I had to start making some changes.

It is amazing how, when we **have** to make changes, we learn that God will anoint someone else to do what we can no longer do ourselves.

I still talk about my tapes in almost every meeting, but now our daughter does most of it before the sessions, and our tape sales have not gone down a bit. She also helps me with the offerings, and they have not gone down.

Do you know why? Because God has taken some of what was on me and has put it on her, just as He did for Moses.[4] He did that because I was just no longer able to perform it all by myself.

Sometimes God cannot give us anybody to help us because we keep looking for perfect people and end up with nobody. Then God has to say to us, "Get a grip and face reality. What were you like when I started with you?"

ENDURE THE STRAIN

Listen now to [me]; I will counsel you, and God will be with you. You shall represent the people before God, bringing their cases and causes to Him,

Teaching them the decrees and laws, showing them the way they must walk and the work they must do.

Moreover, you shall choose able men from all the people — God-fearing men of truth who hate unjust gain — and place them over thousands, hundreds, fifties, and tens, to be their rulers.

And let them judge the people at all times; every great matter they shall bring to you, but every small matter they shall judge. So it will be easier for you, and they will bear the burden with you.

If you will do this, and God so commands you, you will be able to endure [the strain], and all these people also will go to their [tents] in peace.

So Moses listened to and heeded the voice of his father-in-law and did all that he had said.

Exodus 18:19-24

How many times did I tell God, "I don't know how much longer I can endure the strain"?

I learned that if I let somebody else help me with some of the strain, then I could endure it much longer. I also learned that if I was not a people pleaser, always trying to keep everybody happy and give them everything they wanted, then I would be around much longer. I learned that if I was a God pleaser, He would anoint me for what I had to do, but if I started trying to please people, He would not anoint that.

God does not have to anoint anything He does not tell us to do. Jesus is the Author and the Finisher,[5] but He does not have to finish anything He did not start.

Moses' father-in-law told him that if he would do what God commanded him, then he would be able to stand the strain.

God does not give us more than we can stand or endure. If He gives us a job to do, then He gives us the ability to perform it. And I don't mean just dragging ourselves around half dead all the time; remember, Jesus said He came that we might have life and have it in abundance, to the full, until it overflows.[6]

Notice the second half of Exodus 18:23 says, . . . *you will be able to endure [the strain],* **and** *all these people will go to their [tents] in peace.*

I believe that means that when God puts people around us who are anointed to help us, if we do not use them, they will be frustrated; they will have no peace. But if we will use them as God intended, we will be able to stand the strain, and they will be happy and fulfilled because their gifts are being developed and they are making progress.

> ARE THERE ANY
> ADJUSTMENTS
> THAT YOU NEED
> TO MAKE IN
> ORDER TO KEEP
> YOURSELF IN
> BALANCE?

Look around you. Are there any adjustments that you need to make in order to keep yourself in balance? If you will make those adjustments, as Moses did, then you will have much more joy and peace and will be slamming the door in the devil's face.

PRUNED IF YOU DO, PRUNED IF YOU DON'T

So God created man in His own image, in the image and likeness of God He created him; male and female He created them.

And God blessed them and said to them, Be fruitful, multiply, and fill the earth, and subdue it [using all its vast resources in the service of God and man]. . . .

Genesis 1:27,28

Lack of balance hinders fruitful living. And if there is anything that God wants us to do, it is to bear fruit. The first thing God said to Adam and Eve after creating them was, "Be fruitful."

God wants us to be fruit-bearing believers. In John 15:8 Jesus said, *When you bear (produce) much fruit, My Father is honored and glorified, and you show and prove yourselves to be true followers of Mine.* In this same chapter in verses 1 and 2, Jesus talked about pruning, saying, *I am the True Vine, and My Father is the Vinedresser. Any branch in Me that does not bear fruit [that stops bearing] He cuts away (trims off, takes away); and He cleanses and repeatedly prunes every branch that continues to bear fruit, to make it bear more and richer and more excellent fruit.*

To us that word *prune* is a nasty, ugly word because it means to "cut away," "trim off" or "take away." Nobody likes those cutting words.

Sometimes fruit trees get top-heavy or lopsided, and so they have to be pruned. In the same way, sometimes our lives get top-heavy or lopsided, and God has to prune them.

We once had a little tree in front of our house. Every year it put out cute little branches at the bottom of the trunk with lots of green leaves on them. These little branches are called suckers because they suck the life out of the tree. They add nothing to it, but they take nourishment from it and keep it from growing the way it should. So we have to get out the pruning shears and clip them off.

God may have to clip off some things from our lives that are cute, things that we would like to keep babying and nursing along. But God knows what He has in mind for us overall. When He starts dealing with us to let go of something, the best thing we can do is just let it go because He knows His business.

"But, God, if I quit doing that I'll be the only one in the group who is not going anymore." God may be cutting a certain thing out of our life so that we have more time to spend with Him. If we spend that time with God, we might receive what we're really after.

We also have a bush in our yard that gets a lot of pretty branches shooting off in every direction. So we have to get out the pruning shears and clip them off.

God does the same thing with us. It hurts to see those things go, but I have learned a secret about that kind of pruning I would like to share with you.

In John 15:1,2 Jesus says that if we do not bear fruit, God will prune us to make us productive. If we do bear fruit, He will prune us so we bear more, richer and more excellent fruit.

The secret is that whether we bear fruit or do not bear fruit, we are going to be pruned! I don't know about you, but I'd rather be pruned to bear more fruit than be pruned for not bearing any fruit at all.

RESTRICT YOURSELF

Now every athlete who goes into training conducts himself temperately and restricts himself in all things. . . .

1 Corinthians 9:25

The *King James Version* of this verse says that everyone who strives for mastery in anything must restrict himself in all things.

How do we ever hope to achieve balance in our life if we don't restrict ourselves?

I have to strive to achieve balance in my work. Sometimes I will sit at a computer for twelve hours, only getting up to go to the bathroom or get something to drink. It is not good for me to do that because when I am working on something like a seminar or a book, I can get pretty intense. I get into the flow of whatever I am doing and put a lot of spiritual and emotional energy into it.

Dave has told me again and again, "Don't sit there all day long. Work seven or eight hours, but take breaks. When you've worked a good, long day, stop and do something else. If you don't, you will end up paying the price."

He is right. Unless I restrict myself, I will either sit there until I wear myself out or fall asleep in my chair.

I need to use some common sense and get up every two hours or so and stretch. Why don't I do that? Because I want to conquer the project. I hate to stop, even for a little while to rest. Although part of me wants to keep on going, another part of me knows that is not wise.

You and I will never have any real success in life unless we use wisdom. What is wisdom? As previously mentioned, one dictionary I consulted says it is common sense. And common sense tells us that if we don't learn to restrict ourselves, we are going to get into trouble.

AREAS IN NEED OF BALANCE

I have made up a list of areas in which we need to restrict ourselves, areas in which we need balance.

The first of these is **diet.**

If I don't make myself stick to a sensible diet, I will find something I like and eat it all the time. Of course, that is not wise because the human body was not meant to live off of sweets and snacks. We cannot eat only ice cream, cake, candy bars and potato chips and expect to stay healthy.

There are many fad diets out there today. One of them is the no-protein diet. Another is the no-carbohydrates diet.

I am not saying that if you follow one of these kinds of diets you won't lose weight, but ultimately I don't think anybody is going to be healthy without following a balanced diet. If God did not want us to eat from each of the different food groups, He would not have created them.

Each of us needs to know our own body, what it needs and what is best for it.

I have learned that when I need to lose a couple of pounds in a hurry, I can go on a low-fat diet. But I have also learned that my body needs a lot of protein. It probably has something to do with the kind of work I do and the amount of energy I have to put out. I have been told that when I do a long, intense teaching service, it is the equivalent of eight hours of hard labor because of all the emotional and mental stress that goes into it. So by the time I have done five or six teaching sessions, I have expended a lot of energy. I have discovered that in order for me to feel good and recover from such meetings, I have to have a lot of protein.

While I am on a low-fat diet, I may lose weight, but I don't feel well because my blood sugar goes way down.

One day I almost passed out in a hotel room. I didn't know what was wrong with me. When I started praying and seeking God, I realized that I had not been eating any protein for a long period of time.

Now, I love pasta and salad. I could eat it seven days a week. I could go forever without eating any meat. But I need it.

So there I was, sick and going around rebuking devils. But my problem wasn't devils — it was noodles!

Let me give you another example of the need of maintaining proper balance in diet.

My general manager weighs about ninety-three pounds and is just as cute as she can be. Since she has to stay away from sugar and watch what she eats, she discovered something called a Balance® bar and told me about it.

"Oh, it's got just the right balance in it," she said. "It is low in fat, high in protein and full of energy and everything you need. They really make me feel good."

So I bought some of the bars and started carrying them with me on the road for those times when I would get hungry and need something to give me a boost in energy.

Later on, the girl who told me about these things got to eating three or four of them a day and started breaking out in a rash. It turned out that besides eating the honey-peanut butter Balance® bar, she was also eating peanuts and peanut butter. Apparently she was allergic to peanuts, so she began to break out. We all started teasing her that she got out of balance on Balance® bars.

So it is possible to get out of balance in diet. As we have already seen, it is also possible to get out of balance in **spending** or even in **spiritual activity.**

A woman married to an unbeliever or a new believer can ruin her marriage by getting **excessively** involved in spiritual activities like praying, attending Bible studies and talking about God all the time when she should be paying more attention to her husband's needs. It's not that she shouldn't talk about the Lord with him, but she had better talk to him about something else too because he is not where she is spiritually right now.

Men have a great need for recreation, and they want a recreational partner. In other words, they want to have fun.

In our marriage, I can go a lot longer without playing golf than Dave can. I have found out that if I want to have a good marriage, I need to play golf with my husband every once in a while because that is what he likes to do.

Dave is a great man of God, but he would not be happy if I did nothing but walk around and preach to him all the time. He needs other things in his life besides prayer, Bible reading and preaching.

To be honest, we all need other things. Some people, by virtue of their personalities, need a little bit more than others.

If you are married to someone who is not as spiritual as you are, if you try to be spiritual all the time, you are going to have trouble because you are going to be out of balance in that area.

Balance is needed in the area of the **mind.** Some people don't think enough, and some people think too much.

I remember years ago when Dave and I would get up in the morning, and Dave would want to listen to music while I wanted to think. I was thinking, and Dave was happy while I was miserable. That should have been a clue.

Some people plan too much, and some don't plan enough.

Balance is needed in the area of the **mouth**. Some people don't talk enough, and some people talk too much.

It makes me nervous to be around people who don't talk enough because they won't say anything. As a matter of fact, it is work for me to be around them because I feel like I have to do all the talking for both of us. I wear myself out trying to come up with something to say.

Just as I need to discipline myself not to talk too much, some people need to discipline themselves to talk more. They need to give others a break, so they don't have to do all the talking.

Finally, we need balance in **our personal opinion of ourselves.** Sometimes we think too highly of ourselves, and sometimes we think too lowly of ourselves.

In Romans 12:3 we are told not to estimate and think of ourselves more highly than we ought, not to have an exaggerated opinion of our own importance, but to rate our ability with sober judgment. Yet in 2 Samuel 9:8 we see a young man named Mephibosheth who had a dead-dog image of himself, and in Numbers 13:33 we see ten spies who had a grasshopper image of themselves.

We can spend too much time on ourselves, becoming selfish and self-centered. But we can also ignore ourselves and our own needs to the point that it causes deep emotional problems.

Some time ago I talked to a well-known minister who has a powerful ministry. She said that for thirty years she worked constantly ministering, counseling and helping alcoholics and street people while taking care of her own family and many other things.

All this time she kept telling herself, "I'm OK, I'm OK." Then all of a sudden one day she fell apart because she really wasn't OK.

Sometimes strong-willed, determined people can go on for a long period doing for everybody else, then suddenly a scream rises up on the inside of them, "What about **me?** What happened to **me?**"

Every once in a while, we need to do a little something for ourselves, something special to make us feel better. It doesn't even have to be something we desperately need.

For us ladies, it might be something as simple as getting our fingernails done or buying a pair of earrings, anything to just pamper ourselves a little.

For men, it might be buying something to add to the enjoyment of their hobby or favorite pastime. Every so often, Dave likes to buy a new golf club. He already has several of each, but he always enjoys getting another one.

Sometimes we all need to do just a little something for ourselves.

At the end of a long series of conferences, I am worn out physically, mentally, emotionally and spiritually. In those times I have found that one of the things that helps me (and you can laugh if you want to) is to go shopping.

I don't go out and get weird and goofy, trying to see how much money I can spend or putting us into debt or anything like that. Sometimes I don't even buy anything for myself. Sometimes I'll shop for somebody else. But it helps me to get away from my work and get my mind on something else. The change helps me to get back into balance.

Like most women, I enjoy shopping; it ministers to my emotions. God gave us our emotions, and although we should not be controlled by them, we should also not ignore the fact that we have them. We should do what we need to do in order to remain healthy emotionally, as well as physically, mentally and spiritually.

TWO SIDES OF LIFE

Welcome him [home] then in the Lord with all joy, and honor and highly appreciate men like him,

For it was through working for Christ that he came so near death. . . .

Philippians 2:29,30

In Philippians 2:25-30 we find a man named Epaphroditus who got sick due to overwork in the ministry. He was emotionally distressed and homesick. He had probably been gone from home a long time and was possibly lonely. He became so ill that he almost died. But the apostle Paul tells us that God had compassion on him and spared his life. In this passage, Paul was writing to the Philippians to tell them that he was sending Epaphroditus home to rest and recuperate.

I find it interesting that although God healed this man, he still had to take time off to rest.

That same principle is evident in the story of Jesus' raising of a young girl from death. In Luke 8:40-56 we read that a Jewish religious leader named Jairus approached Jesus asking Him to come to his house and heal his twelve-year-old daughter who was dying.

By the time they got to Jairus' home, the girl had already died. But Jesus raised her from the dead. As soon as she got up from her bed, the first thing Jesus told her parents was, "Give her something to eat."

> BOTH THE SPIRITUAL AND THE NATURAL SIDES OF LIFE NEED TO BE KEPT IN BALANCE.

From those two stories I received a revelation that there is a spiritual side to life and there is also a natural side, and both of them have to be kept in balance. Jesus took care of the spiritual side of this young girl's life, but then He instructed her parents to tend to the natural side of her life.

That tells me that God expects us to use common sense as well as spirituality. We see that scriptural principle demonstrated in an incident that took place in the life of one of the great Old Testament prophets.

BEING OUT OF BALANCE CAUSES PROBLEMS

Ahab told Jezebel all that Elijah had done and how he had slain all the prophets [of Baal] with the sword.

Then Jezebel sent a messenger to Elijah, saying, So let the gods do to me, and more also, if I make not your life as the life of one of them by this time tomorrow.

Then he was afraid and arose and went for his life and came to Beersheba of Judah [over eighty miles, and out of Jezebel's realm] and left his servant there.

1 Kings 19:1-3

Why in the world would a man like Elijah, who the previous day had made an absolute fool of 450 prophets of Baal and then personally slain every one of them, suddenly allow himself to become so intimidated by the threats of a solitary woman named Jezebel that he ran away in fear?

I doubt very much that Jezebel was so fearsome that Elijah had to do that. I believe I can prove to you that he responded in such an unbalanced way because he was totally worn out and exhausted.

A man recently told me that he took several weeks off from his ministry. He said after resting seven days he noticed his creativity beginning to return. I saw from this that even our creative ability dries up when we are overly tired. I know from personal experience that my faith is affected when I am too tired; I don't really want to pray at those times either.

> MANY OF THE PROBLEMS PEOPLE HAVE IN RELATIONSHIPS TODAY ARE THE RESULT OF IMBALANCE — JUST BEING WORN OUT.

When we are totally worn out and exhausted, we respond to people differently than we do when we are fully rested. We respond emotionally. We get our feelings hurt easily. We are touchier and more likely to get upset and fall apart at the slightest thing that goes wrong.

Many of the problems people have in relationships today are the result of being out of balance, and often that imbalance is the result of just being worn out.

In many of today's families, both husband and wife have to have jobs just to make ends meet. After working all day long, they then have to come home and take care of the children, fix the meals, do the laundry and housework, go grocery shopping, see to the yard work and on and on.

Sooner or later they start to get more and more exhausted because if they are Christians, they are often taking on church commitments also — and maybe even some commitments that are not Spirit-led. It may be things that they feel they need to do. But if they are not careful, they may end up trying to be everything to everybody, which cannot be done. They may begin to feel that they are being pulled apart because everywhere they look there is someone wanting them to do something.

I know all about this because I have gone through it in my own life. Not only am I a minister with an international ministry to operate, I am also a wife, a mother of four grown children, a grandmother and a friend with many other duties, responsibilities and relationships I have to attend to.

I have so many things to do that sometimes I feel I am being pulled in pieces. In fact, one of my granddaughters writes me notes and sticks them on my car, "Grandma, I miss you, and I want to spend time with you." One time in school she had to write an essay on the subject, "If you could give an invisible gift to somebody you love, what would it be?" Her answer was, "I would give my grandma the gift of time because she is always so busy."

That is true. I am extremely busy. We all are. That's why we need balance in our lives, which may mean having to cut off some things we don't really want to get rid of but which are going to cause us problems if we don't allow God to prune them from our lives.

In some cases, that may mean giving up a second job we have taken, telling ourselves that we took it to do more for our family. The truth may be that the family may need and want **us** more than anything we may be able to give them.

There is a balance that must be maintained in every aspect of life — physical as well as mental, emotional and spiritual — as we will see in the life of Elijah the prophet.

ELIJAH AND THE PROPHETS OF BAAL

Let's examine in detail the story of Elijah we looked at briefly in a previous chapter.

> *Elijah came near to all the people and said, How long will you halt and limp between two opinions? If the Lord is God, follow Him! But if Baal, then follow him. And the people did not answer him a word.*

> *Then Elijah said to the people, I, I only, remain a prophet of the Lord, but Baal's prophets are 450 men.*

> *Let two bulls be given us; let them choose one bull for themselves and cut it in pieces and lay it on the wood but put no fire to it. I will dress the other bull, lay it on the wood, and put no fire to it.*

Then you call on the name of your god, and I will call on the name of the Lord; and the One Who answers by fire, let Him be God. And all the people answered, It is well spoken.

1 Kings 18:21-24

In this story, Elijah the prophet of the Lord has instructed King Ahab, the husband of Queen Jezebel, to assemble the 450 prophets of their god Baal on the top of Mount Carmel.

Once they and the people of Israel have all assembled there, Elijah begins to issue a challenge to the prophets of Baal.

In 1 Kings 18:25-29 (quoted below) Elijah is making preparations for the One True God to demonstrate His power. In the process Elijah puts an enormous amount of physical energy into the challenge.

ELIJAH ISSUED A CHALLENGE

Elijah said to the prophets of Baal, Choose one bull for yourselves and dress it first, for you are many; and call on the name of your god, but put no fire under it.

So they took the bull given them, dressed it, and called on the name of Baal from morning until noon, saying, O Baal, hear and answer us! But there was no voice; no one answered. And they leaped upon or limped about the altar they had made.

At noon Elijah mocked them, saying, Cry aloud, for he is a god; either he is musing, or he has gone aside, or he is on a journey, or perhaps he is asleep and must be awakened.

And they cried aloud and cut themselves after their custom with knives and lances until the blood gushed out upon them.

Midday passed, and they played the part of prophets until the time for offering the evening sacrifice, but there was no voice, no answer, no one who paid attention.

1 Kings 18:25-29

After Elijah issued his challenge to the prophets of Baal, they went about trying to get their god to respond. All morning long they cried out to Baal to answer them, but no answer came.

At noon, Elijah began to mock them, saying, "Cry out louder. Maybe he is musing or has gone aside." One translation says, "Maybe your god went to the bathroom or is gone on a journey. Maybe he is asleep and needs to be awakened."[7] The point is that Elijah was putting a lot into this contest. He was really making a fool of the prophets of Baal, which took a great deal of energy.

ELIJAH'S TURN

Then Elijah said to all the people, Come near to me. And all the people came near him. And he repaired the [old] altar of the Lord that had been broken down [by Jezebel].

Then Elijah took twelve stones, according to the number of the tribes of the sons of Jacob, to whom the word of the Lord came, saying, Israel shall be your name.

And with the stones Elijah built an altar in the name [and self-revelation] of the Lord. He made a trench about the altar as great as would contain two measures of seed.

He put the wood in order and cut the bull in pieces and laid it on the wood and said, Fill four jars with water and pour it on the burnt offering and the wood.

And he said, Do it the second time. And they did it the second time. And he said, Do it the third time. And they did it the third time.

The water ran round about the altar, and he filled the trench also with water.

1 Kings 18:30-35

When it came Elijah's turn, he first had to repair the altar that Jezebel had torn down. Then he had to dig a trench around the altar. Also in the process of the challenge he slaughtered a bull, cut it into pieces and placed its parts on the altar. If I slaughtered a bull, just cutting it up and placing its parts on an altar would wear me out. That alone would finish me off. Elijah did the work of repairing the altar and preparing the bull after making fun of the prophets of Baal all day long.

Then he had the people fill jars full of water and pour it on the altar and the sacrifice — not once, but three times. I was really glad he had somebody else do that because by this time I was really feeling sorry for him because of all the work he had already done.

After all this, Elijah prayed and called on the name of the Lord, which is hard work itself. And Elijah wasn't finished yet.

THE LORD ANSWERS BY FIRE

At the time of the offering of the evening sacrifice, Elijah the prophet came near and said, O Lord, the God of Abraham, Isaac, and Israel, let it be known this day that You are God in Israel and that I am Your servant and that I have done all these things at Your word.

Hear me, O Lord, hear me, that this people may know that You, the Lord, are God, and have turned their hearts back [to You].

Then the fire of the Lord fell and consumed the burnt sacrifice and the wood and the stones and the dust, and also licked up the water that was in the trench.

When all the people saw it, they fell on their faces and they said, The Lord, He is God! The Lord, He is God!

And Elijah said, Seize the prophets of Baal; let not one escape. They seized them, and Elijah brought them down to the brook Kishon, and [as God's law required] slew them there.

1 Kings 18:36-40

After reading all this, are you worn out?

I am.

I never realized how much Elijah did that day. After going through all that day-long contest with the prophets of Baal, he then had to take them all down the mountain to the valley below where he put all 450 of them to death, which was the prescribed punishment for false prophets in those days.[8]

After all that, he had to be exhausted — physically, mentally, emotionally and spiritually.

But as if that weren't enough, he then went on to prophesy to King Ahab and pray for rain.

ELIJAH MAKES A RUN FOR IT

And Elijah said to Ahab, Go up, eat and drink, for there is the sound of abundance of rain.

So Ahab went up to eat and to drink. And Elijah went up to the top of Carmel; and he bowed himself down upon the earth and put his face between his knees

And said to his servant, Go up now, look toward the sea. And he went up and looked and said, There is nothing. Elijah said, Go again seven times.

And at the seventh time the servant said, A cloud as small as a man's hand is arising out of the sea. And Elijah said, Go up, say to Ahab, Hitch your chariot and go down, lest the rain stop you.

In a little while, the heavens were black with wind-swept clouds, and there was a great rain. And Ahab went to Jezreel.

The hand of the Lord was on Elijah. He girded up his loins and ran before Ahab to the entrance of Jezreel [nearly twenty miles].

1 Kings 18:41-46

After everything Elijah had already done, he then ran nearly twenty miles to the entrance of Jezreel — before Ahab in his chariot!

Sometimes the anointing can come upon a person and he can do amazing, astounding things, like those that Elijah did here in this chapter. But that does not mean that he is not tired when it is all over.

Some people have told me they do all the same things I do in ministry and never get tired. I don't want to call anybody a liar, but I do wonder about that because I do get tired, and so does anybody who has a physical body.

I am not exactly an old woman ready for the rocking chair, but I am a grandmother. There are times when the anointing of God comes on me so that I feel like I can run through a troop and leap over a wall.[9] There are times that I feel like I could run twenty miles, as Elijah did in this passage. But then you should see me a little while after I have done those things!

None of us, no matter how anointed we may be, can just go on and on forever without proper rest and recuperation. Trying to do so invites a complete breakdown.

That was the problem with Epaphroditus. He got absolutely worn out from working for God.

So did Elijah.

When King Ahab got back to the royal palace, he told Queen Jezebel everything that had happened and all that Elijah had said and done. That is when Jezebel sent a message to Elijah that she was going to take his life.

What was the reaction of this great man of God who had slain 450 prophets of Baal and outrun a chariot for twenty miles? He got scared and ran away from a solitary woman. He went eighty miles to get away from her and then left his servant there while he went on even farther on his own.

Elijah was out of balance. He was tired, and he became discouraged. He was depressed, and he wanted to be alone. That's an important lesson for all of us to learn. When we get overly tired and out of balance, one of the first things that tries to come upon us is depression and discouragement.

NOTHING LOOKS GOOD WHEN YOU'RE TIRED

But he himself went a day's journey into the wilderness and came and sat down under a lone broom or juniper tree and asked that he might die. He said, It is enough; now, O Lord, take away my life; for I am no better than my fathers.

1 Kings 19:4

Here is where Elijah gets really negative, which is another thing we all often do when we are overly tired.

Nothing in life looks good to us when we are exhausted. It seems to us that nobody loves us, nobody helps us, nobody is concerned about us. We think that we have to do all the work. We think we are being abused, misused, misunderstood and mistreated. Many times when we feel we have deep problems, all that is wrong with us is that we are tired.

> MANY TIMES WHEN WE FEEL WE HAVE DEEP PROBLEMS, THE ONLY THING WRONG WITH US IS THAT WE ARE TIRED.

Elijah was so exhausted that all he wanted to do was die, so he prayed to God to take his life. But God did not answer Elijah's prayer because He knew that was not what he really needed in that situation.

GOD'S ANSWER FOR ELIJAH

*As he lay asleep under the broom or juniper tree, behold,
an angel touched him and said to him, Arise and eat.*

*He looked, and behold, there was a cake baked on the coals,
and a bottle of water at his head. And he ate and drank
and lay down again.*

*The angel of the Lord came the second time and touched him
and said, Arise and eat, for the journey is too great for you.*

*So he arose and ate and drank, and went in the strength of
that food forty days and nights to Horeb, the mount of God.*

1 Kings 19:5-8

When one of my weeklong seminars is over, and I get home late Saturday night or early Sunday morning, I am always hungry. I don't want a cold sandwich or a bowl of fruit. I want a good hot meal because it helps me build myself back up.

How did the Lord through His angel get Elijah back to the place where he was strong enough to go on with the next phase of his ministry? He gave him two good meals and a nice long nap.

That was all He gave him. And 1 Kings 19:8 tells us that in the strength of that food, Elijah went forty days and nights on a journey to Horeb! There was nothing great, spiritual or supernatural about this. Elijah was worn out from everything he had done the day before and everything he had been through since. His body was completely broken down and his emotions had totally fallen apart. He was not handling himself the way he normally would. He was afraid, depressed, discouraged and even suicidal.

AFTER TWO GOOD MEALS, SLEEP AND A FRESH WORD FROM THE LORD, ELIJAH AGAIN SET OFF TO DO THE LORD'S WORK.

The Lord said to him, "You're worn out. You need a couple of hot meals and a good night's rest." And after Elijah was refreshed and made the journey to Horeb, the word of the Lord came to him there. With a fresh word from God, he was sent off again to do the work of the Lord.

CHAPTER 16

COMMON PEOPLE WITH UNCOMMON GOALS

*Now to Him Who, by (in consequence of) the [action
of His] power that is at work within us, is able to [carry out His
purpose and] do superabundantly, far over and above all
that we [dare] ask or think [infinitely beyond our highest prayers,
desires, thoughts, hopes, or dreams].*

Ephesians 3:20

God uses common, ordinary, everyday people who have uncommon goals and visions.

That is what I am — just a common, ordinary person with a goal and a vision. But just because I am common and ordinary does not mean that I am content to be average. I don't like that word. I don't want to be average. I don't intend to be average. I don't serve an average God; therefore, I don't believe I have to be average — and neither do you.

Average is basically OK. It is not bad, but it is also not excellent. It is just good enough to get by, and I don't think that is what God wants us to be.

I believe that any common, ordinary, everyday person can be **mightily** used by God. I believe that we can do great and mighty things, things that will amaze even us, if we believe that God can use us and if we will be daring enough to have an uncommon goal and vision. And what I mean by uncommon is something that doesn't make sense to the mind. We have to believe God for it.

In Ephesians 3:20 we are told that God is able to do exceedingly abundantly above and beyond all that we could **dare** to hope, ask or think, according to His great power that is at work in us. God does it through us according to His power, but it is done through us, so we have to cooperate. That means we need to be daring in our faith and in our prayers.

Some of us are not believing for enough. We need to stretch our faith into new realms. We need to be uncommon people with uncommon goals.

GOD DELIBERATELY CHOSE YOU

For [simply] consider your own call, brethren; not many [of you were considered to be] wise according to human estimates and standards, not many influential and powerful, not many of high and noble birth.

[No] for God selected (deliberately chose) what in the world is foolish to put the wise to shame, and what the world calls weak to put the strong to shame.

And God also selected (deliberately chose) what in the world is lowborn and insignificant and branded and treated with contempt, even the things that are nothing, that He might depose and bring to nothing the things that are,

So that no mortal man should [have pretense for glorying and] boast in the presence of God.

1 Corinthians 1:26-29

Paul tells us plainly what God chooses and why. He says that He chooses what to the world is foolish to put the wise to shame, and what the world calls weak to put the strong to shame.

I am so glad for *The Amplified Bible* translation because it tells me that God **deliberately** chose me. He didn't get me by accident. I wasn't just pushed off on Him so that He had no choice but to carry on this ministry through me because He couldn't get anyone else to do it.

When God got the idea for Life In The Word Ministries, I believe He looked around for the biggest mess He could find, someone who loved Him and had a right heart toward Him, someone who would work hard, someone who would be determined and diligent, someone who would be disciplined and try to use a little common sense, someone who would not quit or give up easily.

I have no special talents. The only thing I do really well is talk. I have a mouth, and I use it. In the body of Christ I am a mouth.

Even so, my voice is a bit unusual. Who would have thought that God would have wanted to take it and blast it all over the place? I don't even always say everything right. I don't always pronounce words correctly or know just the proper phrase to use. It just amazes me that we don't have to be polished and precise according to the world's standards in order to be used by God.

People look at the exterior, but God looks at the heart. What is awesome to me is the fact that whatever God decides to anoint is what works.

People listen to me because I am anointed. It is the anointing that they seek. If He wants to, God can anoint a donkey.[1] He can choose and anoint whomever He wants to. It is not based on our appearance, our education, our possessions or even our talents. It is based on our heart attitude, whether we are willing to fulfill a handful of qualifications a person has to have to be used of God.

Right now, let's look at the qualifications in people on which God bases His choices.

WHO DOES GOD USE?

1. God uses people who are faithful over little things.

A lot of people don't want to do the little things. They want to start doing great things from the beginning.

I cannot tell you how many thousands of meetings I have conducted in the more than twenty years of my ministry. I have file cabinets full of messages I have put together to preach in those meetings. I have spent thousands of hours studying the Word of God. One reason I have the size ministry I do now is that I have been faithful over the little things.

The Bible says that God purposely chooses what the world would throw away, what the world holds in contempt, what the world sees as insignificant, worthless and useless. He takes the things the world considers something and brings them to nothing. The things that start out as nothing, He lifts up and makes them something.[2]

So if we think we are something, we had better be careful and watch out because as we have seen, the Bible says the Lord lifts up and He brings down. It also says the stone that the builders rejected became the Chief Cornerstone.[3]

BECAUSE GOD HAD TOLD ME I COULD DO IT, I WAS ALREADY DOING WHAT PEOPLE TOLD ME I COULDN'T DO.

When I began to preach the Gospel, many of my friends rejected me because in the circles I came out of, people didn't believe in women preaching. They told me I couldn't do it. The only problem was that I was already doing it. I believed I could because God said I could. I experienced a lot of rejection, and it was difficult for me. It was also painful. But now I imagine that those same people who rejected and hurt me cannot flip through their television channels without running into me.

The point is, if you and I will remain faithful to what God tells us to do, sooner or later He will exonerate us and reward us for the hard things we have to go through to be obedient to Him. As a matter of fact, I believe that God will give us double for our trouble.[4]

2. God uses people who will give Him all the glory.

Verse 29 of 1 Corinthians 1 tells us why God chooses the things and the people He does — so that no mortal man can boast in His presence.

I always remember where I came from. If I forget it, God has little ways of reminding me that I am not a big shot. A big shot is just a little shot away from home. When he gets back home, he is not a big shot anymore because everybody there knows him.

People sometimes ask my younger son, Dan, what it is like to have Joyce Meyer for a mother. He just says, "She's my mother." He is not awed by who and what I have become. To him I am just Mom.

The people who know us best don't think we are such big shots; only the people who don't know us think that.

3. God uses people who want to bear fruit for Him.

God uses people who realize that if they are going to bear fruit for Him, they have to be pruned.

If we want to be leaders in God's kingdom, then we must be willing to allow Him to deal with us, and it is not all going to feel good; in fact, it is going to hurt. We are not going to like it at all, but we must trust God.

None of us come ready to use. We all need a little work first. Sometimes we buy products that say "ready to use" because we don't want to mess with having to prepare things. But leaders don't come ready to use.

As I stated in the beginning of this book, I don't believe there is such a thing as a born leader. Leaders have to be developed. There are probably multiplied thousands of people who have the talent in them for leadership, but they won't allow God to do what He needs to do in their lives to prepare them for leadership positions. They won't stay on the Potter's wheel or in the Refiner's fire. They want everything right now.

All of us are impatient. We are like kids going on a trip with their parents in the car. We start asking, "Are we there yet?" as soon as we leave the entrance to the subdivision. What do we tell them? "We will get there when we get there."

That may be a "word in due season" for all of us today.[5] We will get there if we don't give up on God. He knows when the time is right. That is what the Scripture in Galatians 6:9 means that says, . . . *let us not lose heart and grow weary and faint in acting nobly and doing right, for in due time and at the appointed season we shall reap, if we do not loosen and relax our courage and faint.*

Eventually we will get where God wants us to be, **if** we keep being faithful to Him.

4. *God uses people who are willing to finish what they start.*

A lot of people are good at starting, but they are not good at finishing.

The reason is simple. Emotions get us started. They are always there to support us in new things. We get a word from God or someone prophesies to us, and we are off and running. The question is, how long do we keep running once the emotions wear off?

I remember the first time I went to a nondenominational church. I had not been there very many weeks when a prophet came through to minister. He got everybody in a line and was praying for them. I got into the line. He was laying hands on each of us and blessing us. When he got to me, he laid hands on me and said, "Oh, I see you laying hands on multiplied thousands of people, and they are all falling under the power of God."

I went ballistic. To me that word was a confirmation of something I believed God had been speaking to me. I got so emotional about it, I think I scared the poor man. I usually don't get that way, but it was out of excitement. After a few years I was still going ballistic, but it was for another reason. It wasn't out of excitement; it was because I was still waiting for it to happen, and it was like, **I don't think I can stand this waiting another moment.**

The beginning of new things is almost always exciting. But it is not those who start the race in excitement who win; it is those who stick to it and make it across the finish line when nobody is excited anymore, when nobody is cheering them on, when their emotions are no longer supporting them, when they don't feel like going on any longer, when it looks as if they will never make it to the end, when all they have left is that one word from God that got them started in the first place. That's when the ones who will make it are separated from those who won't do anything but talk about it all their life.

We need to learn to walk the walk, not just talk the talk.

5. God uses those who stay on the narrow path.

Matthew 7:13 and 14 are two of my favorite verses. In them Jesus is talking about the kingdom of heaven: *Enter through the narrow gate; for wide is the gate and spacious and broad is the way that leads away to destruction, and many are those who are entering through it. But the gate is narrow (contracted by pressure) and the way is straitened and compressed that leads away to life, and few are those who find it.*

He is saying that it is easy to succumb to temptation, to fall into sin, to be destroyed. It is easy to get into the flow of the world and just float along in the worldly boat with everybody else. One thing is for sure — no one will be lonely on the broad way. There will always be lots of company because many people are going that way.

The world is full of compromisers today, people who are willing to make any concession and live the status quo, be average and just get by in life.

It is easy to relax and "go with the flow." But those who go through the narrow gate are going to have to stand against pressure. Satan is not going to make it easy for those who decide to live righteously — those who attempt to talk right, act right, think right, and put their money in the right place, those who stop living a selfish, self-centered life, who decide to be radical and outrageous for God. The devil will try to keep them from living that way. His purpose, of course, is to pressure us into getting so depressed and discouraged we give up and quit.

That is why we must learn to **resist** the devil and press into the things of God. We resist him by submitting to God and staying on the narrow path.

One way Satan tries to depress and discourage us is by making us feel that we are the only ones who are going through trials and tribulations. The truth is, I don't know too many people who are not going through something.

The Bible never promises us that we will never have to go through fiery trials.[6] It just promises that we will never have to go through them alone.[7] It also promises that when we come through them, we won't even smell like smoke.[8]

God uses people who stay on the narrow path, and sometimes the only people you are going to find on that path are you and the Lord, but just keep going. And don't do what the world does. Even if no one at work will eat lunch with you or talk to you, don't get into office gossip, become a talebearer or be critical and negative like everyone else. Don't get involved in a wrong relationship out of loneliness. Just use that period of time in your life to draw closer to the Lord. Get to know Him better and better.

6. God uses people who make wise choices.

The Bible talks about wisdom and the power of wisdom from cover to cover. I think we need to read Proverbs more often and take it to heart more seriously because it majors on wisdom, and without wisdom we are never going to succeed at anything.

Many people have gifts, but they don't have any wisdom. There are other people who have wisdom, but they don't use it. There are also a lot of people who have gifts, but they don't have character because they won't grow up and allow God to do the things in their life that need to be done.

We all need wisdom in the way we handle other people and in the way we handle ourselves. We need wisdom in relationships. So many people get hurt because they tell a friend what is on their heart, and that friend betrays them. Then they get mad at their friend. If they had kept their mouth shut, they could have avoided that situation. They needed to use wisdom.

I know this is so because it has happened to me many times. God once told me, "Joyce, if you don't want your friends hurting your feelings and betraying you, then just keep your mouth shut. Quit telling them everything I have told you." This is a simple principle of wisdom.

I believe that a lack of wisdom is one of the things that causes many people to not make it to the end fulfillment of their goals. They just don't use wisdom.

If we are going to be leaders and have other people work for us, we have got to have wisdom in knowing how to treat people.

I have discovered that people will not work for you if you don't treat them right. Most people today are not that desperate for a job. So I have to use wisdom in how I treat my employees. I figure that if I treat them well, they are going to want to work for me. For example, if I pay them well, they are not going to go off looking for another job. It is wise to be good to people you don't want to lose.

In Deuteronomy 30:19 Moses told the Israelites, *I call heaven and earth to witness this day against you that I have set before you life and death, the blessings and the curses; therefore choose life, that you and your descendants may live.*

I love that verse because through it the Lord is saying to us, "I am setting before you two pathways — the broad and the narrow. And I am even giving you a hint about which one to choose."

This is like a multiple choice question, and God is even giving us the answer key: "I set before you: A. Life. B. Death. Answer key: **Choose life!**"

> "I SET BEFORE YOU:
> A. LIFE.
> B. DEATH.
> ANSWER KEY:
> CHOOSE LIFE!"

We should all be able to get that.

God wants us to make the right choice because it affects not only us but also those around us, including our children. He makes it clear that we are to choose life so that we and our children may live.

Our children learn from what they see us do. If we are stingy, they will be stingy. If we are critical, they will be critical. If we are negative, they will be negative. We teach more by our actions, by our choices, than we ever do by our words.

7. God uses people who are good examples to others.

One thing you must realize is that some people are good managers, but they still don't lead. Good managers make good decisions because they operate by proven methods. In other words, they go by the book. But good leaders do not just go by the book; they lead by example. God wants good leaders, people who, by their personal example, lead others in the ways of righteousness.

In 1 Corinthians 11:1, the apostle Paul wrote, *Pattern yourselves after me [follow my example], as I imitate and follow Christ (the Messiah).* What a bold, awesome statement!

What exactly was Paul saying in this verse? He was saying the same thing he said in 1 Corinthians 4:16: *So I urge and implore you, be imitators of me.* He was telling the believers in Corinth, "Watch my life, and I will show you how Jesus wants you to live."

That is what God wants us to do. He wants us to have the confidence to know that we are doing everything in our power to obey God to such a degree that we don't feel we have anything to hide from anybody. He wants us to be confident that anyone who models themselves after us will turn out to be like Jesus both in attitude and behavior.

GOD WANTS OTHERS TO LEARN HOW HE WANTS US TO LIVE BY WATCHING US.

I love Romans 5:19: *For just as by one man's disobedience (failing to hear, heedlessness, and carelessness) the many were constituted sinners, so by one Man's obedience the many will be constituted righteous (made acceptable to God, brought into right standing with Him).*

This verse says that just one man or woman can affect the world. If that is so, then surely one of us can affect the neighborhood we live in, the place where we work, the circle of friends we do things with — if we make the right choices.

Adam made a wrong choice and affected millions of people who came after him. Jesus made the right choice and affected millions more who have followed after Him. He got right in the middle of the mess and turned the whole thing around. Everything was going in a negative flow, but He came on the scene and said, "I'm going to teach you a new way to live."

Dave and I marvel at how obvious it is that if we follow God's plan, our life is blessed, and if we don't, it is a mess. That should be evident to everyone. The Bible says it again and again.

In Psalm 119:6, the psalmist writes, *Then shall I not be put to shame [by failing to inherit Your promises] when I have respect to all Your commandments.* In other words, "If I will just read Your Book and do what You say, everything in my life will work out for the best."

Why do we have to rewrite it, adding our little addendum, hoping that some way God will work our plan instead of His? When will we learn that God is smarter than we are and just listen to Him?

Dave and I have been seeing that the Word of God is like borders for our life. It is as though God is saying to us, "As long as you stay within those guidelines, everything will be fine. The enemy won't be able to get to you. I will bless you and take care of you. We will have a good relationship and fellowship together. You will be prosperous, joyous and peaceful. There will be no condemnation because your sins will be forgiven and you will be in constant communion with Me. But outside of those borders are all kinds of wicked, violent, horrible, aggressive enemies who are out to destroy you."

If God has told us that, and we choose to get out of the borders, whose fault is that?

That is what the Israelites did again and again. When the king served God, the people served God and the whole nation would be blessed. Pretty soon the blessings would be so great that the king would think it was because of him. Then sooner or later they would turn away from God and begin to serve other gods. When that happened, every kind of wicked thing would come upon them, and they would realize, "Oh, we have sinned."

If we want to be blessed and used by God, we must stay on the narrow path. One common person's obedient lifestyle can affect many other common people and encourage them to do uncommon things. We need to have an influence on others. We need to teach them that they can have a positive effect upon the world, that they have a God-ordained destiny to fulfill.

> **WE NEED TO TEACH PEOPLE THAT THEY CAN HAVE A POSITIVE EFFECT UPON THE WORLD, THAT THEY HAVE A GOD-ORDAINED DESTINY TO FULFILL.**

BACK ON TRACK

For we are God's [own] handiwork (His workmanship), recreated in Christ Jesus, [born anew] that we may do those good works which God predestined (planned beforehand) for us [taking paths which He prepared ahead of time], that we should walk in them [living the good life which He prearranged and made ready for us to live].

Ephesians 2:10

We are God's Own handiwork. He created us with His Own hands. We got messed up, so we had to be recreated in Christ Jesus. We had to be born again so that we could go ahead and do those good works that God had preplanned and predestined for us before Satan tried to ruin us.

Just because you and I have had trouble in our life or just because we have made mistakes does not mean that God's plan has been changed. It is still there. All we have to do is get back in it.

BE USABLE

I appeal to you therefore, brethren, and beg of you in view of [all] the mercies of God, to make a decisive dedication of your bodies [presenting all your members and faculties] as a living sacrifice, holy (devoted, consecrated) and well pleasing to God, which is your reasonable (rational, intelligent) service and spiritual worship.

Romans 12:1

Do you know what it means to be consecrated to God? It means to be set apart for His use only.

Years ago I began to get the revelation that I don't belong to myself. I have been bought with a price.[9] I have been branded, just like a rancher brands his cattle to show that they belong to him.

That is true of each one of us. We have the brand of the Holy Spirit upon us.[10] We should not have the attitude that God belongs to us and try to tell Him what we want and how He should go about getting it for us. We should not start out every morning by giving God our twelve-part want list of what it is going to take to make us happy that day.

I spent years doing that. I used to pray, "Oh, God, if I don't have more money, I just can't stand it. You have got to do something." Those were the wilderness years of my life. When we are living like that, we are not in the Promised Land. If we want to get from there over into the Promised Land, we have got to get consecrated, dedicated and disciplined.

> GOD REQUIRES SIMPLY THAT WE ARE USABLE, AND ALL OF US CAN KEEP OURSELVES USABLE.

Our problem is that too often we think about what we cannot do rather than what we can do. Whatever God requires of us, we can do. What He requires of us is simply that we be usable, and all of us can do that. We may not be able to do everything, but we can finish what we start. We can stay on the narrow path. We can be committed and disciplined. We can work hard, walk in wisdom and try to make sure our words and thoughts are pleasing to God while we trust Him to work out His good plan for our life.

GOD HAS A GOOD PLAN FOR YOU

For I know the thoughts and plans that I have for
you, says the Lord, thoughts and plans for welfare
and peace and not for evil, to give you hope in
your final outcome.

Jeremiah 29:11

The most important thing is not how we start but how we finish.

Some people get started with a bang, but they never finish. Others are slow starters, but they finish strong.

We find that to be true with people who work in our office. Some come in and after the first three weeks you would think they could run the place single-handed. Before we learned better, we were impressed by such people. We gave them positions of authority before we knew them as well as we should have. Every time it turned out sour. After a short period of time they were ready to go someplace else. They couldn't be controlled. They wouldn't come under authority. They had gifts and talents, but not the right kind of heart and spirit.

On the other hand, some of the people who came into our office were so slow in the beginning that we were not sure we would be able to keep them on because their learning curve was so low. They just didn't seem to get it. But God would say to us, "Just give them a little time."

We would stick with them, and after a while they would suddenly lock in place. Today some of those people are among our key leaders, proving again that it is not how we start that is important but how we finish. It is not really even all that important how many times we fall down in the process. According to Proverbs 24:16, . . . *a righteous man falls seven times and rises again. . . .*

God has a plan for each of us. It is our destiny. But as we have said, it is a possibility, not a "positively." Even when someone prophesies over us wonderful things in the name of the Lord, just as that prophet did with me, what is being prophesied is the heart, the will and the desire of

God for us. That doesn't mean it is positively going to happen just as it is prophesied because if we don't cooperate with God, instead deciding to go the opposite way of what God's will is for us, it is not going to come to pass.

God has a plan for our lives, but we have a part to play in seeing that plan come true. God cannot do anything in our lives without our cooperation.

The first chapter in this book on the subject of leadership was about potential. **I think our number one job is to cooperate with God every single day of our lives to develop our potential.** Every day we ought to learn something. Every day we ought to grow. Every day we ought to discover something. Every day we ought to be a bit further along than we were the day before.

One of the things we must understand is that there is no other human being on the face of this earth who is interested in developing our potential for us. Oh, yes, we all want to help others reach their full potential, especially our children and grandchildren. But the bottom line is that none of us can do that for someone else, and no one else can do it for us. We must each do it for ourselves. We must each discover our own God-given gifts and talents, what we are truly capable of, and then put ourselves to the task of developing those gifts, talents and capabilities to their fullest extent.

> **GOD HAS A PLAN FOR EACH OF US — A GOOD, UNCOMMON, GREAT PLAN, NOT AN AVERAGE, MEDIOCRE PLAN.**

God has a plan for each of us. It is a good plan, an uncommon plan, a great plan, not an average, mediocre plan.

GO AGAINST THE FLOW

John Mason wrote two very good books that I recommend you read. One is titled *An Enemy Called Average,*[11] and the other is titled *Conquering an Enemy Called Average.*[12] I would like to share with you some things that I learned from these books.

"Know your limits, then ignore them."[13] I know what I can't do. But I also know what I can do. I have decided to concentrate on what I can do, not what I can't do.

Too many people concentrate on what they can't do, on everything they do wrong and never on what they do right. They get so caught up in their mistakes that they lose sight of the fact that we serve a great God.

Hebrews 12:2 says, *Looking away [from all that will distract] to Jesus. . . .* Sometimes our own inabilities distract us. We need to stop looking at them and look at Jesus.

If you can only do one thing, make up your mind that you are going to do that one thing well. Decide that you are going to be the best at that one thing you can do.

John Mason says, "The most unprofitable item ever manufactured is an excuse."[14]

One of the main reasons that people don't do anything is that they make excuses: "I can't. It's too hard. I don't have anybody to help me. I don't have any money." Mother Teresa went to India with three pennies and God, and she didn't do badly.

Have you ever heard the phrase *status quo?* It is Latin for an existing condition or state of affairs.[15] In other words, it means the mess we are in. So when we say, "That's status quo," we really mean, "It's a mess."

John Mason also says, "Do what people say cannot be done,"[16] "Never take the advice of your fears,"[17] and "Don't sit back and take what comes. Go after what you want."[18] I am fond of saying, the world is full of people with wishbone, but not many have backbone. Wishing won't get it done.

Take an inventory. What are you doing with your time, your energy, your talents, your abilities, your life? Are you just following everybody else down the broad way?

Go against the flow!

Don't just float downstream because everybody else is. Turn your boat around and start paddling upstream. It doesn't take any energy to float downstream, but it does take some energy and determination to paddle upstream against the flow, especially when everyone else is going in the opposite direction!

Wake Up and Get a Vision!

Therefore He says, Awake, O sleeper, and arise from the dead, and Christ shall shine (make day dawn) upon you and give you light.

Look carefully then how you walk! Live purposefully and worthily and accurately, not as the unwise and witless, but as wise (sensible, intelligent people),

Making the very most of the time [buying up each opportunity], because the days are evil.

Therefore do not be vague and thoughtless and foolish, but understanding and firmly grasping what the will of the Lord is.

Ephesians 5:14-17

Do you know what the will of God is for you? Do you have a vision? Do you know what you are going to do with your life? You should.

Now obviously, when young people are first starting out in life they may not know for sure what their entire future is going to hold, and there is nothing wrong with that. They just need to start doing something, and it will become clear what they are supposed to do with their lives.

But if you are forty or fifty years old, by now you should have figured out what you are supposed to be doing. That's not a put-down; it's a fact.

I have lived more of my life than I have left to live. If I don't have it figured out by now, I am in bad shape. Yet there are people my age who still don't know what they want to be when they grow up!

I got hold of this passage in Ephesians many, many years ago when God first called me into the ministry. In those days I was such a mess that I would sit on my couch after I had put the kids down for a nap, and cry for two hours. That is all I knew to do back then. I was mad at Dave about 90 percent of the time. I had a chip on my shoulder and all kinds of problems in my life, yet I was teaching a Bible study in my home every Tuesday night. I loved God, but I had all kinds of strongholds in my life.

Then the Lord started showing me some of the Scriptures that I have been sharing with you in this book. One of them was this passage about not being *vague*, which Webster defines as "1. not clearly expressed or outlined."[19] Let me quote it to you from another Bible version.

Know What You're Doing — And Why!

You groped your way through that murk once, but no longer. You're out in the open now. The bright light of Christ makes your way plain. So no more stumbling around. Get on with it! The good, the right, the true — these are the actions appropriate for daylight hours. Figure out what will please Christ, and then do it.

Don't waste your time on useless work, mere busywork, the barren pursuits of darkness. Expose these things for the sham they are. It's a scandal when people waste their lives on things they must do in the darkness where no one will see. Rip the cover off those frauds and see how attractive they look in the light of Christ.

*"Wake up from your sleep,
Climb out of your coffins;
Christ will show you the light!"*

So watch your step. Use your head. Make the most of every chance you get. These are desperate times!

Don't live carelessly, unthinkingly. Make sure you understand what the Master wants.

Ephesians 5:8-17 MESSAGE

We need to be people of purpose. We need to know why we are doing what we are doing. We need to make sure we don't lose sight of our goal. We may have had a goal ten years ago and are still just going through the motions. Maybe we were doing something that was anointed, but there is no anointing on it anymore.

If the horse has been dead seven years, it's time to dismount.

Let me share a true story to illustrate what I mean.

"This is a story about Russia in the days of the Czars. In the park of St. Petersburg's Winter Palace there was a beautiful lawn, on that lawn a bench, and next to that bench, two guards. Every three hours the guards were changed. No one knew why. One day an ambitious young lieutenant was put in charge of the Palace Guard. He started wondering, and asking questions. In the end, he found a . . . little old man, the Palace historian.

"'Yes,' the old man said, 'I remember. During the reign of Peter the Great, 200 years ago, the bench got a fresh coat of paint. The Czar was afraid that the ladies in waiting might get paint on their dresses. So he ordered one guard to watch the bench. The order was never rescinded. Then in 1908, all the guards of the Palace were doubled for fear of a revolution. So the bench has had two guards ever since.'"[20]

Occasionally it is wise to ask, "Why am I doing this?"

Regularly I tell our management team, "You have to go over your systems. A couple of times a year, you need to sit back and think through every system in your department. You need to evaluate every report that you are generating to make sure someone is reading it and still needs it. It may have been something that Dave and I needed six years ago and don't even look at now. You may be wasting your time and spinning your wheels doing something that is outdated and unnecessary."

8. God uses people who refuse to give up.

It is easy to drift backward, but we must press on to go forward. Effortless living is never effective. Everyone thinks that the more we can get hold of with no effort, the better life is, but that is a lie.

One thing that is wrong with us Americans today, even with our health, is the fact that we don't have much of anything to do but go through life pushing buttons: get on an elevator, push a button to go to the next floor; put dirty dishes in a washer, push a button and they come out clean; put the laundry in a machine, push a button and they are washed; throw them into another machine, push a button and they are dried — and if they are taken out quickly enough, they don't even get wrinkled enough to need ironing.

Still we gripe and grumble because we have to load and unload the machines!

Speaking of effortless living and its effects, consider this story:

"A number of bees were taken along on a flight into space to see how they would handle the experience of weightlessness. In the weightless atmosphere they were able to float in space without any effort. The report on the experiment was summed up in these words, 'They enjoyed the ride, but they died'"(emphasis mine).[21]

We might think we would like everything to be easy, that we would enjoy an effortless life, but it would kill us. We are created to make effort. Whether we know it or not, we are created for work, involvement, participation and struggle. We are not supposed to struggle with everything, but we are also not supposed to be the kind of people who quit and give up easily.

In Luke 18:1 we read these words: *Also [Jesus] told them a parable to the effect that they ought always to pray and not to turn coward (faint, lose heart, and give up).*

In this parable Jesus told about a widow who kept coming to an unjust judge, annoying and wearing him out by her constant pleas that he give her justice in her case. Jesus' conclusion was, "If this woman could wear out an unjust judge so that he gave her justice, don't you think God will do the same for you, if you will refuse to give up but keep on coming to Him for help?"

What about the woman with the issue of blood who kept pressing through the crowd toward Jesus saying to herself, "If I can just touch the hem of His garment, I know I will be healed"? Jesus commended her for her determination and her refusal to be intimidated by the crowds who surrounded Him and kept Him from her reach.[22]

> ZACCHAEUS DID NOT LOOK AT HIS SHORTCOMINGS BUT SOMEHOW FOUND A WAY TO REACH HIS OBJECTIVE.

What about Zacchaeus who was too short to see Jesus as He passed by on the road, so he climbed up in a sycamore tree where Jesus saw him and told him to come down because He was going to go home with him?[23] Why did Jesus pick Zacchaeus? He recognized in him a trait that he looks for in every individual. He saw that Zacchaeus did not look at his shortcomings but somehow found a way to reach his objective.

Zacchaeus could have said, "I would like to see Jesus, but I'm too short." Too many people stop at but: "I would like to do that, but . . . I wish I had that, but . . . I would like to be a leader, but . . ."

We have got to refuse to give up. Remember, Paul said that the most important thing he did was forgetting what lies behind and **pressing on.**

If we want to be leaders, that is what we must do, too. We must absolutely refuse to give up, no matter what happens.

Don't Become Discouraged

In the fourth year of Jehoiakim son of Josiah king of Judah, this word came to Jeremiah from the Lord:

Take a scroll [of parchment] for a book and write on it all the words I have spoken to you against Israel and Judah and all the nations from the day I spoke to you in the days of [King] Josiah until this day.

Jeremiah 36:1,2

At this time Jeremiah was actually under house arrest. Certain people could come visit him, but he couldn't go out. He was still receiving prophecies from the Lord and writing them down. God would give him a message, and he would record it on parchment. Then one of his servants would come and carry the message throughout the land, since Jeremiah couldn't go himself. So we see that God is not put off by inconveniences; He always finds another way to get the job done.

Since the people of those days did not have computers and printers, typewriters or even ballpoint pens and pads of paper, writing was a tedious job. Everything had to be taken down by a quill and ink on a scroll. If more than one copy was needed, then it had to be made by hand just like the original, which was a long, tiresome and painstaking process.[24]

So God gave Jeremiah a prophecy about Israel and Judah and ordered him to record it on a scroll. Jeremiah called his secretary, Baruch, who wrote while Jeremiah dictated.

When the king heard about the scroll, he ordered it to be brought to the royal palace and read to him. As his attendant Jehudi was reading it to him, the king would take a few pages that had been read, cut them off the scroll with a knife and then burn them in a fire set before him because it was wintertime.[25]

Maybe the king was sitting there by the fire, warming his toes and eating an apple. Whatever the case was, he didn't like what Jehudi was reading because he liked his unrighteous lifestyle, and he didn't want to change it. So he cut up and burned page after page after page until he burned up all of Jeremiah's prophecies.

Can you imagine how Jeremiah must have felt when he learned that all of his hard work had been burned up? Can you relate to that experience? Have you ever worked on something for a long time and struggled and tried and done everything you knew how to do and somehow the devil got in and destroyed it all?

DO IT AGAIN!

Now the word of the Lord came to Jeremiah after the king had burned the scroll with the words which Baruch wrote at the dictation of Jeremiah, [and the Lord] said:

Take another scroll and write on it all the former words that were on the first scroll, which Jehoiakim the king of Judah burned.

Jeremiah 36:27,28

So what was God's answer to Jeremiah's terrible dilemma and discouragement?

"Jeremiah, go get yourself another scroll and write the thing over."

In other words, **do it again.**

If you and I want to be leaders in the kingdom of God, we must be willing to do it — and then do it again and again and again, if necessary — until we get a breakthrough, and we finish what God has called us to do.

CONCLUSION

Conclusion

If you want to be used by God in some level of leadership, you can be. God is always looking for people to promote — and you can be one of them. You have tremendous capabilities and potential; all you need do is fully develop them. That development involves allowing God to change you. The process may hurt at times, but it will benefit you later. As you develop the leadership qualities God has placed in you, remember that you are investing in the future. You **can** fulfill the plan God has for you, but you must be determined to refuse to be anything less than all you can be. The major key to moving from where you are to where you want to be is to keep on keeping on.

Is a good leader born or made? Some people are born with natural leadership qualities that need to be developed. But don't look at leadership as something attainable only by rare individuals with great talents. God delights in using common people to accomplish uncommon things.

Common people with uncommon goals who make an uncommon commitment can help an uncommon number of people who can also lead other common people to do uncommon things.

Develop your potential to the full. And as you do, lead others in developing theirs. Be all you can be. Then help someone else be all they can be.

PRAYER

FOR A
PERSONAL RELATIONSHIP
WITH THE LORD

PRAYER FOR A
PERSONAL RELATIONSHIP
WITH THE LORD

God wants you to receive His free gift of salvation. Jesus wants to save you and fill you with the Holy Spirit more than anything. If you have never invited Jesus, the Prince of Peace, to be your Lord and Savior, I invite you to do so now. Pray the following prayer, and if you are really sincere about it, you will experience a new life in Christ.

Father,

You loved the world so much, You gave Your only begotten Son to die for our sins so that whoever believes in Him will not perish, but have eternal life.

Your Word says we are saved by grace through faith as a gift from You. There is nothing we can do to earn salvation.

I believe and confess with my mouth that Jesus Christ is Your Son, the Savior of the world. I believe He died on the cross for me and bore all of my sins, paying the price for them. I believe in my heart that You raised Jesus from the dead.

I ask You to forgive my sins. I confess Jesus as my Lord. According to Your Word, I am saved and will spend eternity with You! Thank You, Father. I am so grateful! In Jesus' Name, amen.

See John 3:16; Ephesians 2:8,9; Romans 10:9,10; 1 Corinthians 15:3,4; 1 John 1:9; 4:14-16; 5:1,12,13.

ENDNOTES

Introduction

[1] See Galatians 5:22,23.

Chapter 1

[1] Mark 10:27.

[2] See 1 Thessalonians 2:13. One translation of this verse emphasizes God as the One Who does the work in us: . . . *For God is at work in you who believe* (TEV). Many versions of the Bible emphasize that God's work is done in us through His Word: . . . *the Word of God, which is effectually at work in you who believe. . .* (AMP).

[3] Matthew 18:19.

[4] The Holy Spirit is the divine life force of God that comes into our spirit in the New Birth, when we receive His Son Jesus as our Savior. The Holy Spirit prompts, leads, guides and works in us through our own spirit by enabling us to receive and experience the power of God in a greater way. (See John 16:13.) He is powerful and mighty and is able to do in us what we could never do on our own. When we follow after our flesh or our mind, will and emotions, we are depending on ourselves. When we follow after the Spirit, we are depending on God.

[5] *American Dictionary of the English Language,* 10th Ed. (San Francisco: Foundation for American Christian Education, 1998). Facsimile of Noah Webster's 1828 edition, permission to reprint by G. & C. Merriam Company, copyright 1967 & 1995 (Renewal) by Rosalie J. Slater, s.v. "POTENTIAL."

[6] See Galatians 3:16,19.

[7] Webster's 1828 edition, s.v. "DEVELOPMENT."

[8] Zechariah 4:10.

[9] See Genesis 2:7.

[10] See Genesis 1:26,27.

[11] John 10:10 KJV.

[12] John 8:44.

[13] Deuteronomy 1:2.

[14] See James 4:5,6 AMP; Hebrews 4:16; Ephesians 2:8.

[15] See 1 Timothy 3:4,5.

Chapter 2

[1] Roger K. Burke, Consulting Editor, *Health, Physical Education and Recreation Reprint Series* (United States of America: Brown Reprints, 1970), pp. 273, 477.

[2] "Figurative. Oil was a fitting symbol of the Spirit . . . of God, as the principle of spiritual life that proceeds from God and fills the natural being of the creature with the powers of divine life. Anointing with oil, therefore, was a symbol of endowment with the Spirit of God for the duties of the office to which a person was consecrated." *New Unger's Bible Dictionary* (Chicago: Originally published by Moody Press, 1988), s.v. "OIL." Used by permission.

[3] 2 Corinthians 3:2 KJV.

[4] Numbers 20:3-13.

[5] Ephesians 4:22-24.

[6] James 1:2,3.

[7] Exodus 18:21.

[8] 2 Timothy 2:15 KJV.

[9] Matthew 25:20-25.

[10] Philippians 3:14 KJV.

[11] 1 Corinthians 15:58.

Chapter 3

[1] Matthew 24:27-44; Revelation 19:11-16.

[2] See "Acts 2:17." "The expression [the last days] then properly denoted 'the future times' in general. But, as the coming of the Messiah was to the eye of a Jew the most important event in the coming ages . . . the phrase came to be regarded as properly expressive of that. . . . The last days, or the closing period of the world, were the days of the Messiah. It does not appear from this, and it certainly is not implied in the expression, that they supposed the world would then come to an end. Their views were just the contrary. They anticipated a long and glorious time under the dominion of the Messiah, and to this expectation they were led by the promise that his kingdom should be forever; that of the increase of his government there should be no end. . . ." Albert Barnes, D.D., *Barnes' Notes*, Electronic Database (copyright © 1997 by Biblesoft). All rights reserved.

[3] *Webster's II New College Dictionary* (Boston/New York: Houghton Mifflin Company, 1995), s.v. "stability."

[4] *Wycliffe Bible Commentary,* edited by Charles E. Pfeiffer and Everett F. Harrison, Electronic Database (Moody Press, copyright © 1962). All rights reserved. See "Romans 8:4-15."

[5] Joyce Meyer, *Managing Your Emotions* (Tulsa: Harrison House, 1997).

[6] Matthew 23:1-3.

[7] See Hebrews 13:7.

[8] See Proverbs 16:18.

Chapter 4

[1] See Romans 5:8-10; 1 Corinthians 15:3,4.

[2] See Hebrews 13:8.

[3] See Ephesians 1:11,12.

[4] See *Jamieson, Fausset and Brown Commentary, Electronic Database* (copyright © 1997 by Biblesoft). All rights reserved.

[5] Romans 8:29.

[6] 1 Peter 5:8.

[7] Psalm 62:8.

[8] Proverbs 17:17.

[9] See Romans 6:10,11.

[10] Matthew 26:41.

Chapter 5

[1] 1 Peter 3:4.

[2] See 1 Corinthians 9:4-12.

[3] See 1 Corinthians 3:13-15.

[4] See 1 Chronicles 28:9; Revelation 2:23.

[5] See 2 Samuel 11; 24:10.

[6] Hebrews 11:6.

[7] ". . . on the one hand, He [God] put their unbelief to shame by the miraculous gift of water, and on the other hand punished Moses and Aaron for the weakness of their faith"; *Keil & Delitzsch Commentary on the Old Testament: New Updated Edition,* Electronic Database (copyright © 1996 by Hendrickson Publishers, Inc.). Used by permission. All rights reserved.

[8] Romans 1:17 KJV.

[9] See Psalm 23:3 KJV and other versions.

[10] John 8:32.

[11] James 1:22.

[12] Andrew Murray, D.D., *Humility: the Beauty of Holiness* (Fort Washington, PA: Christian Literature Crusade, Edition of 1961, Reset 1980, Pocket Companion Edition, Unabridged, Edited and Reset 1991).

[13] Webster's 1828 edition, s.v. "PRESUMING."

[14] 1 Samuel 16:7.

[15] Titus 1:15.

[16] See Matthew 5:13,14.

Chapter 6

[1] Matthew 6:14,15.

[2] Luke 6:27-38.

[3] Genesis 37,39.

[4] Genesis 41:40.

[5] Genesis 42-45.

[6] 2 Chronicles 16:9.

[7] Acts 7:59,60.

[8] 1 Corinthians 13:4-8.

[9] Numbers 12:1,2.

[10] Matthew 7:12.

[11] Genesis 12:1.

[12] Philippians 3:13,14.

[13] Isaiah 43:18,19.

[14] "No person with a physical defect or disqualifying disease could serve as a priest (Leviticus 21:16-21). Bodily perfection was to symbolize the priest's spiritual wholeness and holiness of heart." *Nelson's Illustrated Bible Dictionary* (copyright © 1986 by Thomas Nelson Publishers). All rights reserved. Used by permission.

[15] Matthew 15:14.

[16] Proverbs 28:1; 2 Timothy 2:24.

[17] Psalm 18:39.

Chapter 7

[1] Isaiah 61:3.

2   Hebrews 11:6.

3   James 1:22.

4   1 Corinthians 14:33 KJV.

5   Luke 1:26-38.

6   Luke 2:19.

7   Psalm 138:8.

8   Hebrews 11:6.

Chapter 8

1   See Matthew 25:31-40.

2   Psalm 115:17.

3   See John 11:44.

4   2 Timothy 1:6,7.

5   Ecclesiastes 9:10.

6   Haggai 1:7.

7   Romans 12:5,6.

8   See 1 Samuel 16:1-13.

9   1 Samuel 2:6,7.

10 W.E. Vine, *Vine's Complete Expository Dictionary of Old and New Testament Words* (Nashville: Thomas Nelson Inc., 1984, 1996), "An Expository Dictionary of New Testament Words," p. 223, s.v. "FAITHFUL, FAITHFULLY, FAITHLESS," *pistos.*

11 Matthew 25:21,23.

12 Romans 8:37.

13 Philippians 4:13 KJV.

14 2 Corinthians 2:14 KJV.

15 Revelation 1:18; Matthew 28:18-20; Ephesians 1:17-23; John 8:44; Deuteronomy 28:13; John 3:16.

16 1 Timothy 6:12 KJV.

Chapter 9

1   Nehemiah 8:10.

2   See Matthew 23:27 NIV.

3   See John 3:3-15 KJV.

4   Mark 9:21 (author's paraphrase).

[5] 1 John 3:8 NKJV.

[6] Galatians 5:22,23.

[7] Luke 1:26-38 (author's paraphrase).

[8] Matthew 6:14,15.

[9] Matthew 6:12 (author's paraphrase).

[10] See Psalm 133:1-3 AMP, TLB.

Chapter 10

[1] "Lydia was . . . 'one that worshipped God.' . . . The phrase which describes her religion . . . is the usual designation for a proselyte [author's note: a convert to Judaism]. . . . She was in the habit of frequenting a place of prayer by a riverside, a situation convenient for the necessary ablutions required by the Jewish worship, and there Paul and his companions met her." *International Standard Bible Encyclopedia*, Original James Orr 1915 Edition, Electronic Database (copyright © 1995-1996 by Biblesoft). All rights reserved.

[2] "The character of Nazaraeth was proverbially bad. To be a Galilean or a Nazarene was an expression of decided contempt (John 7:52). . . . Nathanael asked, therefore, whether it was possible that the Messiah should come from a place proverbially wicked. This was a mode of judging in the case not uncommon. It is not by examining evidence, but by prejudice. . . ." *Barnes' Notes*, John 1:46.

[3] Ephesians 6:5-8.

[4] Deuteronomy 28:1-14.

[5] *Nelson's Illustrated Bible Dictionary*, s.v. "fear."

[6] Matthew 12:34 NKJV.

[7] Numbers 13:30.

Chapter 11

[1] Webster's 1828 edition, s.v. "TEST" (noun).

[2] Webster's 1828 edition, s.v. "TEST" (verb).

[3] Matthew 26:34-75.

[4] James 1:12.

[5] Isaiah 61:3 KJV.

[6] *Adam Clarke's Commentary*, Electronic Database (copyright © 1996 by Biblesoft). All rights reserved. "Psalm 118:22"; "Matthew 21:42."

[7] John 7:5.

[8] See Hebrews 9:28.

[9] John 15:18-20.

[10] See Hebrews 10:30.

[11] Proverbs 18:24.

[12] "Throughout the Old Testament period he [Satan] sought to destroy the messianic line. When the Messiah became a man, Satan tried to eliminate Him (Revelation 12:4,5). . . . Satan leads people into sin by various means. Sometimes he does it by direct suggestion, as in the case of Judas Iscariot (John 13:2,27) . . . sometimes through a person's own weaknesses (1 Corinthians 7:5)." *Nelson's Illustrated Bible Dictionary*, s.v. "SATAN."

[13] Matthew 26:48,49.

[14] 2 Samuel 15:1-14.

[15] Genesis 37,39.

[16] Miriam, as a prophetess . . . no less than as the sister of Moses and Aaron, took the first rank among the women of Israel; and Aaron may be regarded as the ecclesiastical head of the whole nation. But . . . they challenged the special vocation of Moses and the exclusive authority which God had assigned to him. Miriam was the instigator, from the fact that her name stands conspicuously first (Numbers 12:1), and that the punishment (Numbers 12:10) fell on her alone. . . ." *Barnes' Notes*, Numbers 12:1.

Chapter 12

[1] John 11:4 KJV.

Chapter 13

[1] Isaiah 14:15.

[2] Matthew 26:39.

[3] See 1 Corinthians 16:9 KJV.

[4] Hebrews 12:3 KJV.

[5] See 1 Samuel 24:1-7.

[6] "Job is a model of spiritual integrity — a person who held fast to his faith, without understanding the reason behind his suffering." *Nelson's Illustrated Bible Dictionary*, s.v. "JOB."

[7] See Mark 6:16-27; "John was a forerunner of Jesus not only in his ministry and message (Matthew 3:1; 4:17) but also in his death. *Nelson*, s.v. "JOHN THE BAPTIST."

[8] Luke 2:46,47.

[9] Luke 2:40.

[10] Luke 2:52.

[11] William Smith, LL.D., revised and edited by F.N. and M.A. Peloubet, *A Dictionary of the Bible* (Nashville: Thomas Nelson, 1962), s.v. "Jesus Christ," p. 308. "Jesus began to enter upon his ministry when he was 'about thirty years old. . . .'"

[12] See Luke 2:51.

Chapter 14

[1] "The image and likeness must necessarily be intellectual, his mind, his soul, must have been formed after the nature and perfections of his God. The human mind is still endowed with most extraordinary capacities, it was more so when issuing out of the hands of its Creator. God was now producing a spirit, and a spirit, too, formed after the perfections of his own nature. God is the fountain whence this spirit issued, hence, the stream must resemble the spring which produced it." *Adam Clarke's Commentary*, Electronic Database (copyright © 1996 by Biblesoft). All rights reserved. "Genesis 1:26."

[2] Romans 9:20,21.

[3] ". . . the brilliant concluding piece of Part II of Handel's *Messiah*," *The Columbia Encyclopedia*, Sixth Edition (copyright © 2000, Columbia University Press); available from <http://www infoplease.com/ce6/society/A0822457.html>.

[4] Webster's II, s.v. "charisma."

[5] Webster's II, s.v. "character."

[6] Ephesians 6:6 KJV.

[7] 1 Samuel 2:7.

[8] Luke 8:18.

[9] Deuteronomy 28:2.

[10] Matthew 7:16.

Chapter 15

[1] Webster's II, s.v. "balance."

[2] Webster's 1828 edition, s.v. "BALANCE."

[3] Philippians 4:13 KJV.

[4] Numbers 11:16,17.

[5] Hebrews 12:2 KJV.

[6] John 10:10.

[7] 1 Kings 18:27 TLB (author's paraphrase).

[8] "Elijah's act is to be justified by the express command of the Law, that idolatrous Israelites were to be put to death, and by the right of a prophet under the theocracy to step in and execute the Law when the king failed in his duty." *Barnes' Notes*, 1 Kings 18:40.

[9] See Psalm 18:29.

Chapter 16

[1] See Numbers 22:21-33.

[2] See 1 Corinthians 1:27,28.

[3] As we saw in a previous chapter, the *chief cornerstone* of Psalm 118:22 seems to have originally referred to David. David, rejected by Saul and the other Jewish leaders, was later chosen by the Lord to rule Israel. Jesus, the Chief Cornerstone (see Matthew 21:42), was rejected and crucified by the Jews then rose from the dead as the Atonement for the sin of the world. Based on *Adam Clarke's Commentary*, Electronic Database (copyright © 1996 by Biblesoft). All rights reserved. "Psalm 118:22"; "Matthew 21:42." Also Ephesians 2:20.

[4] Isaiah 61:7.

[5] See Proverbs 15:23 KJV.

[6] See 1 Peter 4:12,13.

[7] See Isaiah 43:2.

[8] See Daniel 3:27.

[9] See 1 Corinthians 6:20.

[10] See Ephesians 4:30.

[11] John Mason, *An Enemy Called Average* (Tulsa: Harrison House, 1990).

[12] John Mason, *Conquering an Enemy Called Average* (Tulsa: Insight International, 1996).

[13] Mason, *Conquering*, p. 15.

[14] Mason, *Conquering*, p. 35.

[15] Webster's II, s.v. "status quo."

[16] Mason, *Conquering*, p. 77.

[17] Mason, *Conquering*, p. 93.

[18] Mason, *Conquering*, p. 117.

[19] Webster's II, s.v. "vague."

[20] Paul Lee Tan, Th.D., *Encyclopedia of 7,700 Illustrations* (Rockville, MD: Assurance Publishers, 1979), p. 1504.

[21] Dave Grant, *The Great Lover's Manifesto* (Eugene, OR: Harvest House Publishers, 1986), p. 13.

[22] Matthew 9:20-22.

[23] Luke 19:1-5.

[24] "Ancient surfaces, such as animal skins and stone, on which information was recorded in Bible times. . . . A reed pen (3 John 13), a metal pen, or a brush-like tool was used to write on softer materials (Job 19:24; Jeremiah 17:1). The ink used was black, sometimes of metallic content. Usually it was made of soot, mixed with oil and gum of balsam." *Nelson's Illustrated Bible Dictionary,* s.v. "WRITING MATERIALS."

[25] Jeremiah 36:22,23.

BIBLIOGRAPHY

American Dictionary of the English Language, 10th Ed. San Francisco: Foundation for American Christian Education, 1998. Facsimile of Noah Webster's 1828 edition, permission to reprint by G. & C. Merriam Company, 1967 & 1995 (Renewal) by Rosalie J. Slater.

Burke, Roger K. *Health, Physical Education and Recreation Reprint Series.* United States of America: Brown Reprints, 1970.

Grant, Dave. *The Great Lover's Manifesto.* Eugene, Oregon: Harvest House Publishers, 1986.

Mason, John. *An Enemy Called Average.* Tulsa: Harrison House, 1990.

Mason, John. *Conquering an Enemy Called Average.* Tulsa: Insight International, 1996.

Murray, Andrew, D.D. *Humility: the Beauty of Holiness.* Fort Washington, Pennsylvania: Christian Literature Crusade, Edition of 1961, reset 1980, Pocket Companion Edition, Unabridged, Edited and Reset 1991.

Tan, Paul Lee, Th.D., *Encyclopedia of 7,700 Illustrations,* Rockville, Maryland: Assurance Publishers, 1979.

Vine, W.E. *Vine's Complete Expository Dictionary of Old and New Testament Words.* Nashville: Thomas Nelson Inc., 1984, 1996.

Webster's II New College Dictionary. Boston/New York: Houghton Mifflin, Company, 1995.

Recommended Reading on Leadership

Blanchard, Ken. *The Heart of a Leader.* Tulsa: Honor Books, 1998.

Briner, Bob and Ray Pritchard. *The Leadership Lessons of Jesus: A Timeless Model for Today's Leaders.* Nashville: Broadman & Holman Publishers, 1997.

Cathy, Truett. *It's Easier to Succeed Than to Fail.* Nashville: Oliver Nelson, 1989.

Damazio, Frank. *The Making of a Leader.* Portland: City Bible Publishing, 1988.

Hammond, Mac. *Positioned for Promotion: How to Increase Your Influence and Capacity to Lead.* Tulsa: Harrison House, 2000.

Maxwell, John C. *The 21 Irrefutable Laws of Leadership: Follow Them and People Will Follow You.* Nashville: Thomas Nelson, 1998.

Ziglar, Zig. *See You at the Top.* Gretna, Louisiana: Pelican, 1977.

Joyce Meyer has been teaching the Word of God since 1976 and in full-time ministry since 1980. Previously the associate pastor at Life Christian Center in St. Louis, Missouri, she developed, coordinated, and taught a weekly meeting known as "Life In The Word." After more than five years, the Lord brought it to a conclusion, directing her to establish her own ministry and call it *"Life In The Word, Inc."*

Now, her *Life In The Word* radio and television broadcasts are seen and heard by millions across the United States and throughout the world. Joyce's teaching tapes are enjoyed internationally, and she travels extensively conducting *Life In The Word* conferences.

Joyce and her husband, Dave, the business administrator at *Life In The Word*, have been married for over 34 years. They reside in St. Louis, Missouri, and are the parents of four children. All four children are married and, along with their spouses, work with Dave and Joyce in the ministry.

Believing the call on her life is to establish believers in God's Word, Joyce says, "Jesus died to set the captives free, and far too many Christians have little or no victory in their daily lives." Finding herself in the same situation many years ago and having found freedom to live in victory through applying God's Word, Joyce goes equipped to set captives free and to exchange ashes for beauty. She believes that every person who walks in victory leads many others into victory. Her life is transparent, and her teachings are practical and can be applied in everyday life.

Joyce has taught on emotional healing and related subjects in meetings all over the country, helping multiplied thousands. She has recorded more than 200 different audiocassette albums and is the author of 39 books to help the body of Christ on various topics.

Her "Emotional Healing Package" contains over 23 hours of teaching on the subject. Albums included in this package are: "Confidence"; "Beauty for Ashes" (includes a syllabus); "Managing Your Emotions"; "Bitterness, Resentment, and Unforgiveness"; "Root of Rejection"; and a 90-minute Scripture/music tape entitled, "Healing the Brokenhearted."

Joyce's "Mind Package" features five different audio tape series on the subject of the mind. They include: "Mental Strongholds and Mindsets"; "Wilderness Mentality"; "The Mind of the Flesh"; "The Wandering,

Wondering Mind"; and "Mind, Mouth, Moods, and Attitudes." The package also contains Joyce's powerful book, *Battlefield of the Mind*. On the subject of love she has three tape series entitled, "Love Is..."; "Love: The Ultimate Power"; and "Loving God, Loving Yourself, and Loving Others," and a book entitled, *Reduce Me to Love*.

Write to Joyce Meyer's office for a resource catalog and further information on how to obtain the tapes you need to bring total healing to your life.

To contact the author write:

Joyce Meyer Ministries
P. O. Box 655
Fenton, Missouri 63026

or call: (636) 349-0303

Internet Address: www.joycemeyer.org

Please include your testimony or help received from this book when you write. Your prayer requests are welcome.

To contact the author
in Canada, please write:

Joyce Meyer Ministries Canada, Inc.
Lambeth Box 1300
London, ON N6P 1T5

or call: (636) 349-0303

To contact the author
in Australia, please write:

Joyce Meyer Ministries-Australia
Locked Bag 77
Mansfield Delivery Centre
Queensland 4122

or call: (07) 3349 1200

To contact the author
in England, please write:

Joyce Meyer Ministries
P. O. Box 1549
Windsor
SL4 1GT

or call: 01753 831102

Do It! Afraid

*Expect a Move of God in Your Life...**Suddenly***

Enjoying Where You Are on the Way to Where You Are Going

The Most Important Decision You'll Ever Make

When, God, When?

Why, God, Why?

The Word, the Name, the Blood

Battlefield of the Mind

Battlefield of the Mind Study Guide

Tell Them I Love Them

Peace

The Root of Rejection

Beauty for Ashes

If Not for the Grace of God

By Dave Meyer
Nuggets of Life

Available from your local bookstore.

Harrison House
Tulsa, Oklahoma 74153

THE HARRISON HOUSE VISION

Proclaiming the truth and the power
Of the Gospel of Jesus Christ
With excellence;

Challenging Christians to
Live victoriously,
Grow spiritually,
Know God intimately.